In the Heart's Last Kingdom

In the Heart's Last Kingdom

ROBERT PENN WARREN'S MAJOR POETRY

Calvin Bedient

Harvard University Press
Cambridge, Massachusetts, and London, England   1984

This book is printed on acid-free paper, and its binding materials
have been chosen for strength and durability.

Library of Congress Cataloging in Publication Data

Bedient, Calvin.
   In the heart's last kingdom.

   Includes bibliographical references and index.
   1. Warren, Robert Penn, 1905–   —Criticism and
interpretation.   I. Title.
PS3545.A748Z58   1984   811'.52   84-6674
ISBN 0-674-44546-5 (alk. paper)

Page 245 constitutes an extension of the copyright page.

Designed by Gwen Frankfeldt

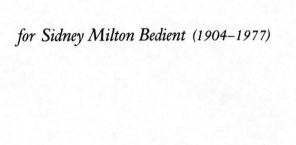

for Sidney Milton Bedient (1904–1977)

Contents

Yeats had it backwards—he thought that the shudder comes from a flight out of nature. It comes from a flight into nature.

Robert Penn Warren, *Flood*

Art as freedom from moral narrowness and corner-perspectives . . . Flight into nature, where its beauty is coupled with frightfulness. Conception of the great human being.

Friedrich Nietzsche, *The Will to Power*

O N E

His
Grand
Last
Phase

*N*othing in Robert Penn Warren's long career as a man of letters has so distinguished it as has the final act, which opened in the late sixties, when he himself had entered his sixties (he was born in Guthrie, Kentucky, in 1905). His greatness as a writer began with his determination to concentrate on poetry as the extreme resource of language-knowledge, language-being—began with *Audubon: A Vision* (1969), forty-six years after he started publishing poems as a student prodigy at Vanderbilt, under the tutelage of (among others) John Crowe Ransom and Allen Tate. What seized him then was a heroic effort to present himself as a man whose passion for the adventure of living is his sole, his imposing identity and glory. (One might say he had finally recognized, without shrinking from, his passion for passion.) Just as he had with Audubon, he created a type out of himself, acting out a demand for knowledge of himself and the world, performing a hunger for consummate meaning and distinction (a nobility and glory based on reverence for distinctions and exemplifying the quality), while recognizing, while heaving against, everything dark and heavy in the truth. At moments he has seemed merely stagy (an image of his own heroic image of man), but volume by volume no one could doubt the strength of his appetite for glory and truth, with beauty trailing after as "the fume-track of necessity."

Audubon rose above his previous volumes like a curiously abrupt, grand escarpment, a repudiation of the scrub country of uncertain poetic purpose. Two proud differences announced themselves: an assured voice (at last his own, and major) and a personal and passionate knowledge of values. Warren may have been writing about a nineteenth-century Frenchman who became the very type of the "natural," wood-wholesome American, and he may have shown an equally unfashionable longing for majestic beauty and glory, but he invented a convincing contemporary manner (and structure), and there was no dismissing his grand sensibility: like the Rockies, it was there.

Casting off the regal diction with which he had earlier tried to warm himself, he began to blaze inwardly with a direct and passionate pursuit of the real. What he lived for was what he could not live without, and his words, at their best, seemed resonant with actual life. The joy he was after—namely, "knowledge based on the empathic imagination"—may have been jettisoned by "the world of science, technology, big organization—and of course the business culture"; but he would have it, singlehandedly he would replant it in America, if passion could do it, if anyone could do it. Both retreating and advancing to nature, like some latter-day Thoreau, Ishmael, or Whitman, he sought to reconcile, in Rilke's words, "the Individual and the All"—sought "the moment of exaltation, the artistically important Moment, . . . in which the two scales of the balance counterpoise one another."

Warren had always manifested, if at first murkily, a tragic hunger for "Truth," one that made him formidable, set him apart. That passion grew until it could scarcely be slaked. With *Audubon* it became clarified, beautiful, essential. If this Sisyphus of certain questions—What is Truth? What joy? Where lies glory?—even now only rolls them near to the summit of perfect understanding before they crash down again, still his evocations of the labor can seem blessed as well as sinewy; the effort itself is happiness and appears touched by a rare and difficult light. Warren is that very unusual thing, a poet of tragic joy—indeed the first such among American poets.

"Truth" is everything inescapable in any given life, a life potentially perceivable as a unity, a fate. In particular, truth is the bruising hardness we and the world bring to one another, but this is not the whole truth; for ultimately truth—or such is the devout hope—is the same as glory: the apprehension that fate is, or can be, spectacular, a noble splendor. Truth is redeemed in glory, or glory is the lenity of truth, evidence that our existence is justifiable, that we can turn back cosmic "contumely."

For a writer, glory has, as well, a special meaning—that of making oneself worthy of regard through acts of creation. And primarily, of course, worthy of human regard. But not solely of that: in sacral creativity something more vast and indefinite—say, the heavens—seems to deserve, if not expect, a human effort at a self-exalting. "To write something that will be worthy of that rising moon, that pale light. To be 'simple' enough, as one would be simple before God"—so Katherine Mansfield put it in her *Journal*. Writing, Kafka said, is a form of prayer, and all Warren's questing poetry (not all his poetry has been questing) is prayer: his way of attempting to scour himself into truth and charity, become self-lightened, raised up.

If tragedy is (as the young Georg Lukács said) "a revelation of God before the face of God," then prayerful creation, creative prayer, gravitates toward the tragic. Beginning as one certain of the "unuprootable ferocity of self," Warren must have known as well as anyone the terror of Ibsen's question, "But can he who has been seen by God continue to live?" Yet, American in this, or perhaps simply human, he has held out for the possibility of an earthly human redemption. He has not explained the violent contradiction; he has only borne it. "Truth's glare-glory"—nowadays who but Warren would wrestle this difficult, awkward concept onto the page, offering it as a frightening promise to those who, though without any understanding of God, would yet be blessed?

This poet whose mature love of the physical world is second to none, whose art is almost religiously intent on mimesis, who seldom doubts the truth-grasping capabilities of words, makes you feel that, if he only could, he would take on himself all desire, devour all experience, all action, all beauty, all magnificence. And not only out of love, but because to incorporate all would be to survive all, be magnified beyond all dying. So he would convert fate into power, truth into the everlasting name of glory (glory for him not being quite "that bright tragic thing" it was for Emily Dickinson):

> Question: What can you do with stars, or glory?
>   I'll tell you, I'll tell you—thereof
>   Eat. Swallow. Absorb. Let bone

Be sustained thereof, let gristle
Toughen, flesh be more preciously
Gratified, muscle yearn in
Its strength. Let brain glow
In its own midnight of darkness,
Under its own inverted, bowl-shaped
Sky, skull-sky, let the heart
Rejoice.
                    What other need now
Is possible to you but that
Of seeing life as glory?

Not the least prodigious aspect of his passion is its almost ghoulish feeding on the passions of others. Passion always wants more of itself, wants itself seconded everywhere. Maybe no poet since Dickinson has looked on others with such "narrow, probing eyes," but whereas she weighed their grief, he almost grieves "To know what postulate of joy men have tried / To live by, in sunlight and moonlight, until they died." The reverse side of his Audubon-like self-sufficiency (a caricaturist might show him swinging off alone toward the craggiest wilderness with a rifle-sized pen on his shoulder) is this emotional cannibalism, this headlong and primal inquisitiveness (especially naked in his poems about his son). When he says, "You / Must eat the dead . . . bone, blood, flesh, gristle, even / Such hair as can be forced . . . Immortality is not impossible, / Even joy," he deliberately makes an ogre of himself, would make one of you.

To poets the vexing question always, and all the more so in a scoffing age, is how to reconcile truth and glory in the line. Truth wants to sink, glory to rise. The one dulls, the other dazzles. What must be created is a credible, self-qualifying mixture, a self-validating continuity. Until *Audubon*, Warren's taste was for the overglorious, the highfalutin. "We may endeavor definition," "the bosom's nocturnal disquiet," "the fanged commotion rude," "an unreviving benison"—Warren could make you want to reach for Whitman, or any writer of rude invigorating slang (for the truth, of course, can quicken as well as drag one down). The unsettling, occasional swings into bitter or rub-it-in forthrightness only betrayed his justified anxiety about his style and added commotion rude (the title "Go it, Granny—Go it, Hog!" was the nadir).

Warren was schooled in, and virtually parodied, the precious rhetoric that an injured but high sensibility applies to itself as a balm. Youth in particular is drawn to this mode, once it tastes the idea of mortality (without yet suffering any of its poison). Dreamily piecing together a quilt of terms and rhythms from Marvell, Yeats, T. S. Eliot, Auden, Ransom and others, the young, and later not so young, Warren pulled it up over his jutting country-boy knees, presenting himself as an invalid of virtue, a casualty of the collapse of the sublime. He had yet to see that a certain rawboned vigor (both of attitude and word) was to be his salvation. His gathering "rage of joy" was, in any case, scarcely credible in the staled gestures of yesterday; only yesterday is ever credible in them. What we want from new poets is a voice exact to the time. Today, Thursday, the sun rises and somehow the right things remain to be said; the sun rises and the net of language dries on the dock . . .

After a long partial failure, Warren learned to speak from the unmistakable authority of his own native testings of words. Probably what he found hardest to leave behind was Eliot's alienly impersonal, alienly fastidious, all but ritual model. He was inclined to defer to Eliot's cutting condemnation of man; but his own disposition was more expansive and generous, and Eliot's example chafed. "At the hour when the ways are darkened"—this sort of mincing elegance sat uncomfortably and paled beside the lyric grandeur of "The salmon heaves at the fall, and, wanderer, you / Heave at the great fall of Time, and gorgeous, gleam / In the powerful arc." Warren's sweat-soured novels displayed with seamy convincingness a moral acuity that his verse, when posturingly superior, took too much for granted and, when sublime, displaced with wonder. Because he was really much happier than Eliot ever was to be a "creature of this world" (he could even speak of "the deep delight" and "nobility" of the flesh), his true manner had to be earthier than his mentor's—more prosaic, more eager. It was in *Audubon* that, suddenly, and as if by grace of identifying with his buckskinned subject, he developed a straight-out voice, with a grand yet honest range of tones.

Others have singled out *Incarnations: Poems 1966–1968* as marking the significant change, several finding the book, for reasons insufficiently specified, "transitional";* still others look even further back, James R. Justus (for instance) naming *Promises: Poems 1954–1956* "his greatest single volume of poems." What I would argue is this: in all the earlier volumes, without exception, the calibration of the style is repeatedly off, now too golden throated, now too gritty. A line, even a whole stanza, might dazzle, or simply serve, but in any given poem something (and often a great deal) will be amiss. The manner rarely sits well with the subjects because it is too much a manner, with too much aspiration or too much ego. The correspondence of the term to its import isn't "absolute," to echo Pater, or even decent: it is usually a little condescending. Both the pretentiousness and the bitter high spirits confess and complain that there is really not enough sublimity to go around.

Looking back at the warm reviews of *Promises* (especially those of Leonard Casper, James Wright, and James Dickey), one wants to cry out: "Wait! *Audubon* and *Or Else* and *Can I See Arcturus from Where I Stand?* will be much more deserving of exactly the same praise." I think, for example, of Dickey's claim that "Warren's best poems . . . give us . . . the sense of the thing done right." And yet Dickey's description of the "obvious imperfections and near sublimity" of "the massive, slow-moving, and leonine writing" of "To a Little Girl, One Year Old, in a Ruined Fortress" makes one reflect that to write in a "leonine" fashion about a little girl, even one situated in a ruined fortress, even one's dearly beloved own, is to wrap a lion's skin around a toddler: the sense of propriety is out of whack. "Near sublimity" is

---

*   Harold Bloom, reviewing *Selected Poems: 1923–1975* in *The New Republic* (November 20, 1976, p. 30), declares that "Warren's greatness has been palpable at least since his three previous books, *Incarnations, Audubon* and *Or Else.*" And J. D. McClatchy, reviewing the same volume in *Poetry* 131 (December 1977): 169–175, and dubbing *Audubon* "one of the best long poems ever written by an American," honors *Incarnations* as "transitional," finding in it "the bold intellectual and sensuous command that has marked his poetry since that time."

here so shaky a proposition that "obvious imperfections" are the inevitable price. The poet's throat seems ready to burst with the burden of history, the benediction of beauty, the ache of all hearts, the filth of fate, and so on. Alliteration, assonance, and full rhyme embroider an already purple robe. (None of Warren's mature successes, by the way, is in rhyme; for this poet, rhyme is an invitation to oversing.) Of course, I am not doing "justice" to the poem; when I read James Wright on it I think, "How wonderfully he gives himself over to Warren's purposes." My point is that it is *all splendid and too much*:

> But at your laughter let the molecular dance of the stone-dark
>   glimmer like joy in the stone's dream,
> And in that moment of possibility, let *gobbo, gobbo's wife*, and
>   us, and all, take hands and sing: *redeem, redeem!*

The sensitive and critical point in Warren's poetry was and still is tone, and the chief fault has been a tendency to hysteria: the wish to escape from the limitations of what is being said, to oversay it. What we want is an intelligent, honest relation to the material; Warren's posturing puffs or curdles it, and his impulse to instruct, to inflict judgment, chokes it up. Because of the strained sublimities and the sour discursiveness, I miss what Heidegger called the purity with which the great poet "submits what he says to an ever more painstaking listening," an openness and a readiness "for the unforeseen."*

Take one more example of this failure, "Masts at Dawn," perhaps the best managed, most resounding poem in *Incarnations*. Attractive as this poem is (it contains one of the most ringing and quotable of Warren's frequent "modal" pronouncements: "We must try / To love so well the world that we may believe, in the end, in God"), it is mostly nervous; it is "talk." Thus, after the first line, "Past second cock-crow yacht masts in the harbor go slowly white," little failures begin to mount: the tendentiousness, for instance, of "the stars show

---

* Quoted by Christopher Middleton in "Ideas about Voice in Poetry," *PN Review 9*, no. 6 (1983): 15–18. In speaking of "the prattle of everyday speech" that often spills over into poetry, of "expressions linguistic but voiceless," Middleton names part of what is objectionable in Warren's early volumes.

a certain fatigue," or the spell-destroying didacticism of "They with-draw into a new distance, have discovered our unworthiness," or the merely decorative owl "in the dark eucalyptus, dire and melodious," or the after-Eliot pulling-up of "Long since the moon sank and the English / Finished fornicating in their ketches." And so on, till one is grateful, despite and in part because of the rude, vigorous inversion, for "Red died the sun, but at dark wind rose easterly, white sea nagged the black harbor headland." (But "Poundian," one may think.) The sea, the poet will later say, "doubts its own mission," but so does the poet, whose writing hand is shaky. Even here, in this poem of gorgeous description and mood, he is a little anxious to project both a moral and a philosophical authority. He all but looms over his subject, as if to keep from being intimidated by it ("You must learn to accept the kiss of fate").*

But suddenly, in *Audubon*, you hear, in Dave Smith's fine phrase, "the human need to prevail by witness," indeed by "celebration." The language, as Smith adds, becomes "what it had been in fits and starts, a voice-instrument calibrated to final experience."† The tone lets itself go out to adventure like the seeding cottonwood. His pride relenting, his heart submitting, Warren here writes lines that are experience-honoring, experience-blessed. Your eye has but to alight on

---

*   The habit of too hastily taking charge may be traced back to Warren's poetic school-ing. In his overgenerous but (characteristically) highly intelligent review of Warren's *Thirty-Six Poems* (*Poetry* 48 [April 1936]:37–41), Morton Zabel praised Warren for "growing beyond . . . the formidable influences" that supervised "his studious youthful efforts." "To belong to the Fugitives was one of the best fortunes that could befall, in America at that mo-ment, any young poet interested in craft and its uses. But schools of style offer as much risk as benefit; a premature forcing of the intellectual manner, while essentially more profitable than the flaccid impressionism encouraged among most beginners, can breed as deluding and pre-tentious an ambition in a poet as the visionary arrogance or lyric softness which it aims to correct." Zabel goes on to convict Warren of refracting pathos through "elaborate preco-sity"; of the "strenuous effort" to make phrases "encompass more than their context allows"; of "forcing a poetic theme with too many stimulants"—in short, of a fussily intellectual man-ner, "elaborate subterfuges and disguises."

†   "He Prayeth Best Who Loveth Best," *American Poetry Review* 8 (January/February 1979): 4–7. Smith further remarks, I think with perfect rightness, that "we have no poet truer to a comprehensive, sustained evocation of the nature of existence."

> Dawn: his heart shook in the tension of the world.

> Dawn: and what is your passion?

to feel the thrill of a direct and deep vitality. The colons themselves seem aquiver, marks of confrontation and expectation, two fingers taking a pulse.

Warren has a romantic and heroic idea of Audubon that exalts and chastens his own way of seeing and writing. Even as he all but alters Audubon out of recognition (sweetening and deepening him, and tightening him like a bow), so he is simplified and tautened in turn, in a reciprocal refashioning. Something of frontier sturdiness, of frontier plainness, independence, curiosity, and a love of living on the edge, comes into his poetry to stay. "He embodies one of the deepest American traits, the courage to plunge into the unknown . . . seeking the new"—these words, a mere ironic tink in Warren's novel *The Cave* (1959), resound when his recent poems are made the clapper. With *Audubon* he became heroic and large-scaled without straining, without wondering how he dared. Simply, he set out to repioneer the sort of "love knowledge" he associated with Audubon and the wilderness, its pristine invitations, its diverse creatures and intimate interiors. Philosophically, too, he has put on seven-league boots; has "starward . . . stared / To the unnamed void where Space and God / Flinch to come."

Warren began to confront the great undomestic things—time, nature, truth, fate, glory, the "all"—in a way that made his earlier relation to them seem like viewing a distant river; now he was in the river. His words entered experience, or appeared to, fully and tragically and happily, impatient of defenses and eager for unambiguous truth (however rashly eager). No longer anxious to exude authority, Warren gained it at once, held it by the good faith of his relation to, his demands on, experience. His voice became as flecked as a forest floor with inimitable personal lights, his idiosyncrasies almost as marked as before, but more fragrant, more assuredly his, tried now and true, knowing their purpose. There was nothing dressy in the manner now, nothing wild, temperamental, and skittish; it was broken in, like a good mount, and fit for travel.

If before *Audubon* Warren seemed incapable of writing a master-piece, he has since to write anything to equal it. Indeed, he has contin-ued to publish some jarringly bad poems, if with a different badness than before, an aping of his worst fears about the draining of life into memory, banal or nightmarish Truth, and the like. Portentousness and pretentiousness still abound. But he has written several superb poems as well, poems that anyone ought to revere, and numerous poems with a tone so passionately and gravely serious, a manner so plunging and plangent, that the poetry is like the rumor of a still un-seen waterfall: poetry whose strength feels elemental, makes you at-tend, whatever its chance limitations.

In part what became established with *Audubon* was a deeper and firmer respect for realistic circumstance, event as the print of fate.* "I would . . . start with the world," Warren said in an interview: this, rather than descend to it with a rescuing gospel, or any stoop of tender idealism. To the question "What has been denied me?" the "question is the only answer," and the world itself is the question.

* The prominence and importance of narrative in Warren's recent poetry have been stressed by a number of critics, including the present writer ("Greatness and Robert Penn Warren," *Sewanee Review* 89 [Summer 1981]: 332–346). Cleanth Brooks addresses the mat-ter in "Episode and Anecdote in the Poetry of Robert Penn Warren" (*Yale Review* 70 [Sum-mer 1981]: 551–567); James R. Justus stresses it in *The Achievement of Robert Penn Warren* (Baton Rouge: Louisiana State University Press, 1981). Back in 1969, George Core, in his essay "In the Heart's Ambiguity: Robert Penn Warren as Poet" (*Mississippi Quarterly* 22 [Fall 1969]: 313–326), aptly applied to Warren's own poetry the following words from Warren's essay "Melville's Poems": "The lyric mood, or unmoored emotion, or abstraction, was not for him; his feelings responded to, and his imagination took fire from the collisions and ten-sions of experience as life offered specific, realistic images of them." In fact, as the date even of Core's piece begins to suggest, Warren has long been praised for his "realistic" textures. In "Robert Penn Warren: The Drama of the Past," a review of *Selected Poems: 1923–1966* (*New Republic*, November 26, 1966, pp. 16–18) John Wain was already finding that "Mr. War-ren's gift, in poetry, is mainly autobiographical and descriptive . . . his craft shows to best ad-vantage when he is bringing a scene before our eyes with sure, deft touches of detail. And the scenes he paints best of all are from memory"—words, however, a good deal truer of War-ren's subsequent poems. Still earlier, M. L. Rosenthal, in "Robert Penn Warren's Poetry" (*South Atlantic Quarterly* 62 [Autumn 1963]: 499–507), concluded that "a dramatic or narra-tive structure is almost always necessary to enable Mr. Warren to realize his poem . . . It is in the concrete evocation of scene and atmosphere that Mr. Warren excels."

That the world provides not only the black-toothed horizon for heroism, the space and the time in which the thaw-stream can heave "In the deep certainty of its joy, like / Doom," but sudden joys of connection as well, is justification enough. Warren's gulls, hawks, eagles, and buzzards rise and take to themselves the offered light.

As he had in "Masts at Dawn," so Warren would again and again consecrate perception in a sense of mortal finality. His poetry bears the spikes of the here and now, of fate, in its hands and feet. To the tragic mind, circumstance is sanctified merely by taking place, as if under necessity. How blasphemous its absence would be. The premise that limitation, or pain, is the basis of happiness is "the appalling logic of joy." The wound of "Time's irremediable joy" has become Warren's most lyric subject. The circumstantial and forgetful imagination of time itself is his harsh, irreplaceable muse.*

Warren's sensibility flames at moments to a bluey ethereality ("Platonic"), then subsides, grows red or golden, moted, storied. Usually it is the opposite of bleached, static, beached, Platonic. This poet lives, "Man lives," by images that "Lean at us from the world's wall, and Time's." For him, nothing redeems life so much as a heroic appreciation of it. Earlier he had noted (I quote from *Brother to Dragons*) how we need to

> lift our eyes up
> To whatever liberating perspective,
> Icy and pure, the wild heart may horizonward command,
> . . . the glimmering night scene under
> The incalculable starlight serves
> As an image of lethal purity—
> Infatuate glitter of a land of Platonic ice.

* M. M. Bakhtin notes in "Epic and Novel" (*The Dialogic Imagination: Four Essays by M. M. Bakhtin*, ed. Michael Holquist, tr. Caryl Emerson and Michael Holquist [Austin: University of Texas Press, 1981], p. 7): "In the process of becoming the dominant genre, the novel sparks the renovation of all other genres, it infects them with its spirit of process and inconclusiveness." In poetry the result—as in *The Waste Land* and many of Warren's poems—is "a novelized poem." Speaking of his own work, Warren says: "There's been some kind of cross-fertilization. And more and more since I quit writing stories. Even in poems as old as those in *Promises*, the germ is mostly anecdotal." See *Robert Penn Warren Talking: Interviews 1950–1978*, ed. Floyd C. Watkins and John T. Hiers (New York: Random House, 1980), p. 16.

But better to be an infatuate (so the later, tragic Warren implies) of the sun-touched earth itself: "Tell me a story . . . The name of the story will be Time."

If the earlier Warren thought this too (he thought many things, contrariwise), he lacked muscled conviction; his celebrations trembled in his throat. Even where incident is vivid, as in "The Ballad of Billie Potts" and "Dark Night of the Soul," its nakedness is dressed in rhymed commentary, and a potent summation seems to be the real concern. By and large, action and scene were pretexts for hanging language, sentiment, reflection, and homiletics. Past incidents represented not the unforeseen, but the seen again; they were still unexhausted only as packets of old seed are, seed that will never be planted. An unusually beautiful and intriguing example is this stanza from "What Was the Promise that Smiled from the Maples at Evening":

> What was the promise when, after the last light had died,
> Children gravely, down walks, in spring dark, under maples, drew
> Trains of shoe boxes, empty, with windows, with candles inside,
> Going *chuck-chuck*, and blowing for crossings, lonely, *oo-oo*?
> But on impulse you fled, and they called, called across the dark lawn,
> Long calling your name, who now lay in the darkness to hide,
> While the sad little trains glimmer on under maples, and on.

This is as sealed off as it is well turned. A set piece, it is like a slide slotted into a viewer. Nothing could be more different from Warren's later, heroic mode and still be narrative. This curious episode of childhood delicately radiates disturbing suggestions, not least of the imagination's perverse abandonments of its own creations (and in the early volumes Warren's own imagination was precisely that restive); solipsism, pride, furtiveness, anarchy, and sadness characterize the gravely dreaming child. Even so, the stanza is like a wingbacked armchair; it invites only a contemplative repose. Abandoned by the next stanza as the shoebox train is by the impulsive child, it remains an isolated, melancholy little happening. Nothing ever came of it, unless it was the poet's early poetry.

In the later work, story is less an occasion for swelling language with mood, mood with music and design, than a joy of experience ("This is happening. / This is happiness") or a puzzle that may perhaps still be resolved, if only questioned hard enough, attacked with an unknotting bravery or anguish. The verse is now all passional engagement, even as it urges it: "Continue to walk in the world."* There are quick, fluid interchanges between objects and sensations, actions and thoughts. Life is viewed not as a melancholy entrapment, but as a call for the ancient *arete* ("virtue"; "courage"; a natural yet spectacular ability, in W. R. Johnson's words, "to fulfill one's special function, to exercise one's gifts and thereby become and be oneself").† Warren had been raised on stories—those told, for instance, by his grandfather of legend-provoking name, Gabriel Telemachus Penn, a cavalry captain and hangman of bushwhackers; he had caught fatal tales of courage, defeat, and glory out of the Southern auricular air. Now he began to breathe living story; he himself was the story, and fate was the even now and yet to be, more momentous than sealed.

The empowering incident need be nothing more than a narrative bloodspot—a moment fraught with temporal dynamics, instinct with a potential for discovery, even transfiguration. For example, on the one hand not much happens in "Heart of Autumn" and on the other what takes place is astonishing, a Dionysian metamorphosis. A beginning: the speaker looks with longing at wild geese flying. A middle: he reflects on the long pathlessness of human life. An end: he assumes a sublime destiny at last, his new miraculous powerful body lifting off toward sunset. It ought not to work, but so skillful is the transition, so matter of fact the transformation, so perfect and terrible a flowering

---

*   Warren might have been writing of himself when he said of David Bottoms that "he is temperamentally a realist. In his vision the actual world is not transformed but illuminated, and in his language the tang of actuality whets his compelling rhythms. Of few can this be said." Press release, Academy of American Poets, April 20, 1979.

†   W. R. Johnson, *The Idea of Lyric: Lyric Modes in Ancient and Modern Poetry* (Berkeley: University of California Press, 1982), p. 57.

of the desire for destiny, that it seems real beyond hallucination. It just is. The actual sorrow and the imaginable joy of being alive, alive to die, are sharply evoked. Nothing more could be wanted. Nor does the poem wait until the close to become an action; something is already happening at the start, where the wind escapes an article: "Wind finds the northwest gap, fall comes."*

As intimated earlier, once Warren concentrated on the "tang of actuality," once his poetry bore the stings of empirical narrative, his language grew sparer and swifter and harder. "Story" kept him from heaping on sickly grandiloquence, and it incited an enactive, line-tormented syntax. The union of the freer yet firmer manner with the drama of incident and "anguished" lineation made possible a signature of struggle, bravery, passion, and quest, and added up to the poem as a "vital image." In his best work the ready prose of life and his own strenuous passion, limiting circumstance and lyrical feeling, mingle in a live reaction. Each poem is unique with an individual, profound experience, and each is held up to our inspection like some unnamable river creature luminously trapped in a jar. When Warren knew what his earlier random loosened line had been seeking, knew how to tighten it with his metrical training, knew what his line-breaks like cracked kindling were for, he knew what *he* was for: he became a true poet.

It was long before Warren could step simply, humbly, if at the same time ambitiously out of his Fugitive cloud of glorious rhetoric. We find Leonard Casper, in a review of *Promises*, already warming to an "abandonment of anonymity," but until *Audubon* the man behind the

* By contrast, the celebrated early anthology piece "Bearded Oaks" may contain "adumbrative narrative," as James R. Justus says, but, as he adds, here "meditation replaces action": "The oaks, how subtle and marine, / Bearded, and all the layered light / Above them swims (in *Selected Poems: 1923–1943*, rpt. in *Selected Poems: 1923–1975* [New York: Random House, 1975], p. 308). This is lovely stasis and promises more of the same. Nothing dynamic disturbs the time. The language is free to be music, pattern, ritual.

Comparing this poem with the recent "Trying to Tell You Something," Stanley Plumly, in his review "Warren Selected," noted the "obvious and important difference of the abstracted passion of the one poem and the passionate inquiry of the other . . . 'Bearded Oaks' ruminates its philosophical position, while 'Trying to Tell You Something' directly dramatizes its position." See *Robert Penn Warren: A Collection of Critical Essays*, ed. Richard Gray (Englewood Cliffs: Prentice-Hall, 1980), p. 133.

poet remained hidden in a sort of verbal high-shine. His medium was so self-conscious it sealed everything off as "verse." The speaker of the poems was more a verbal organism, more an ephebe of the sublime, that what Monroe K. Spears was later to call him (in *The Sewanee Review*, Spring 1970)—a "representative man." Now more "representative" than anonymous, though more heroic "image of man" than representative, Warren had first to learn to approach himself with "curiosity and communicativeness," in Michael Hofmann's words,* before he could even begin to edge toward and benefit from the new frankness in postwar poetry. Perhaps he had also to like himself a little more, to forgive himself still more his "failures" and "folly." (His unhappy first marriage, his first wife's mental illness, may have helped impel him to an Eliotic obliqueness.)

Perhaps he had also to be persuaded that the novel would never satisfy his tragic passion for inwardness and ultimacy. Fine schooling though his fiction was for the eventual narrative tempering of his poems, solid performances that they are (in one sense all too solid), they yet delayed his creative fulfillment; they proved a hairshirt to his poetic sensibility. As the poetry is about the hunger for happiness, so the fiction is about moral failure and a grim redemption, the tone a settled drizzle of self-disapproval.† "The awful responsibility of Time," *a little more virtue* . . . the message dies of joylessness, inanition. Nor is

---

*   In *PN Review* 9, no. 6 (1983): 57–59, Hofmann speaks of Warren as approaching himself thus in *Rumor Verified* and adds that he is nonetheless "as far removed from self-pity as it is possible to be."

Hofmann associates Warren with Berryman and Lowell admiringly: "When Berryman published *His Toy, His Dream, His Rest* on his fifty-fourth birthday, Lowell wrote to him, 'What I like is your ease in getting out everything—I mean everything in your experience, thought, personality etc. mills thru the poetry. I think age helps; but most poets are dwindled by age. Like you I want to go out walking.' Robert Penn Warren, older by a decade than Berryman and Lowell, is still getting out everything, is still walking."

Exceptions like Hofmann apart, it would still seem true that "Robert Penn Warren's reputation . . . has never really penetrated to England," though it was an applauding Englishman, John Wain, who said it.

†   Some of Warren's protagonists are mean-proud, smarting, and ungenerous, and strangle the poet in him. As early as 1944 (*Saturday Review*, May 20, 5 pp. 10–11), John Crowe Ransom complained of this, concluding, "I wish we had a way of holding this poet, whose verse is so beautiful when it is at his own height of expression, to a level no lower than this height."

there any genius of conception or attack. A Faulkner pitches us toward his "subject" with a tricky imaginative arm and the meaning, at least the poetry, is the alarmed getting-there; a Eudora Welty, a Flannery O'Connor, a James Agee transports us hardly less bewitchingly. But on much the same country road Warren offers mostly a prosaic, foot-on-the-bumper presentation. Despite occasional virtuoso passages of description (in *All The King's Men* particularly), there is no thrill of passage.*

The aim of the film director in Warren's novel *Flood* (1964) is "to give the impression of the mysterious inwardness of life, not the obvious plottiness"; but though the fiction of other writers may have realized this goal (in *The New York Times Book Review*, March 2, 1980, Warren notes in Welty the "something" that "on occasion seems to take the place of plot, a flow of feeling"), Warren's own novels, save for the Lawrentian sexual romance *Meet Me in the Green Glen* (1971), seem too disgruntled to attempt it. An inwardness of which event and circumstance, character and speech, form the living organs eluded him—became the missing all. Fiction in his hands remained a relative thing, he wanted the lyrical and the absolute. He wanted himself: "There's a lot of things you don't notice in town," Lucille Christian remarks in Warren's first novel, *Night Rider* (1939), ". . . yourself, for instance. . . . when I was in St. Louis . . . I did things, and I never knew why." It was this not knowing that seemed to drive Warren out of the city of the novel into the country of poetry,† which he entered as a postlapsarian Adam who, though he had eaten of the apple, sought, all the same, an earthly peace.

Whereas Warren's novels pass the hat of joy among unlikely crowds, his poetry is sometimes the spruce-fragrant promise of what

---

*   The novels are, of course, distinguished in their several ways and degrees. But in a strict reckoning they fail of greatness. F. R. Leavis stated the proper criteria justly if clumsily: "The major novelists [are those] who count . . . in the sense that they not only change the possibilities of the art for practitioners and readers, but they are significant in terms of the human awareness they promote; awareness of the possibilities of life" (*The Great Tradition* [Garden City: Doubleday, 1954], p. 10).

†   Significantly, *Meet Me in the Green Glen*, his first novel after *Audubon*, is set in an isolated rural home, till city forces send the hero to the deathchair, the heroine to an asylum.

Rousseau and Wordsworth called the sentiment of being (if in War-
ren usually an invalidated promise). In the poems, the real begins
where the last concrete walk gives out and the smart-weed crawls in
the cracks ("The Mad Druggist"). Soul-stillness increases with each
step away from the human clot, the human swarm. Tramps (the one
in the story "Blackberry Winter" and those in the poems "Dark
Night of the Soul" and "Convergences")—ornery, lone-wolf tramps—
know best. To move "past contumely of stars or insolent indifference
of the dark air," to achieve *that* distance from the human, would be
"awfulness of joy." Or so bitterness prompts. Better yet, because still
worlded, would be to breathe "with the rhythm of the stars." Nature
at least is grand and open, not clenched upon the hollow of itself like a
man making his way among men. So it was that Warren, solitary on
vertiginous cliffs of verse, began to assume postures of tragic expostu-
lation and prayer.

His costly impulse to write fiction nearly exhausted, his self-esteem
improving, and the internal history of modern poetry working to pry
him loose from verse habits that were bad for him (frigid impersonal-
ity, judgmental writing, smart irony, royal phrasing, rhyme), Warren
was at last ready to take up his own life, or something like it, with the
inwardness that (as he noted in *The New York Times Book Review*, Au-
gust 23, 1953) "is the central fact of poetry." Inwardness meant "the
heart," to him an unembarrassing, essential phrase. It meant becom-
ing transparent to the beautiful hieroglyphs surrounding and entan-
gling us at each moment (just to watch a leaf fall, suggested the film
director, ought to be enough). It meant a constant delicate and strenu-
ous appraisal of the adequacy of existence for "total reverence."

Selected Poems: 1923–1975 (since followed by *Now and Then, Being
Here, Rumor Verified,* and *Chief Joseph of the Nez Perce*) forms an implic-
it story of a writer's growth into existential humility, bravery, awe.
How remarkable it is that a poet already much lauded at sixty should
nonetheless have set out to become an even stronger and truer poet,
almost as if he thought he had still to write a single worthy line. Soon
he would be seventy. His passion for greatness grew. Yes, seventy! His
courage doubled. Then he was seventy and the first masterpieces had
come.

Beginning with *Audubon*, Warren put to his talent hard new de-
mands of the sort that alone makes greatness possible. And how
much, once it was written, his poetry appeared needed. For who else
could match his capacity for loving the world and enduring the brunt
of experience, his virile awareness of limits and his "rage" (a favorite
and even overworked word) to know them in joy? He might almost
have perceived a tremendous gap in American poetry and set out to
fill it, so happily did his work meet our deficiencies. Robert Lowell
was then the reigning American poet, our exemplary nihilist, a focus
even so for our hero worship, the nihilist as hero. Then John Ashbery
ambled along with his ironically smiling indifferent grace. Dizzying
possibility: Was this the new Poet? No sooner had many begun to
think so (for to most, Warren's witching transformation was still in
the shadows) than James Merrill sprang on us his trilogy, huge section
by section, as if opening to a jaded public the doors of a laboratory
still smoking and blinking with magnesium glare after an extravagant
experiment. But greatly as one admired these poets, something was
yet missing. Of poetry Lowell made a revelation of nonbeing, Merrill
of higher realms, Ashbery of the mystery still possible to language;
but where was the poetry of earthly existence itself? Who mirrored
with passion the world's body? Where was the poet as weighty as
these others but their coarse and necessary complement, the poet
writing with brains, bones, heart, sex and courting in the American
landscape original moments of being? Philip Levine, then Louise
Glück, then Carolyn Forché would prove as pained and passionate,
Ashbery at once as prosaic and extravagant, A. R. Ammons as lucidly
grand and impersonal; but none has rivaled Warren's broad normality
and balance, his nerve for both necessity and largeness.

So Warren is, if not the Poet,* a poet of whom we have need. He
has been candid about the terror in his heart, but jubilation has

---

* Yet Stanley Plumly said of Warren (in his review "Warren Selected") that, despite
"terrifically bad lines," he has become, "in the sum, poem by selected poem," "our great
poet" (*Robert Penn Warren: A Collection of Critical Essays*, ed. Richard Gray [Englewood
Cliffs: Prentice-Hall, 1980], p. 133). And Harold Bloom, also in a review of *Selected Poems:
1923–1975*, remarked: "Our nation, necessarily slow to recognize its own sublimities, again
has a living poet comparable in power to Stevens or to Frost" (*New Republic*, November 20,
1976, p. 30).

coursed in his limbs. He takes us back to Yeats and Synge and "all that heightens the emotions by contrast, all that stings into life the sense of tragedy." With his great question concerning the adequacy of existence for the total reverence of the heart, he has made determined casts into memory, the slipstream of the now, dream, the heart, Truth, to find whatever joy, fate, blessedness, or nightmare awaits him. His fears have been great, but his capacity for admitting and confronting them has been quickening, and his yearning has never abated. Here is a poet who has found the right relation (right for him and in general seemingly right) between struggle and submission, glory and truth, nobility and self-knowledge, joy and pain, quest and common sense, art and experience: a relation of strong and poignant accord. There are other ways to be a writer of rank, but for Warren perhaps only the one. His hardihood before the truth, his moral and aesthetic respect for realistic narrative, his happy discovery of Audubon, his hunger for beauty and glory—all combined to propose greatness; and as he became older he had more reason than ever to honor his love of existence and more need to make his art its salvation. The way was opened. He continues along it.

T W O

*His
Mature
Manner*

The inwardness "central" to poetry is imperious. Nothing is allowed to remain outside it, as waste motion, dead matter. The form seizes hold of everything, but from within, in the name of a kind of feeling intelligence: an intelligence that lives in form, and only in form.

Even Warren's most sensitive prose, that of *Meet Me in the Green Glen,* lacks it, merely has it on the tip of its tongue:

> But that secret world of no-Time, which had seemed to be safely boxed inside the walls of the house, and which he entered only at night when he set hand to the knob of the kitchen door—that world had begun to bleed out into the outside world. It spread slowly outward from the kitchen door, as though the fluid seeped under the door all night. It spread out like a stain, on the grass. When, in the morning, he opened the door to go out, it followed him like thin smoke. It spread around him. You could see through it so easily you did not at first realize it was there. But things seen through it looked different. They would curl and waver, like paper being burned by a flame invisible because of the brightness of the sunshine.

"Poetic" as is the conception of the ethereal and treacherous spread of "no-Time," it cannot of itself make the language inward. Much of the passage remains matte. Its genius is not verbal. The words do quite well, but other words might do even better. That is not what you feel of, say, "October: and the bear, / Daft in the honey-light, yawns." Here everything is irreplaceable, including the line-break and the punctuation. The words are more than right; you feel that they could have found their way to where they are through aeons of interference and distraction. They have arrived, they know it, and they are happy.

The general point may be clarified by a direct comparison of two passages, one in prose, the other in poetry, which deal with like material. The first is from Warren's novel *The Cave:*

> And they came streaking over the cold, buttermilk-blue and saffron sky, which was the inside of his enormous head, moiling in the sky, streaking down with the nervous twitch of wing, necks out, necks out in longing—yearning like lost hearts—streaking in, plunging toward the unwavered water, which was the color of sky, waiting for the boom of the .12 gauge.

The other is the opening stanza of "Heart of Autumn":

> Wind finds the northwest gap, fall comes.
> Today, under gray cloud-scud and over gray
> Wind-flicker of forest, in perfect formation, wild geese
> Head for a land of warm water, the *boom*, the lead pellet.

The first passage certainly affects to be psychologically inward, even reelingly so; its maudlin moiling quality is in character for the banker Mr. Bingham. Neck out, the prose moves in a gangly, unguarded fashion. But as an expressive maneuver this feels slack. It amounts to gestural, not intelligent, form. We find verbosity, not delicacy; a crowded looseness facilitated by the present participle. Nothing quite works: "streaking" is overvivid, "buttermilk-blue" overpacked, "saffron" literary, "nervous twitch" strained, "unwavered" dull yet unnatural, and "waiting for the boom of the .12 gauge" melodramatic even for a pathetic fallacy.

By contrast, the quatrain is balanced between its own and an imaged vitality.* It takes thought as to its form and so gains not a van-

---

* If I had to say what I would try to hunt for in a poem . . . it would be some kind of a vital image, a vital and evaluating image, of vitality. That's a different thing from the vitality you observe or experience. It's an image of it, but it has the vital quality—it's a reflection of

ity of structure, but an austere, impersonal beauty. It displays a formal remorselessness toward its content even as it graces data with design. Think of "necks out in longing—yearning like lost hearts" trying to survive in its creative furnace. Of course, language has the advantage, here, of being not in or around the self-pitying head of Mr. Bingham but in (as it were) the mind of the world. The inwardness is of that thrill-cold kind.

It begins with the brisk omission of the definite article before "Wind." It continues with the subdued animism of "finds." The end of "Heart of Autumn," with its ecstatically freed energy, is already stirring in this tense and terse beginning, this hint of pent-up force raging to disperse itself. The butting emphases of "Wind finds" are repeated at the end of the line in "fall comes." All obstacles must give way, finitude be broken: the season, the writing, will have it so. Everything seems caught up in the same desire for self-abandonment. The gray wind-flicker of forest repeats in longing the gray cloud-scud. The verse answers this gusting symmetry with its own, as in the re-echoing accents already noted; the formation of frictional *f*'s in "flicker," "forest," "perfect," and "formation," and of the "-er" in "under . . . over . . . flicker . . . perfect . . . water"; and still other patterns, including the familiar, satisfyingly four-fold quatrain.

If such V's of sound, such honkings back and forth, are expectable in verse, it is an analogical and dramatic, an inward imagination that makes them "perfect," arrowing them toward a common destination. The syntax, too, is instinct with desire, the syntax that, with the long interruptive clause beginning with "under," makes you feel the great distance still to be traversed; it sighs with delay, is "gray . . . gray." But placed where it is, and with its almost comic literalness, its hint of a piercing stubbornness, "Head" reinvigorates the syntax—and at last the way to the longed-for "land of warm water, the *boom*, the lead pellet" feels assured.

Freud might have been commenting on the delicately envious description of the destination when he said, "One group of instincts

---

that vital quality, . . . but it has its own kind of assurance, own kind of life, by the way it's built." *Robert Penn Warren Talking: Interviews 1950–1978*, ed. Floyd C. Watkins and John T. Hiers (New York: Random House, 1980), p. 16.

presses forward to reach the final goal of life as quickly as possible." He added that another group "flies back at a certain point on the way only to traverse the same stretch once more from a given spot and thus to prolong the duration of the journey"; and of course the poet might have entertained this latter meaning, instead, had autumn not been so deep in his heart.* But he himself is full of a scudding desire for the final goal. His yearning it is that speeds the geese toward the absolvingly and dissolvingly inanimate. The phrase "warm water" even sounds maternally warm and watery. The series of *a*'s in "a land of warm water" combines with the *w*'s and nasals to hint of a sweet and intimate landing place, a welcoming home.

Pitilessly destined, to be sure, is "the *boom*, the lead pellet." Yet this is indicated with a suspicious matter-of-factness. The humorless dull concreteness of specification places us in the uncomprehending wild-goose mind (so, then, the poet is *there*). First the boom, then (with no causal inference) the lead pellet. It is, so to say, written; it will be. There is a logic to it, as to the season. But it is the logic of the autumnal heart. Understanding is something else, neither sought for nor provided.

Heavy and self-affirming in sound, "lead pellet" hints of sharp pain and a rude end to flight. Perhaps something in the poet still resists extinction; perhaps the joy of dying is as yet no more than an exciting rumor. But by the end of the poem this excitement will turn to ecstasy as the "I" lifts itself to the last word, "height," with the strokes of several long *i*'s. The stupid literalness of "the *boom*, the lead pellet" is a transitional characterization, one subtler by far than anything in the prose presentation of Mr. Bingham.

From the first already-fled article to the dying fall of "pellet," this autumnally heavy quatrain, with its traveling, gradually lengthening lines, is as inward as narrative writing can be. Here, to use Pater's words, "it is impossible to distinguish the form from the substance or matter, the subject from the expression." We find the "absolute corre-

---

* Throughout this book, when referring to the speaker of a poem as "the poet" I mean simply that the speaker speaks as a poet, that he speaks as poets do, that he speaks as Warren does when Warren speaks as a poet—and not that Warren is necessarily being autobiographical.

spondence of the term to its import" that Pater hailed as the hallmark of "good art." So defined, good art is synonymous with inward art, "inward" implying an exact fit, an inspired and unique subtlety of precision.

"People nowadays imagine that art is like a fountain, whereas it is a sponge. They think art has to flow forth, whereas what it has to do is absorb and become saturated. They suppose it can be divided up into means of depiction, whereas it is made up of the organs of perception."

—Boris Pasternak

I bring back "Bearded Oaks" to ask: Is it inward? Here is the concluding quatrain:

> We live in time so little time
> And we learn all so painfully,
> That we may spare this hour's term
> To practice for eternity.

To ask if this is inward entails asking if it is sincere. Its logic seems askew: if we live in time so little time, can we spare any part of it? If in time "we learn all so painfully," should not our being eternal be put off till (easy) eternity? Not genuine, the stanza is only imitated inwardness—the model, of course, Marvell. You could say to the author, how can you get to inwardness over so outer, so historical, a model/obstacle? Inwardness has to be the start.

Reading the early Warren is like visiting the ranch of a poet-rustler, whose roaming herd keeps flaunting, now on this flank, now on that, his neighbors' brands. His own voice may have been already equally in evidence: the interruptions already marked; the use of "you," sleeve-nabbing and needling; the directives bullying ("Go to the clinic. Wait in the outer room"); the compounds tormented ("sun-torment of whitecaps"); space or time unraveling in the lines ("Or it goes to the backyard and stands like an old horse cold in the pasture"). Yet, derivativeness aside, inwardness was still hampered. Rhyme led the lines by the nose; it fussed. There was too much prissy prattle, as in the lines telling of "The hunchback on the corner," who "Has his own wisdom and pleasures, and may not be lured / To divulge them to you." And behind both rhyme and palaver lay a desire to impose the manner on the matter: if life itself was not sublime, words would have to compensate, be superior.

There was strength, but it tried too hard. Heroism and anguish both postured. Even in the impressive

> All day there was picnic and laughter,
>   Bright eye and hair tossing, white foam and thigh-flash,
> And up from some cold coign and dark lair of water,
>   Ectoplasmic, snot-gray, the obscene of the life-wish,
> Sad tentacles weaving like prayer, eyes wide to glare-horror of
>   day-wash,
> The nightmare was spread out on stone. Boys yelled at the
>   knife-flash

—even here the touches ("the obscene of") lunge and grind; a panting, wide-eyed, primal Anglo-Saxon quality startles the verse. The poems and volumes are heavy; one longs for more subtlety, paring, and purity. (One wants this of all the volumes except *Audubon* and *Chief Joseph of the Nez Perce*, but in the recent work less often and less desperately.)

Warren's temperament required strenuousness; he had only to avoid the overstrenuous. His manner would not become mature, or inward, until he listened harder. He had first to reject not only rhyme but the trivializing idea of the poem as a longish decorative bead-chain of identically carved stanzas. He had to treat torment as less than a lyric absolute. And he had to be less importantly melancholy about the wisdom he could not attain.

At length, a small range of intense but unexcessive tones and styles emerged, a variable and credible verse agon. He was still not good at performing anguish: except for the den of frail characters in *Brother to Dragons*, he never could do "nerves" convincingly. What he called "lip-biting, and spasm," existed too much in its own right, as an act. Courage and ecstasy were his bone-truths, his crests. (The latter required something of the former; the former itself tensed into joy of a heroic kind.)

One of the first inwardly strenuous passages occurred at the close of *Tale of Time* (1966):

> Suddenly. Is. Now not what was *not*.
> But what is. From nothing of *not*
> Now all of *is*. All is. Is light, and suddenly
> Dawn—and the world, in blaze of *is*,
> Burns. Is flame, of time and tense
> The bold combustion, and
> The flame of *is*, in fury
> And ungainsayable updraft of that
> Black chimney of what is *not*,
> Roars . . .

Faulkner's influence flashes here; the simply worded but strenuous brainwork is akin to wise-mad Darl Bundren's. But now the syntax is fully concentrated, is doing the lion's share; both syntax and diction are disciplined by their consecration to a mighty (a would-be-precise) description—one, again, involving intense cerebration.

All that *is*, says the passage, is self-assertive but doomed: it flames forth from nothing, but in a form already reverting to it. (To *be* is the positive of nothingness.) This stirring, Faulknerian-naif concept, which will survive as Warren's radical sense of world violence, commands from point to point a direct and abrupt attack of language. The style at first says "suddenly," then in the longer sentence "ungainsayable," and throughout "bold combustion," "updraft," "fury": it seeks to match the subject in pure momentousness, to be equal to, brave enough for, tragic but glorious transiency. (The sharply cracked sticks of grammar and lineation recall those of another poem on Dionysian, holocaustal renewal, William Carlos Williams' "Burning the Christmas Greens.") But I shall put by the temptation to examine the lines in detail. The point I would make is a general one: compared even to the words on the octopus and knife-flash, this writing is serious. What it says *means* something to it. It is less self-display than strict incarnation; less mood than intelligent feeling, felt thought.

"What makes one heroic?" asked Nietzsche, and answered: "Going out to meet at the same time one's highest suffering and one's highest hope." In the metaphysical furnace opened by "Suddenly. Is," Warren had no choice, short of hysteria, but to be heroic. His mature verse is clear-eyed, fateful, and ecstatic.

Not that the going is smooth. Often he is both curt and copious, both checked and current-strong, like a stream torn by snags. The style is violent—violence being, in Heidegger's words, "the use of power . . . against the overpowering." So we find (1) lines sprung beyond the poise and breath-measure of pentameter: "From behind a beech deadfall, the doe, it had leaped, / Cow awkward on earth, but magically airy in flight, / And weightless as wind, forelegs airward prowing"—lines in which the style races the subject; (2) the gasp-for-breath catch-up of a pronoun: "The flashlight, / It slipped"; (3) various forms of ellipsis, suggesting hypnotic fixation ("Stared long"), shortness of breath ("But / Cannot, breath short"), or scattered wits ("One moment, / Bewildered"); (4) compounds groaningly crowding perception with feeling: "the *groan-swish* of magma"; (5) frequent cocking of syntax, which gives explosive force to the clause-resuming word: "While the heart, like a trout, / Leaps"; (6) hot-cumulus pile-ups of nouns and adjectives, evoking what Karl Jaspers calls "the irremediably dark origin"; (7) rhetorical interruptions—for instance, jerks of iteration: "Never—yes, never—before"; (8) exclamations; (9) anxious or insidious questions; (10) ticklish sound-patterning, as if language were picking a path through its own barbarous brush: "I warily handled the sweet-smelling squaw-fruit"; (11) and not least line-breaks that lift the verse to a feared or wonderful place: "Is light, and suddenly / Dawn."

In all, the poetry is action-loud, will-loud, thought-loud, as distinct from I-loud. On the steep grade of longing or nightmare, it grinds in low gear under thunderhead terms such as Time, Truth, Fate, and Dream. The style has scarcely more than its determination to keep it going. It takes to motion with a lump in its throat.

Even though a depiction of dumb vegetal struggle, the first quatrain of "No Bird Does Call" will serve as a paradigm of Warren's agon:

> Bowl-hollow of woodland, beech-bounded, beech-shrouded,
> With roots of great gray boles crook'd airward, then down
> To grapple again, like claws, in the breathless perimeter
> Of moss, as in cave-shadow darker and deeper than velvet.

The heroic epithet "great"; the heroic-pathetic "crook'd," with its mutilated elision; the warrior word "grapple"; the primeval and desperate "claws"—these oppose, with combative strenuousness, the insidious "hollow," "bounded," "shrouded," and "breathless"; these resist the seductive "cave-shadow," the void of repose. Life roots and rises and then, sent back, roots again with a vengeance, even if in the devouring earth. Heroism is qualified by pathos, pathos by heroism.

Pall that it is, the first line asserts no verb among its deadweight compounds. The absence of articles is no less oppressive. The language wants air. The falling rhythm of "hollow," "woodland," "bounded," and "shrouded" keeps sloping the woodland back into its hollow. But then the rhythm of the stanza begins to rise, opposing nothingness. (Even the first line was aggressive with bunched compounds.) The greatness of the boles resounds through the loud and stately phrase "great gray boles crook'd airward." The monosyllables feel strenuously raised. However "downward" the struggle, the grappling in the third line rides rhythmic upswings: "To grapple again, like claws." Though the agonized roots may confess the pain of individuation, not least the failure of the male to stand free of females, including mother nature, they fight for life even in the dark and breathless void, with its "feminine" endings: "in the breathless perimeter." They emblematize what Yeats called an athletic joy. When the poet concludes, "And now when I wake in the night to remember, no bird ever calls," you hear his depression. Better the vital note of yearning or self-activation than a shrouded silence.

The Warren agon is a stark conflict between phallic verticality, or the air-borne phallus, and passivity. It is a pitched battle for mortal *life*.

On this subject, Warren is almost unbearably inward. Nothing will ever rouse him to equally stringent passionateness, equally clawed words, except his imaginings of death itself as the final opening of experience, the last dimension of being on which to seize.

In English the poetic norm is a line like a freshet, a straight run. Turns, rips, resistances are the exception, if one that often crowds the rule, as in Keats. Hopkins makes the standard exception his rule. So does Warren. Rarely does serenity or discursive confidence see him untroubled to the end of the line.

His internal pauses combine with his line cuttings to form characteristic configurations, linear voiceprints. In the brief catalogue that follows, I have given the various line-types (in Puttenham fashion) "vulgar," perhaps mnemonic names.

1. *The kicker.* Here a strong pause toward the end of the line; whereupon a new clause starts up worriedly or restlessly, as in these lines from "Marble," which, at the time of this writing, is the most recent of Warren's poems to appear:

> Paradox coils in *time* like
> The bull snake in fall's yet-leafed growth. *Then*
> Uncoils like *now. Now*
> Like *then*. Oh, it
> Was long ago—the years, how many?
>
> .
>
>   Her eyes,
> From one to another of those who
> Stand by, move. You hear,
> Almost, the grind in the socket.
>
> .
>
> Her eyes, after each effort, fix
> On the ceiling of white plaster above them. The pink

Of sunset tints the ceiling. I stare
At the ceiling.

    •

No word. My father
Sits rigid on a bench. His loneliness
Is what he seems to insist on. As though
He were stone.

    •

        Why
Didn't I laugh *then?* I
Feel like laughing *now* . . .

The pain of this poem is excruciating, and in part enforced by the prod of the line past its achieved pause. You feel it even where the line is not forced to run on to the next: "I stand on the gravel of the parking lot, alone." Again: "I stare at the moon. *Now.*" The kicker often says that life is a forced condition. At times it may suggest that one is half-willingly led or pushed on, as in another recent poem, "Why You Climbed Up":

    Like substance hangs the silence of
    The afternoon. Look—you will see
    The tiny glint of the warbler's eye, see
    The beak, half open, in still heat gasp, see
    Moss on a cliff, where water oozes.

Less often, but importantly, the compulsion is transformed into a constructive tragic urgency, as in "Trying to Tell You Something":

          The wind,
    Northwest, is steady, and in the wind, the cables,

    In a thin-honed and disinfectant purity, like
    A dentist's drill, sing. They sing

Of truth, and its beauty. The oak
Wants to declare this to you, so that you

Will not be unprepared when, some December night,
You stand on a hill, in a world of whiteness, and

Stare into the crackling absoluteness of the sky. The oak
Wants to tell you because . . .

2. *The tripper.* The opposite of the kicker, a marked pause near the beginning of the line. The effect jolts, all the more so if syncopated by enjambment:

Path of logic, path of folly, all
The same—and I stand . . .

Or it is all let down:

and saw
The first lamp lit behind a window, and did not know
What he was.

It may suggest being at a loss, if perhaps still in the game: "I / Stopped. At the edge of the high mountain mowing, / I stood. Westward stared / At the half mile of white alabaster unblemished." The tripper is fate-shadowed, all but dire.

3. *The dipper.* Here 1 and 2 combine to bracket an isolated middle, which may seem a dead center, a twitch, an aside, or a sudden collapse. A few examples, from different poems:

Got back. Back to the bank. But
One morning was not there.

.

Spat on it. As a child would. Next day
The buzzards.

.

The great coin . . .

. . . . .

Balances. Suddenly is gone. A gull
Defiles at last the emptiness of air.

"Back to the bank" might seem a neutral enough notation, were the fragment, significantly resting on the commercial "bank," not lacking in all living connections. The monotonous dead bell of "Back" and "bank" intensifies the funereal dead-pause. "As a child would" says, in a deprecatory aside, "folly, futility." "Suddenly is gone" is like a stomach-fluttering dip in a road, the abruptest discontinuity. If syntax is vocal strength and declaration, the fragmentary sealed-off middle is the next thing to silence: "*Tap-tap.* Silence. Then anguish / Of band-saw on white oak."

4. *The nipper.* Another medial enclosure, but less disjunctive than in the dipper, and giving a fillip to the following word: "Her eyes, after each effort, fix." Again: "Raw-ringed with glory, like an ulcer, God's / Raw face stared down." The form takes to irony. But at times the effect is spacious and lovely, as with the subtle evocation of distance in "A crow, somewhere, calls."

5. *The snipper.* A line-bisecting pause, particularly suitable when proposing alternatives or detailing binary oppositions, discords, doubts:

Are you
Real when asleep? Or only when

·

But what use that? The sea comes back.

·

The door opens. Is shut.

The snipper may hint of scissoring time:

And flesh is grass, the season short.

·

But
Cannot, breath short.

6. *The rippler.* Multiple caesuras, usually commas, like wind-marks on water. The note may be troubled, as in

> Yes, sky was blue, but water, I suddenly felt,
> Was black, and striped with cold, and one cold claw
> Reached ghostly up

The form may bear the brunt of a nauseating profusion:

> like a hurricane of
> Camellias, sperm, cat-squalls, fish-smells, and the old
> Pain of fulfillment-that-is-not-fulfillment . . .

But it is equally ready for rapture:

> That voice
> Is vaulted in—oh, arch on arch—redundancy of joy, its end
> Is its beginning . . .

When more strongly marked, it gives pause:

> Off in Wyoming,
> The mountains lean. They watch. They know.

Often shading into one another, sharing lines, these six typical patterns combine in shifting permutations. An early instance of their cooperation occurs in the first stanza of "Fox Fire: 1956"—an uncanny mimicry of Warren's mature manner before the fact:

> Years later, I find the old grammar, yellowed. Night
>   (*rippler, kicker*)
>
> Is falling. Ash flakes from the log. The log
>   (*dipper*)

Glows, winks, wanes. Westward, the sky
  (*rippler, snipper, kicker*)

In one small area redeemed from gray, bleeds dully.
  (*with the line above, an extended nipper*)

Beyond my window, athwart that red west
  (*snipper*)

The spruce bough, though snow-burdened, looks black
  (*nipper*)

Not white. The world lives by the trick of the eye, the trick
  (*tripper, weak kicker*)

Of the heart. I hold the book in my hand, but God
  (*tripper, weak kicker*)

—In what mercy, if mercy?—will not let me weep. But I
  (*rippler, kicker*)

Do not want to weep. I want to understand.
  (*snipper*)

The internal and terminal interruptions of the lines are adapted, as always, to the momentary situation—to flaking, winking, waning, athwartness, and so on. The line-composition combines a system of marked habits with the flexibility of a fix-it shop. Inwardness finds ready to hand a number of broadly expressive, interconnectable forms. The not-always-avoided danger is Parnassian facility. The potential gain is the continual refinement of expression (aesthetic precision) through patterns congenial to a specific temperament.

The same patterns, or approximations, occur at random in a great many poets—in Alexander Pope as well as in Robert Lowell. But in Warren they insist on themselves, even as they mingle pell-mell. They scratch, like inescapable crystallizations of experience. They articulate fated rhythms, including the inner quarrel with fate: twistings, defiances. They account for the flinching and flaring so characteristic of his lines and, at the same time, together with his syntactic control, the firmness, the unyielding "I / Stand" of his art. After all, if even the tripper can be seized by elation, as in "and the world, in blaze of *is*, / Burns," anything is possible; necessity itself can "bloom." Agonistic as the line-types may seem, the poet searches their every rhythm-thistle for the budding outlines, surprisingly elegant, of the rose.

For a heroic poet, the resistance offered by the turning or terminating line is a productive irritant. He is put on his mettle: he must get by the guards, find a way to come up elsewhere. Or if he feels rudely pushed on, he must somehow keep his dignity. The poem is a temporal space he crosses as if it were life with all its hazards.

In a review of the original version of *Brother to Dragons*, Hugh Kenner observed that Warren's "natural medium isn't the word or the line but the sonorous mass"; and though this was not exact even then, it is true that we associate Warren with massed energies. He would put language like a boulder in the path of death (of guilt, weakness, silence, and isolation). But just for that reason he is especially attentive to the limits of the line. He encounters the line-end as a potentially revocable, or at least negotiable, prohibition. If he chooses to see it as a form of opposition—his temperament requiring this contest—he delights in overriding it, like water topping a dam. Many things would stop him short, force curtness on him, challenge his "rage" for copiousness. But the line-end is one he can turn to his own advantage. It provokes and renews his energy. If it is like a dry click in the throat, the voice, protesting this choking up, may break out again all the more impassioned. The new line may seem sped forth with a determined impetus.

A splendid example of heroic lineation is the opening portion of "Evening Hawk":

> From plane of light to plane, wings dipping through
> Geometries and orchids that the sunset builds,
> Out of the peak's black angularity of shadow, riding
> The last tumultuous avalanche of
> Light above pines and the guttural gorge,
> The hawk comes.

His wing
Scythes down another day, his motion
Is that of the honed steel-edge, we hear
The crashless fall of stalks of Time.

The tugs of resistance have been imagined, heard, dealt, to perfection.
They dramatize the conquering energy of the bird. Compare:

From plane of light to plane,
Wings dipping through geometries
And orchids that the sunset builds,
Out of the peak's black angularity of shadow,
Riding the last tumultuous avalanche of light
Above pines and the guttural gorge,
The hawk comes.

By comparison, this is boneless gentility. The form fails to accent the
meaning. The flight is merely named, not enacted. A way is cleared
for the hawk and dully, duly, it comes. Our kinetic imagination, our
emotions, are scarcely implicated. We are not required, as in the more
interrupted version, to reintegrate the single scene from its strenuous
division into planes.

Our passionate coactivation is the thread that brings the hawk tri-
umphantly out of the maze of the lines. We master the air with him,
we ride the light. The space not only of the flight but of the verse
seems cubic, an arena for action, a dimension in which to journey.
The two sorts of passage, of proceeding on, merge into one, just as
the eye, the ear, and the empathic or analogical imagination combine
to consolidate these spatial leadings and angularities, these aural
pauses, these dramatic and physical tensions.

I quote again from "Marble":

The doctor comes in. Slowly nods.

Soundless, as though from an axe-butt
Set suddenly to temple, the tall man falls
Sidewise. Rigid.

His daughter stoops to hold his rigid hand.

At last he kisses her hand. Rises:
Face severe, nose outthrust, eyes
Glittering, cold.

Until "Rises:" the line-breaks are either rigid as death or rude with it ("axe-butt / Set"; "falls / Sidewise"). Matching "Rigid." syllable for syllable, capital for capital, rasping "R" for "R," and mark for mark, "Rises:" challenges the total hegemony of death. Its placement, its colon, enact a resolve of the will. If scarcely less "set," "eyes" differs in not looking forward, except mechanically, through the run-on. What is there to look forward to? The eyes must be fixed, but by a human determination, not by death.

If run-ons focus Warren's copiousness, fragments focus his curtness. A clipped quality, attained through the omission of articles, subjects, or verbs, is as characteristic of him as anything is. Yet just as every line-end is to some degree severing, so in spirit Warren's fragments enjoy, to borrow a phrase from William F. Baker, "an orthodox location with respect to other words," whatever their violation in the letter.* Thus, "Rises: / Face severe, nose outthrust, eyes / Glittering, cold" is so mindful, indeed so overwhelmed by an apprehension, of the preceding "he" that it would be waste motion to spell out the subject. The syntactic abruptness argues an excess, not an absence, of felt relation.

Yet here, as often, the elision serves a double function. On the part of the father himself it enacts disorientation, the need to take one thing, make one move, at a time, and so try to get through the ordeal. What seems, and in one sense is, narrative briskness is, even more, a near-stymying of the mastering potential and habit of the ego. In "I Am Dreaming of a White Christmas: The Natural History of a Vi-

---

*   " 'Fragmentation' is an unusual alteration in location; it occurs when a word or word group is without an orthodox location with respect to other words." *Syntax in English Poetry, 1870–1930* (Berkeley: University of California Press, 1967), p. 18.

sion," in which the old family home is viewed "Through / Air brown as an old daguerreotype fading," syntactic atomization may approach still another tonality, that of awe, as in:

> The rings. They shone.
>
> Shine now.
>
> In the brown air.

But the transfixion is touched by terror, which waxes in

>   Approaching,
> See.
>
>   See it.
>
>   The big head. Propped,
> Erect on the chair's leather pillow, bald skin
> Tight on skull, not white now, brown
> Like old leather lacquered, the big nose
> Brown-lacquered, bold-jutting yet but with
> Nostril-flanges gone tattered in Time. I have not
> Yet looked at the eyes. Not
> Yet.
>
>   The eyes
> Are not there. But,
> Not there, they stare at what
> Is not there.

The syntax picks its way forward as if on broken glass, cutting itself each step of the way. Often syntactic deletion puts Warren's words out on a dramatic edge, leaving consciousness a little behind and a gap where the world breaks in:

> The cave wandered on, roof lower and lower except
> Where chambers of darkness rose and stalactites down-stabbed
> To the heart of my light. Again, lower.

I cut off the light. Knew darkness and depth and no Time.
Felt the cave-cricket crawl up an arm. Switched light on
To see the lone life there, the cave-cricket pale
As a ghost on my brown arm. I thought: *They are blind.*
Crept on. Heard, faintly, below

A silken and whispering rustle. Like what? Like water—so
   swung
The light to one side.

"I thought: *They are blind*"—the terror incipient in this thought, already crawling in the syntactic dislocations, finally breaks out:

Thought: *Me—who am I?* Felt
Heart beating as though to a pulse of darkness and earth, and
   thought
How would it be to be here forever, my heart
In its beat, part of all. Part of all—
But I woke with a scream. The flashlight,
It slipped, but I grabbed it. Had light—
And once more looked down the deep slicing and sluicing
Of limestone where water winked, bubbles like fish-eyes, a
   song like terror.

The grammar, with its paradoxical absorption in other locations (the subject *elsewhere*) is a countersign to feeling metaphysically, and blindly, "Part of all." With a cold precision it measures the discomfort and, indeed, the inconclusiveness of this state: *"Is this all? What is all?"* We hear the confusion when the knowing subject lags behind, is displaced by, itself as an opaque object—grammatically figured in "Thought: *Me—who am I?*"

Warren's omission of articles can make one appreciate what thresholds, linchpins, and cushions they usually are. Song, a soft subject in itself, becomes Platonically severe in "Song is lost / In the blue depth of sky" (and the sky no less severe), where the song is, after all, that of a particular lark in a particular location ("over meadows of Brittany").

Not for mortal ears, this song, nor for mortal transit, that sky. The elided articles help hold them off from us. Or consider "Night comes. Eyes stare." The night seems the more looming and inescapable for overriding the definite article. And out of it eyes stare—eyes that, so says the syntax, drill.

Not a few of the fragments are depressed. They say neither "my wits are about to be scattered" nor "this is beyond my control" but, instead, "I barely exist; what exists is nothing." So it is in "What left / To do but walk in the dark, and no stars?" And again in the glum "More snow that night." Or where the reference is to the speaker's own hand, "I can vaguely see it. The hand." Silence is already devouring these expressions. Silence will get the last word in anyhow, standing free of syntax, the very perfection of ellipsis:

> And it is not certain that the world will not be
> Covered in a glitter of crystalline whiteness.

> Silence.

There are many compounds in Warren, and a compound is a form of ellipsis. It eliminates such relational words as "of" and "with." Not the height of the barn, but "barn-height." Not bound with brass, but "brass-bound." Several of Warren's are compacted similes, quashing "like"—for instance, "blood-wet," "ice-eyes," "petal-pink," and "cloud-stone." Even "White-splintered" or "white-crashing" (though no word is eliminated) feels tight. In each, two words are pressed together and ready to serve as a single, economical adjective. By contrast, in "splintered white" and "crashing white" (the references are to water), "splintered" and "crashing" expand into verbs and take up more grammatical space.

Warren's compounds often seem fisted with the world's foreign energy or opacity. Thus, in "swish-hiss" two qualities gang up and strike the senses simultaneously. "Stab-jab" (less successfully) manufactures two assaults out of one. "Slip-tilt" doubles a jeopardy. Many compounds suggest a primitively susceptible and vital perception, the sec-

ond term like a violence of the first: "sun-torment," "sun-stung,"
"rock-rent," "snow-tangled," "snow-sly," "death-gaudy," "fur-prick-
led," "cliff-thrust," "rain-slash," "spray-roil." Where Hopkins, find-
ing God in all things, graciously lifted even an auxiliary word to hy-
phenated heights in "very-violet-sweet!" Warren notices clottedness
(he even speaks of "fog-clots") and allows his poetry to be infested
with little compound-plots. To him the world rears a Medusan head
of entanglements.

Yet with his tragic temper he can long to get nearer to even such a
world as that (he must have a world, and there is no other; even art
must be its transparency). His compounds take hold now of this tuft,
now of that. What George Steiner says of Heidegger—that he "twists
and compacts the sinews of vocabulary and grammar into resistant,
palpable nodes" in an effort to "get language and his reader inside the
actual world, . . . to make luminous and self-revealing the obstinate
opaqueness of matter"—may be said of Warren, too, for whom lan-
guage is, no less than for Heidegger, a blessed violence.

Consider how, in the following, the compounds fix an empathy
pure as compassion:

> Nothing
> But the wing-flurried snow. Then, small as a pin-head, the
>   single
> Bright-frozen, red bead of a blood-drop.

Here the snow seems the more cross-hatched for the first compound.
The hyphen hints of a cross-movement. More, it intimates a collision.
The compound is like shocking evidence of a crime entered into
court. The figure of the "pin-head" keeps the drop of field-mouse
blood pinned against, not to, the snow; pinned to Appearance, to life.
The struggle to *be,* even if literally over, is imaged as the blurt of one
hue against another. The frozen bead keeps its own spherical integrity
against the white waste that would absorb it. "Pin-head," "Bright-fro-
zen," and "blood-drop" all gather language against the dispersal of the
drop. "Bead" all but claims for it a sacral substance. Both "red bead"
and the compounds seek to be inward with "living" matter.

Another, still more moving example of the adhesive compound comes in "Old Nigger on One Mule Cart Encountered Late at Night When Driving Home from Party in the Back Country":

> He enters
> The dark shack, and I see
> A match spurt, then burn down, die.
>
> The last glow is reflected on the petal-pink
> And dark horn-crust of the thumbnail.

The compounds are like the sudden flare-up of the light of language before light and language fail, as they must. They combine words with a fond and protective redundancy. Each cups hands around a faltering flame. As horizontal extensions, they seem to reflect more of appearance than a single small word could (and indeed each has a double meaning). Because of and despite their tenderness, they are subtly ambitious: between them they detail and span the polarity of pink infancy and crusty age, the organic inside and the protective epidermis, vulnerability and callousness, beauty and the beast ("horn-crust" is primordial, like a talon), life and death. "Petal-pink" moves reassuringly from organic softness to rosy health; "horn-crust," threateningly, from barely organic hardness to the corruption and covering-over of sensitive tissue. The movement is deathward, the emotion ambivalent. (In "dark horn-crust" the "inorganic . . . hides out within the organic," as F. W. Dupee observed of Warren's early images of stone and bone.) But primarily the passage corroborates the old man's human existence, down to the horn-crust of his thumbnail. The lines linger (the separation of the last two abetting) on the wonder of a living appearance.*

Warren's most brilliant use of compounds may be the daring string of clichés at the end of "Acquaintance with Time in Early Autumn."

---

* There is racial astonishment in the wonder, for, however faintly, the first compound registers the white man's naive surprise at pink in a black man. This note appeared, greatly magnified, in Warren's second novel: "his thrust-out, puckered, peeled-back lips were like a little, astonishingly pink-hearted flower." *At Heaven's Gate* (New York: Harcourt, Brace, 1943), p. 273.

The heart, the poet says, has "picked today as payday, the payment /
In life's dime-thin, thumb-worn, two-sided, two-faced coin." Weary
alike in their familiarity and profusion, not to mention their aural
peas-in-a-pod similarity, these compounds yet hint, in series, of a clat-
ter and a sum, as of several coins spilling out of a slot-machine at
once—several, not one; something, not nothing. The compounds are,
to be sure, ironically "two-sided": divided yet single, as desire is, de-
sire that wants life, wants death. Yet here is a measurable return, a lit-
tle clutch of heart's knowledge, wisdom itself as a hard little reward.

If not curt, Warren's occasional "oral" outcries are spasmic,
abrupt. Spasmic, for instance, is the beginning of the greatest passage
in *Audubon*, perhaps in all Warren:

> The blessedness!—
>
> To wake in some dawn and see

Following, as it does, logic-chopping lines,

> His life, at the end, seemed—even the anguish—simple.
> Simple, at least, in that it had to be,
> Simply, what it was, as he was,
> In the end, himself and not what
> He had known he ought to be

the exclamation is the acutest rise of feeling. It is an imaginative self-
launching toward the furthest ripening of destiny, when destiny
turns, not a moment too soon, to fate:

> To wake in some dawn and see,
> As though down a rifle barrel, lined up
> Like sights, the self that was, the self that is, and there,
> Far off but in range, completing that alignment, your fate.
>
> Hold your breath, let the trigger-squeeze be slow and steady.

The quarry lifts, in the halo of gold leaves, its noble head.

This is not a dimension of Time.

This is not logic-fretting, but gratefully lucid. Where "The blessedness!— / To wake . . . and see" recalls the root of the word "utterance," *ut,* or "out" (to speak is to *out*), the remainder is serenely written (to write is to compose). The design of a life, at last to be seen complete, is itself a composition, exterior to, removed from, time. The writing leans over a life as if reading a map by its own steady glow. The flamey exclamation and infinitive, by contrast, are inside time, seeking to break out.

If writing is (at its maximal) Olympian, the "oral" is purest as outcry. As it is, joyously, in these two examples from "Red-Tail Hawk and Pyre of Youth":

> Then
> In widening circles—oh, nearer!
> . . . . .
> And at last a red-tail—
>
> Oh, king of the air!

Rational discourse is subverted by a spurt of subjective, almost forgetfully private ecstasy. (Of course, the reader is instantly jealous of this ecstasy, instantly appropriates it.) Even in the painful case of "When the tooth cracks—*zing*!—it / Is like falling in love," the interruption breaks free of the time-locked horizontality of regular (written) syntax. Intense sensation, like intense feeling, is absolute. Loud with immediacy, it is all impatience with the diffractions of discourse.

Other of Warren's "oral" interruptions are spasmic without trying to yank away from time. Carried over from the country dialogue in his novels, for instance, is the jerky pronominal backup, as in "the earth— / It shakes," or "The sun, / It is gone," or "The lips, / They were trying to say something very important"—a jittery instance of percussion. Similar to this oral stumble, hard swallow, syncopation, is the stuttery repetition in "But what can you say— / Can you say—

when *all-to-be-said* is the *done?*" or "She wept. / She wept and she prayed" or "Never, never, a face" or "unless, unless what? Unless." The mind is inside such language only as a florid actor is inside a role. Related, too, are the expletives "No" and, still more common, "Yes," which sometimes means "No": "the city / Was totally unprepared for such a crisis. Nor / Was I—yes, why should this happen to me?" The poetry talks to itself, grumbling, seconding, hopping about on the hot stones of language, or milking words for sympathy.

An interruption that is also an elaboration may begin as the curt but ends as the copious: ends as writing. To go back to the example from *Audubon*: "The blessedness!" interrupts the discourse of the poem, but only to usher in the most *written* of its passages, the most elegantly elaborate. If writing is aligned, here, with the timeless, it is no less writing *against* time from a position necessarily within it—an effort to draw it out, keep time going. Imagine saying simply, "To wake in some dawn and see your fate": put this way, the awakening sounds disagreeable. So the sentence must gather defenses against its own unspoken core word, "death." The gracious precision of "and see / As though down a rifle barrel, lined up / Like sights, the self that was, the self that is, and there, / Far off but in range, completing that alignment, your fate" is postponement disguised as perfect equanimity. (Clandestinely, "rifle," "lined," "Like sights," and "alignment" re-echo "I," and "self" is spread out luxuriously, as by multiple mirrors, in space.) "And there / Far off" is doubly distancing ("there," "Far"). "Was . . . is" leads, through prayer, to "ever shall be." The open-tensed infinitive pulls away from "completing," and "down" joins with "up," "Far off" with "in," to confuse the sense of location, to keep space free for life. Even in the later line "The quarry lifts, in the halo of gold leaves, its noble head," the interruption creates a lovely delay, something additional to bare necessity, a sanctifying surround. Until the crack of doom we remain creatures of place, the place our own, the scene of our unfolding; we are not taken naked; we have about us what we have adopted, what has blessed us.

How reluctant Warren is to arrive at the dead end of a sentence. If he is not too breathless from combat, he is likely to pause and open up the time-vault of an introductory phrase, a parenthesis, or a series of adjectives displayed like valuables in a case. To dwell a little on this last: in "Enormous, smoky, smouldering, it stirs" (this of the "arrogant" harvest moon), the line rejoices first in the ruddy superiority of beauty to the burial horizon, even if beauty itself has caught fire. Or take the evocation of the pain-thrill of chance and its blessed surprises in "Loss, of Perhaps Love, in Our World of Contingency":

> Think hard. Take a deep breath. As the thunder-clap
> Dissolves into silence, your nostrils thrill to the
>
> Stunned new electric tang of joy—or pain—like ammonia.
>
> We must learn to live in the world.

The hot crowd of adjectives seems to have been impelled ("Stunned") into near-fusion. "Tang" alone would undershoot the sensation. "Stunned," "new," and "electric" galvanize it, make it taste of tragic contingency. As a metaphor, "tang" itself is like a modifier, and together these modifiers form a massive quantitative counterpart to an astonishing and swift qualitative change. That a stunned tang is nonsense, an electric tang dubious, hardly matters: hugger-mugger, the attributes dash in strong and sure and excited, not stopping to question their harmony with one another. The phrase is at once as single and splayed as forked lightning. It anatomizes the sensation—thoroughly savors it while abruptly evoking it. So Warren would retrieve qualities from even terrible accidents and necessities. What else is there to harvest under a harvest moon "Enormous, smoky, smouldering"?

Sometimes Warren's nouns and adjectives are in cahoots, standing off from verbs, helping each other to the illusion of absoluteness. For example, charmed by music and awash with alcohol they flow together indiscriminately in the opening lines of "Old Nigger on One-Mule Cart:

> Flesh, of a sudden, gone nameless in music, flesh
> Of the dancer, under your hand, flowing to music, girl-
> Flesh sliding, flesh flowing, sweeter than
> Honey, slicker than Essolube, over
> The music-swayed, delicate trellis of bone
> That is white in secret flesh darkness.

Like a nervous suitor the verb doesn't know when to cut in, and remains a wallflower. The various verbal echoes and pairings—"Flesh . . . flesh," "flowing . . . music," "Flesh sliding, flesh flowing," "music," "flesh"—combine with the pedal-holds of weak rhyme (for instance, the lovely "delicate trellis") to enfold us in a musical sphere, apart from mortality. The swaying and sliding and flowing argue an erotic infinite.

Later in the same poem a verb is again elaborately avoided, so that memory can pour forth from the cornucopia of nostalgia, as if yesterday were still today, were always:

> No moon, but stars whitely outrageous in
> Blackness of velvet, the long lane ahead
> Whiter than snow, wheels soundless in deep dust, dust
> Pluming whitely behind, and ahead all
> The laneside hedges and weed-growth
> Long since powdered whiter than star-dust, or frost, but air
> Hot . . .

The scene centers upon itself through the deep-intervaled verbal repetitions, the deep lanes of sibilance and resonance, the dust of *d*'s and *t*'s, the colluding compact compounds, the pliant punctuation. Here too the adjective, Orpheus to Eurydice, would bring the world's noun forward out of nothingness.*

---

* Warren recalls William James's description of the "entire man" who "feels all needs by turns," who "takes nothing as an equivalent for life but the fullness of living itself," and who will always return gleefully from ideal regions "into the teeming and dramatic richness of the concrete world" ("The Sentiment of Rationality," *Essays in Pragmatism*, ed. Alburey Castell [New York: Hafner, 1960], pp. 3–36).

Two small forms of elaboration are the *like*-phrase and the *of*-phrase. Because of his predilection for a *teeming* world, Warren favors the *like*-phrase over metaphor. The latter binds two things into a tight, circular relation, one that rotates and blurs the contours of each. It gains unity at the expense of diversity. By contrast, the *like*-phrase gestures from one thing to another, in a "by the way." Its rainbow of connection is full of distance. *The heart, a trout, leaps* does exciting violence to both the heart and a trout. *The heart, like a trout, leaps* merely offers, as against extorts, a comparison. Each entity maintains its own integrity. The metaphor says that the world contains a heart-trout, the simile that it contains a heart and a trout—not two-in-one but two, which at least in the numerical sense is more.

Compared to metaphor, the *like*-phrase refuses to press, is detachedly observant, cheerfully extroverted. In "Stunned new electric tang of joy—or pain—like ammonia," the closing phrase stands relievingly aside from the already overcharged electric hubbub and pile-up of attributes. Descriptively important as it is, it comes almost as an afterthought in the line (*is* thought, not a burst of sensations). Its periphrastic form forbears to make an assault of its information. At the same time, it swells the verbal and rhythmic copiousness of the line (even if its feminine ending suddenly eases the rhythmic intensity).

The periphrastic elaborateness of the *like*-phrase attracts it to lines detailing distance, travel, lulls, slow change. Elsewhere in "Loss, of Perhaps Love, in Our World of Contingency" it is effective in the depiction of

> the dark little corner under your bed, where God
>
> Huddles tight in the fluff-ball, like a cocoon, that He,
> All knowing, knows the vacuum won't find!

"Like a cocoon" is not only more precise than "a cocoon" would be; as an out-flung verbal and imaginative form, it helps convey the clever evasiveness of God, whose very presence is like a circumlocution. Or consider how the trail in "The trail / is like a decisive chalk mark that disappears / In penetrating a drift of cloud" is more trail-long than the one in "The chalk-mark trail disappears / In . . ." Similarly ex-

tending evening time is the *like*-phrase in "The evening slowly, sound-
lessly, closes. Like / an eyelid." And combined with alliteration, how
lulling the *like*-phrase is in "With the tire song lulling like love, gaze
riding white ribbon, forward / You plunge."

Warren frequently makes elegant use of the expansive *of*-phrase,
too. It contributes notably to the sublime effect of

> From plane *of light* to plane, wings dipping through
> Geometries and orchids that the sunset builds,
> Out *of the peak's black angularity of shadow*, riding
> The last tumultuous avalanche *of*
> *Light* above pines and the guttural gorge,
> The hawk comes.
>
>   His wing
> Scythes down another day, his motion
> Is that *of the honed steel-edge*, we hear
> The crashless fall *of stalks of Time*.

"From plane of light to plane" is epic, magisterial in its ease: the
hawk's highway. By contrast, and its crudity aside, "From light's
plane to plane" is wrong for the bird, stiff as if to avoid stumbling.
Then the shadow in "of the peak's black angularity of shadow" seems
the longer and more would-be-engulfing for the double use of the *of*-
phrase. In the otherwise crashy "tumultuous avalanche of light" the
upward-inflected *of*-phrase comes like a glorious release, the tumult
harmless. As for "the crashless fall of stalks of Time," it is appropriate-
ly hushed as well as slow, thanks to the suspended, repeated sounds in
"—less fall of stalks of" and the slow-motion iambs. By comparison,
"The crashless fall of Time's stalks" is brutally unceremonious; the
close could even be thought dismissive. If wordy, "His motion / Is
that of the honed steel-edge" sounds flatteringly formal, majestic, and
sustained. So it is that, throughout, the sublime elaborations of phys-
ical space, the profusion of its planes and forms, and the floating mo-
tion of the hawk find in the *of*-phrase their phrasal correlate.

Warren's lines contract or expand according to the veerings of what he describes, his tight shudders and unravelings, his rebuffs and joy. Analyzing the ceiling over a deathbed, a short line in "Marble," "It roofs all *time*," is architecturally succinct; the confinement is extreme, the surrounding white space an *X* of blank:

> I stare
> At the ceiling. It is *infinity*.
>
> It roofs all *time*.
>
> From his vest pocket the doctor draws
> The old-fashioned gold-cased watch.

In Warren, if with little importance in the line "To one side," if with barbed puzzlement in the line "Thereof?" the short line-length is gestural. And the long no less so. Stanley Plumly links the long line with Warren's peculiar way of seeing things: "Warren was to learn . . . that he needed *time*, time across as well as down the page, in order to accommodate the pace and size of his statement." Supporting "pace" but undercutting "size," he adds that when the method is one "of perception as opposed to conception, finding what will suffice . . . can take a line as long as the arm." What this description omits is the strenuous enactive element that accounts for the extreme variation in the length of Warren's lines. Few are the long lines that form a kind of exhibition shelf for a prized observation: "and at / Dawn I have seen the delicate print of the coon-hand in silt by the riffle." The long lines usually follow disappearing space or groan with time. "The red cabooselight disappears into the distance of the continent" is all swallowing distance, the *of*-phrase assisting. "Over the green interstices and shambling glory, yet bright, of forest, / Distance flees westward" is a more characteristic, because more muscular, example. The length of "With what painful deliberation he comes down the stair" suffers the painful deliberation, the sharp accents of "*pain*ful" and "de*libera*tion" like sudden increases of pain.

Whether long or short or of medium length, the line is an undergoing. It is a fine graph of the action at a particular point. A final example, in which a short and long line work in tandem: "Now with glasses, I see / The squabble and pushing, the waggle of wattle-red heads." The first line holds steady, while (thanks to the caesura, the grammatical shift, and the run-on) directing itself forward in anticipation. All the concentration, the breath-holding of spying, is in it. The second, by abrupt contrast, unleashes a flurry of motion. It seethes with instinctual strife; its crowd of action-denoting nouns ("squabble," "pushing," "waggle") and its similar, pushing-for-first-place sounds evoke, rather horrifyingly, the bustle and competition of carrion-feeding buzzards. Poets know by imaginative enactment, becoming what they know.

In part 3 of "Rattlesnake Country" the vigor of the enactment, its accumulative *copia*, takes a lovely quasi-cinematic form. Indeed, everything exists in a wonderful copiousness in this section, hearing no less than seeing, action no less than contemplation. And swelling the empathic, narrative, and sensory plenitude is a temporal wealth of memory: the past recaptured by the vital present tense; a past, moreover, that had already prized and represented within it a still more distant past: "what I have, / Literally seen, I now in my mind see"—this double seeing now redoubled as the poet sees himself seeing what he saw then, when he saw what he had already seen. The poem brings its multiplying mirror to an action already multiple with self-mirrorings: repeated cries, leaps, plunges, flickerings, seeings, hearings; a riding that will lead to still more riding; everything "Like quicksilver spilled," self-proliferating:

> *I-yee!*—
>   and the wranglers, they cry on the mountain, and
>   waking
> At dawn-streak, I hear it.
>
>   High on the mountain
> I hear it, for snow-water there, snow long gone, yet seeps
>   down

To green the raw edges and enclaves of forest
With a thin pasturage. The wranglers
Are driving our horses down, long before daylight, plunging
Through gloom of the pines, and in their joy
Cry out:

> *I-yee!*

> We ride this morning, and,
Now fumbling in shadow for *levis*, pulling my boots on, I hear
That thin cry of joy from the mountain, and what I have,
Literally, seen, I now in my mind see, as I
Will, years later, in my mind, see it—the horsemen
Plunge through the pine-gloom, leaping
The deadfall—*I-yee!*—
Leaping the boulder—*I-yee!*—and their faces
Flee flickering white through the shadow—*I-yee!*—
And before them,
Down the trail and in dimness, the riderless horses,
Like quicksilver spilled in dark glimmer and roil, go
Pouring downward.

> The wranglers cry out.

> And nearer.

This is luxuriant yet athletic writing, ecstatic, rapid, volleying, volu-
minous, tumbling, flowing. Here narrative is lyric: the expression of a
state of the soul. It celebrates that classic moment of vital exuberance
when you feel that all life is in motion forever. Many of Warren's
typical devices for suggesting a flaring intensity of feeling and a sense
of emotional plenitude are brought into play: the verbal backup ("and
the wranglers, they cry"), verbal repetition, syntactic parenthesis, the
of-phrase ("of forest," "of the pines," and so on), the long line and the
run-on, the *like*-phrase ("Like quicksilver spilled in dark"), participial
additives, the spasmic cry (here quoted but repeated and salient), and
near-riot crowds of identical or similar vowels and consonants.

Remarkable in itself, the passage is all the more extraordinary in
the context of the four other parts of the poem, which surround it,

two by two, and contradict its evidence of vital joy. No poem of Warren's has in it more of the pitiless objectivity we associate with the novel—more of the "knowledge," in Georg Lukács' words, "that meaning can never quite penetrate reality." In the parts preceding (but not leading up to) the wrangling episode, there is no body-world, I-world, we-world, wish-world, or "nameless" world in evidence; for the most part, there is only brute world. The "anger of sun on the mountains," the forest fire on Mount Ti-Po-Ki, the "mesquite, wolf-waiting," the lake "stretched / Tight as a mystic drumhead" and glittering "like neurosis"—all rebuff the spirit, driving it back into the void from which it issued, like a rattlesnake into a rock-pile. "Matter is supposed to be in space," wrote Bergson in *Matter and Memory*, "spirit to be extraspatial." But here spirit merely suffers the flaming violence at its "mouth-hole," the sky shivering "white with heat." True, "extraspatial" memory is able to revisit the scene, indeed through beautiful subleties to reconstitute it in the present tense and as a "here" (though the poem begins "Arid that country and high"). But why spirit would want to crawl once more into the furnace of that long-ago matter is the great puzzle of the poem. What compulsion tries to "convert what now is *was*"—and such a "*was*" as that arid time—"Back into what was *is*"? Is it the traumatic need to exhaust, and so master, the shock of an experience? Or a metaphysical, even masochistic heart-wish to home to all that time has offered as our own, the country of what the heart has undergone, however rattlesnake-infested: the tragic superposition of "had to be" on "what has been"?

In part 2 the poet briefly breaks away from the brute world into nonworld; floating, he dreamily dissolves his identity in the moon-silvered lake:

> Swam miles out,
> Toward the moonset. Motionless,
> Awash, metaphysically undone in that silvered and
> Unbreathing medium, and beyond
> Prayer or desire, saw
> The moon, slow, swag down, like an old woman's belly.

But what is this if not a "naughtening" (*Nichtung*, Heidegger's word for the eruption of nothingness into the world) as complete as that of the "red eyes of fire" that "Wink at you from / The black mass of the mountain," if as defleshed as the other is demonic? "Swam miles out" already melts the "I" (which was slow to appear in the poem at all) under the moonset; and the long-sustained but self-slowing word "Motionless" speaks of a gorgeous pall in the lifeless medium from which life once rose, spurred by its foolish inability to keep still. The swimmer is deliciously passive—adrift—in what is itself the passive reflector of a passive and passing reflector. "Since prehistoric times," notes Mircea Eliade in *Patterns in Comparative Religion*, "water, moon and woman were seen as forming the orbit of fertility both for man and for the universe." But here where "the moon, slow, swags down, like an old woman's belly," fertility is routed. What holds sway is the ancient renunciatory meaning of immersion in water, that of "a return to the pre-formal, . . . for immersion means a dissolution of forms, a reintegration into the formlessness of pre-existence." This moon and this water unmake desire, even the desire to pray, and without desire man is undone. Beautifully the many *m*'s murmur Being into indistinctness.

What could be more opposite than the wranglers' shouting flesh? Their "*I-yee!*" rises steep with vitality, is a world-hailing cry. In this episode those petty demons of the fallen world, the phallic rattlesnakes, give way to the plunging horses, ancient symbols of passional force. Here water flows, grass greens, flesh acts, motor power is released, and memory—which might well have absented itself in the face of this spontaneous leap of happiness—plunges into a creative activity of its own. Riding on the pouring energy of the morning, under a pristine first light that cancels both the sun (that explosion) and the moon (that exhausted womb of Being), it proves a free energy added to a free energy, a happy redundancy of spirit, converting the rude life of the body into the mind's directorial debut in this new beginning of time. The "lower" mimetic of reaching for "*levis*" in the shadows, and listening, is accompanied by the "higher" mimetic of the mental film of the (otherwise unseen) high wrangling, a film instantaneously edited to perfection, the creative mind's self-enthrallment.

It is the imagination that sees, seeing by heart and putting it-
self muscularly into the action on the mountain. What a lovely
rhythm—springy, strong, and original—is in "the horsemen / Plunge
through the pine-gloom, leaping / The deadfall—*I-yee!*— / Leaping
the boulder—*I-yee!*—and their faces / Flee flickering white through
the shadow—*I-yee!*" Compelled to convert *was* into what was *is*,
memory has at last found a congenial theme and runs for joy. Now
memory itself can do the compelling (from the Latin *compellere*, "to
drive cattle together").

No wonder the passage is exuberantly inward, passionately whole.
Everything harkens to everything else, as if each thing were the first *I-
yee!* of a wrangling; everything finds itself impelled along in the same
rhythmical stream, in which it is at once part of the current and a gid-
dy chip. For instance, in "what I have, / Literally, seen, I now in my
mind see, as I / Will, years later, in my mind, see it," the concealed vi-
tal boast of "I" in "*I-yee!*" reappears in a cooled ecstacy, together with
a spate and progeny of *i*'s and *e*'s—raising, in all, a subdued *I-yee* of
memory. Or take the cycle of return in "I . . . in my mind see, . . . I . . .
in my mind, see," which is potentially as illimitable, is in the same
spirit, is still as fresh, as the plunge and leap, plunge and leap of the
horsemen at this earliest moment of the long mountain mourning.
And how naturalistically engaging the specification of "*levis*" and
boots, how genially they link the waking poet to the already-
vigorous wranglers as one with the same blood for adventure: "We
ride this morning."

The whole "image" is "vitally built" in the sense expounded by
Eisenstein and Pudovkin in their writings on montage (which may
have inspired Warren's notion of a "vital and evaluating image . . . dif-
ferent from the vitality you observe or experience"). Through every
"and" and present participle, every "through" and "down," every re-
echoing repetition, the passage spills and returns on itself in an incre-
mental pattern, as a dynamically emerging sequence. As memory un-
rolls its visual reel on the cycle of the repeated rapturous cry, "*I-yee!*"
steps down and down the page, graphing the wranglers' own descent
and moving from margin to margin till it becomes virtually ubiqui-
tous in the episode, coextensive with all the vital motion and joy. At
the same time the camera distance shifts and the image of the wran-

gling sharpens: first a long shot, with a minimum of detail (simply, wranglers "plunging / Through gloom of the pines"); then, as memory warms to its subject, a medium shot with successive flashes of specification (plunging horsemen, a leap, a deadfall, a cry, a boulder, a leap, and so on).

Everything is right; the tensions are all curve and surprise. With each phrase, line, and punctuation mark Warren rivals Eisenstein's "severe responsibility for each shot," his concern to admit each "into a montage sequence with as much care as a line of poetry is admitted into a poem." For instance, the first "leaping," which is end-placed,

> the horsemen
> Plunge through the pine-gloom, leaping
> The deadfall—*I-yee!*

is kinetically fierce. The poet could have risked placing the second one at breakneck line-end, too, regardless; but instead he lets "*I-yee!*" geyser into space (in tension with "The deadfall") and waits to present "their faces," with true-and-deceptive calm, in unqualified portrait-stillness, in end position ("Leaping the boulder—*I-yee!*—and their faces")—this before plunging the faces back into change and motion ("Flee flickering white through the shadow—*I-yee!*"). In consequence, the fleeing and flickering seem the more what they are, if reigned in by the forceful alliteration and contiguous stresses in "Flee flickering" (as earlier the repeated *p* and resonance in "Plunge" and "pine-gloom" had bridled the plunge). The impetuousness is all under control. In the rest of the sentence the tension is at last eased, first through the prepositional latitude of "Down the trail and in dimness," then through the reprieve from human hazard in "the riderless horses," then through the comparison with indestructible metal in "Like quicksilver spilled in dark." At once firm and fluid, the writing churns with interruptions and multiple verbs, yet rolls:

> And before them,
> Down the trail and in dimness, the riderless horses,
> Like quicksilver spilled in dark glimmer and roil, go
> Pouring downward.

Satisfyingly dim is the short *i* and the shadowy *es* in "in dimness, the riderless horses," and quick the short *i* and liquid, sheeny, light the *l* in "Like quicksilver spilled in dark glimmer and roil."

"Montage," said Eisenstein, is a "juxtaposition of [certain] *elements*" that will "evoke in the perception and feelings of the spectator the most complete *image of the theme itself*." So Warren juxtaposes "*I-yee!*" with "I hear," "the horsemen" with "I see," till one is driven to hear and see with him, hear his hearing, see his seeing. He shapes and intensifies the emotion through the interplay between not only the poet below and the wranglers above but the static "*I-yee!*" and the plunge and pour, the single cry and the visual pell-mell, the prod-cry (which is hardly less a response cry, a gut response to the cool freedom of the morning and the physical challenge of the wrangling) and the seductively enactive narrative language, as he does also through the differentiations effected by the *italics* and dashes, the exclamatory, accelerating rhythm of the alternation between "*I-yee!*" and the rest (the cry seeming at once part of the narrative and an irruption into it), and the drama of the advent of so much energy, the ever-nearing plunging herd, which will break out of memory and into the actual bottomland of the morning:

> The wranglers cry out.
>   And nearer.

The reader is, in Eisenstein's words, "compelled to proceed along that selfsame creative road that the author traveled in creating the image."

The paradox of vitality is that it seems the more indomitable the more it voluntarily puts itself at hazard, expends itself greatly. It *is* in the teeth of death, its quality self-apprehended in the opposition. Film, the undeclared metaphor in the passage, catches its spirit with its galvanic pulsations of light. The director in *Flood* "was glad he was not a writer. He had been spared that. He had been spared the yearning for immortality. . . He knew that he worked in evanescence . . . Now he had for an instant the vision of a great screen, like a blank screen in an empty theater, a screen flickering and pulsing with subdued waves of silvery light, then the shadow of a human figure drifting across it, dim and without feature. Evanescence—if you knew you worked in that you could have joy." The goal of immortality is cruel; evanescent mortality, by contrast, is joy, a tragic expense of life in the self-delighting moment. Like the fleeing faces of the wranglers, joy flickers: "Joy flickers . . . in the heart's / Cold fatigue. But joy is energy. There is one germ for joy. / Its name is vision."

What vision, if any, underlies the life-affirming leaps and plunges of the mountain wrangling? Perhaps the peculiar "immortality" implicit in life itself. When successive leaps of vitality come fast and thick, they deny the law of gravity; they form their own law apart. So with the pulsations of light on a movie screen. The light appears exultant. You would think there was nothing but light. To a planetary eye, vitality leaps, subsides, leaps again—is always present. To a metaphysical eye, nonbeing is like a screen on which blackness is "Slashed by stab-jabs of white," the attack repeated and vicious (for being is an impurity). It is a sympathetic illusion that construes passionate successiveness as a calm continuity.

To Schopenhauer, only the negative rhythm of vital flickerings is the real illusion:

> We ourselves recognize in the lowest forces of nature an eternity and ubiquity with regard to which the transitory nature of their fleeting phenomena never makes us err for a moment. So much the less then, should it come into our mind to regard the ceasing of life as the annihilation of the living principle, and consequently death as the entire destruction of the man. Because the strong arm which, three thousand years ago, bent the bow of Ulysses is no more, no reflective and well-regulated understanding will regard the force which acted so energetically in it as entirely annihilated, and therefore, upon further reflection, will also not assume that the force which bends the bow to-day first began with this arm. The thought lies far nearer us, that the force which earlier actuated the life which now has vanished is the same which is active in the life which now flourishes: nay, this is almost inevitable . . . taken simply as a force of nature, the vital force remains entirely undisturbed by the

change of forms and states, which the bond of cause and effect introduces and carries off again, and which alone are subject to the process of coming into being and passing away, as it lies before us in experience. Thus so far the imperishable nature of our true being can be proved with certainty.

Something in the repristinating morning air—something about being on horseback, about driving thundering horseflesh down the mountain—seems to awaken in the wranglers, or if not in them in the poet, a confidence in the indestructibility of vital force. Perhaps "the force which earlier actuated . . . life" is still early, "now flourishes"? "Nay, this is almost inevitable." The "vision" vitality carries within it like a clue to joy is a vision of its own "imperishable nature." The tragic shadow, the "cold fatigue," lies in the perishable, changing "forms and states." To be plunged in the vegetable gloom as the wranglers are and yet *be*, indeed leap and yell with exuberance, awakens in the poet a tragic knowledge of both the transitory and the indestructible. Yeats wrote of "the orgiastic moment when life outleaps its limits." In Warren's novel *A Place to Come to* a woman jumping her horse "imperially" floats "into a dimension beyond gravity, time, and contingency." Even the woman of whose "essential incapacity / For experience" part 5 of "Rattlesnake Country" complains—even she approaches an apotheosis when she puts "her mount to the jump," her "beautiful figure . . . poised forward," her "face / Thrust into the cleansing wind of her passage." And yet the faces of the wranglers flicker; they flee. All the leaping and plunging is but a descent. Vital vision may awaken joy but determines it as cold. The joy itself flickers. Again cinema offers itself as an emblem. With its horror of sclerosis, its flash and flow of frames within the enduring rectangle of the screen itself, its figures starting into being and snapping away, its hint of a force "entirely undisturbed by the change of forms and states, which the bond of cause and effect introduces and carries off," it echoes the shadowed indestructibility, the imperishable evanescence, of "our true being."*

* In Warren's numerous black-and-white scenes (for instance, "birch-whiteness, black jag / Of shadow, black spruce-bulks snow-shouldered") there is perhaps a memory of the old black-and-white cinema (the intuition of the stabbing relation between being and nonbeing

Memory, too, is like the silver screen, flickering, remembering what was, letting it pass again—an arm that, though not the same arm, eagerly bends again the bow, though not the same bow.

The looping verbal repetition in the passage is itself the flickering of a force that, however intromitted, comes back, its vitality unabated. The series of ejaculatory cries (beginning thin, coming nearer), the string "cry... Cry out ... cry... cry out," or "I hear it ... I hear it ... I hear," or any of a half-dozen more, argues a fertile power of renewal. The redundancy is, in the words of *Audubon*, "redundancy of joy," whose end is "its beginning"—in which necessity blooms "like a rose." Such energy vaults "oh, arch on arch" like the wranglers in their leaps or the verse with its dashes and springing returns line by line, same word by same word—spilling like quicksilver, which as it shatters spurts and multiplies with an indestructible glimmer.

"It is essential to be hungry but impermissible to be merely that; you have to take your time, the imagination must work; the first rule is to pay attention to what you are doing."
—Eleanor Clark, *The Oysters of Locmariaquer*

"In poetry a supplementary statement is framed by a precise marshalling of . . . latent meanings . . . the reader would not be aware of more than the manifest statement were it not for the heightened sensibility induced in him by the rhythmic intoxication of verse."
—Robert Graves, *The Common Asphodel*

---

perhaps coming to him in some darkened moviehouse in Kentucky or Tennessee)—this as well as the racial tensions of the South and the robust man's love of "strong relief" (William James); hence, too, his added jabs of red.

Marshall Sahlins observes that in any given culture the most rudimentary distinction—perhaps universally significant and semantically motivated—is the discrimination of lightness and darkness; "in the evolution of basic categories" the next state is the additional opposition of red, which "has the most color" and which "is to the human eye the most salient of color experiences." So a "triad of red-white-black" results from "the crossing of the basic dark/light dualism by a second contrast of hue/neutrality." See Roman Jakobson and Linda R. Waugh, *The Sound Shape of Language* (Indianapolis: Indiana University Press, 1979), p. 191.

"The idea has come to me that what I want now to do is to saturate every atom. I mean to eliminate all waste, deadness, superfluity: to give the moment whole; whatever it includes. Say that the moment is a combination of thought; sensation; the voice of the sea . . . Why admit anything to literature that is not poetry—by which I mean saturated?"

—Virginia Woolf, *A Writer's Diary*,
entry for November 28, 1928

"Criticism when it really functions in the full sense of the word leads to a creative act in the sense of appreciating the work of art, whatever it is. You have to redo the work. You repaint the picture, rewrite the book, recompose the music, by going inside, if you are really experiencing it properly. You are writing the book; you are painting the picture; you feel the whole process is yours. This is clearly a creative act, and it's a very difficult creative act.

—Robert Penn Warren, *Robert Penn Warren
Talking*, p. 145

Warren's most identifying manner is a strenuously marshaled response to the threat of naughtening, to blows dealt by death. Powerful forces of dispersion declare themselves; the poet clenches himself into a heroic withstanding. "There isn't much vital imagination," he has said, "that doesn't come from some sort of shock, imbalance, need to 'relive,' redefine life."

The result can be at once a muscular realization, enactment, and *stand*, as in the first of the four sections of "Sunset Walk in Thaw-Time in Vermont":

> *Rip, whoosh, wing-whistle*: and out of
> The spruce thicket, beating the snow from
> Black spruce boughs, it
> Bursts. The great partridge cock, black against flame-red,
> Into the red sun of sunset, plunges. Is
> Gone.

In the ensuing
Silence, abrupt in
Back-flash and shiver of that sharp startlement, I
Stand. Stare. In mud-streaked snow,
My feet are. I,
Eyes fixed past black spruce boughs on the red west, hear,
In my chest, as from a dark cave of
No-Time, the heart
Beat.
      Where
Have the years gone?

Eventually, panic will subside into *Angst*, which in turn will steel itself to become what Heidegger called *Sorge*, or care—in Warren's difficult phrase, "the loving immortality of death." But this first part, beginning in shock and imbalance, ends in the same. An inner "*whoosh*" follows from the outer one: a partridge flies off; where have the years gone? Nonetheless, the verse is a notable coping, equal to its trial of strength.

"Explosition," in a word from *Finnegans Wake*, it yet sternly registers ear-shock, eye-venture, heart-terror of the most unshielded kind. In it the world proves, first to the ear, then to the eye, as all along to the heart, a fearful going already bearing the fate of "Gone." Immediacy: the thin end of the wedge of death. Abruptly in the darkening wood the air pumps loudly with pure departure. A drumming and rushing vacuum, a shuddering ghost of sound almost *lingers* behind a crazily escaping mass. Even so, it rips into, rips up, time. Not yet connected with an identifiable object, it invades the ear like hysteria, the ear being especially vulnerable to such assaults, less on guard than the eye, relatively primitive in structure, feminine in that it is open to violation—a sensitive cave or vial. (In any case, everything the ear perceives is, as Walter J. Ong says, already "going out of existence.") Not yet spiritualized or ghosted into a concept ("pure perception," as Bergson notes, ". . . is really part of matter"), the "*rip*" and "*whoosh*," if in strict auditory order, strike outside of syntax, are neither nouns nor verbs, though resembling both. They are time in the form of a flagrant naughtening.

Less quasi-raw than *"whoosh,"* tipped by a familiar visual image, and categorizing the genus of the object, *"wing-whistle"* begins a taming process, even as the italics oppose it and syntax continues to be flouted—what came first in experience insisting on taking first place in the line. But then a colon shores the rush of sensations; the mind is regathering itself to make a disposition of this flurry of material. The eye comes to the blind ear's assistance. "Out of" begins to track the bird, and "it" spots it as a brute appearance, till memory fixes it as a partridge cock, species settled, no great terror. Some of the wildness still vibrates in the epithet "great," but the denomination "the partridge cock" is as near to a stabilization, a resolution, as language at this point can get.

Meanwhile, "Bursts" has lit the fuse of presentness. "Burst" would have eased us; "bursts" is pure problem. Adopting the convention that he is writing, or speaking, in the very moment of the original experience, the poet finds himself again at its knife-point. (The not-said is that he now has writing as a resource; writing is now his armor— transparent, and not.) Licensed by the present tense, all going—the snow dropping from the black spruce boughs, the partridge plunging into "the red sun of sunset"—seems to become manifest with a vengeance. The eye, in acute reaction, attempts a freeze, the accents co-operating: "The great partridge cock, black against flame-red," might be describing a scene on an illuminated sportsman's lampshade. Though supported by the line-break, the strategy is doomed: "black" hints at a charring, speaks of a savage reduction to a silhouette. The holding "against" almost instantly gives way to the sacrificing "Into" (as in "into the flames"): "The great partridge cock, black against flame-red, / Into the red sun of sunset, plunges. Is / Gone." "Plunges," exactly like "Bursts" before it, detonates in unfended terminal position in the sentence—the more explosive for being held off by the feeble, momentary stay of the syntactic interruption.* Antiseptically isolated at the end of the line, the copulative "Is" might be

---

* More strictly, in all such instances there is a simultaneous qualification of the force of the verb (the connection of the verb with the subject has been loosened, and syntax has demonstrated that the verb can be delayed) and a subtle enhancement of it, since it kicks up after the caesura with the *wham* of heavy machinery being started up.

trying to pass itself off as a categorical, wide-eyed declaration of "Being," but is undermined by the gap at its foot, then dashed by the blunt, unmusical, remorselessly capitalized "Gone," which, arrogating a line to itself, abrogates both adjunct and sequel.

At each point the battle is lost: the line-break after "out of" cannot prevent the naming of what is left behind ("The spruce thicket"), nor can the one after "from" ("Black spruce boughs"); "Bursts" *will* follow "it"; the *abaaab* rhyme pattern of "the red sun of sunset" (a magical plot to retain the pattern-nurturing light) and the play-dumb explicitness and touch of redundancy in the phrase fail to stop that disappearing act, that fiery self-consumption; and so on. But still the poem continues. If in a world of fleeing phenomena stability cannot be found in perception (and by the end of the poem perception will yield to prophetic moral vision), the poem must attempt to be its own "in," opposed to the "out of" and "into" of evanescence. Mindful of this, it begins the next verse-paragraph with the trap-laid "In," which it sneaks in again two syllables later in "ensuing." "Ensuing" is an earnest of reasserted sequence; we are back in a world where one thing duly follows another, however "abrupt"—a world where time lasts, permits, can be counted on. "Silence" provides the dubious void in which the poem now attempts to create duration, a human space: "In the ensuing / Silence, aburpt in / Back-flash and shiver of that sharp startlement." After the noisy departure, this silence is at once an absence and a positive concentration of nondeparture. The sounds of "-su" and "Si" are soothing in contrast to the harsh agitation of "Back-flash and shiver of that sharp startlement." In this new, soft continuity a rebounding "I" finds a standing place. Thanks in part to the line-break, however, it feels almost as abrupt as the back-flash silence, and is schizoid in relation to its own standing and staring: "I / Stand. Stare." If the "I" twice takes a strong stand at the end of a line, the tactic is costly, for the isolation momentarily robs the inner man of a grammar of relationships:

> I
> Stand. Stare. In mud-streaked snow,
> My feet are. I,
> Eyes fixed

To be here becomes a brute, unblessed, stubborn self-assertion. How stiff is this standing; how fixed the staring. How stolid the expression "My feet are." This last forms a determined counterweight to "Mud-streaked snow," which, as the object of "in," had sent the scene reeling once again into transiency. "My feet are" competes with it accent by accent. But the feet seem curiously distanced from the "I," all the same; the reappearance of "I" after a period almost insists on it. The regathering of the "self" is, then, touch-and-go. The language seems to be rigid, in casts; is still sorely recuperative. Repetition, as in a slow learning to walk again, is its chief hope, at least a way of getting on. The alignment of one "I" above another at line end argues persistence. "Stand" harks back to "back-flash"; "Stare" seems to have crystallized out of "sharp startlement." "Past black" re-echoes "back flash." And "Past black spruce boughs on the red west" makes the earlier paragraph sound again. What can be recovered is not altogether "Gone."

But then comes an "In" that, involving an ominous echo of "red west" in "chest," and likened to "a dark cave of / No-Time," is all but entombing: an unexpected interiorization of the alien, stony-hearted world:

> I,
> Eyes fixed past black spruce boughs on the red west, hear,
> In my chest, as from a dark cave of
> No-Time, the heart
> Beat.

The heart reveals itself not as part of the "I," but simply as a brute "Beat," also essentially alien; and "Beat" is as savagely isolated and capitalized as "Gone" was, and apparently as unsubduable. (This intractable, unrevelatory "Beat" has been a subtext for some time—sounding for instance in the staccato "I," "Stand," and "Stare." In fact, since "startlement," only words of one syllable have struck.)

What is "the heart" if it can thus be reduced or become so painful, so prodigious? What are the years if they are years of such a heart? What is time if it can be ripped in an instant, laying bare the primal darkness of No-Time? (As always in Warren—a metaphysically violent writer—nonbeing hides in the bosom of being, ready to unleash Original Night.)

Of the question "Where / Have the years gone?" one could think: "It is really an exclamation muffled by dismay." But the lower case of this "gone" and its civil placement argue a stalling till the mind can think of something . . . something human that lasts. The question at least keeps alive the possibility that the poem can continue, that some reason for trust can be reconnoitered from its base. As "closure," it is tentative, all unsatisfied. And indeed the actual close of the poem will contain (violently wrested out of the ice-forming night) the powerful word "immortality," which, moreover, it will triumphantly bond to the human word "loving."

The section sustains a microscopic examination because it is all imaginative enactment. It has been refined with both hammer and blaze, as is all inward art—"Until," in Emily Dickinson's words, "the Designated Light / Repudiate the Forge." Though everything is as if painfully and severely announced, the effect is tremendous and unitary. And individual: for at his best, Warren improvises his technique (it is chosen by the situation) and his good things are never twice alike. "Sunset Walk" is not like "Rattlesnake Country"; *Audubon* is not like "Sunset Walk." What all have in common is a concentrated vigor (and, to varying degrees, a volume) of response that seems in itself an elemental force as great as the one, now in crisis, now in delighted greeting, they address.

For Warren, rhythm is destiny—"an affirmation that our being may move in its totality toward meaning." He finds in rhythm "the abstraction of experience by imagination." Rhythmically, his poems (at least the best) are unique draftings and graphings of being here. The rhythm is at once lifelike (situational, impulsive, mood-rich) and a heuristic: a reading of experience, a diagnosis, a gnosis.

Yet not only are certain line-rhythms (noted earlier) characteristic of him; his rhythms are uniformly virile, *marked*. He always accentuates; his voice knows no hesitations but those he wants to emphasize.

He knows exactly what he wants to stress and how to stress it and is behind everything he says.

Consider the close of "Have You Ever Eaten Stars?":

> What other need now
> Is possible to you but that
> Of seeing life as glory?

Like some raw rock formation, this is indifferent to being scanned: it insists on being heard as a vigorous utterance whose shape is merely the sign of its vigor. Syncopation lies in the spacing of the chief accents: "What *o*ther need now is *pos*sible to you but *that* of seeing *life* as *glory?* The other accents, adding density, and the fragmenting line-breaks hold it all down to serious delivery. "Other" has a vaulting force; "need now" raps for your attention; "Is possible to you" is first like a crack in the voice, then provides a little thaw-flood of rhythm (the *p* spurting); "but that" is joyously assured (its accents and terminal *t*'s matching the accents and initial *n*'s of "need now" just above); then after the springing tension of "Of seeing" comes the exalted double peak of "life as glory," the three words almost radianced into one.

There is no holding Warren to tame pattern. Paul Breslin regrets its absence in the following:

> Below all silken soil-slip, all crinkled earth-crust,
> Far deeper than ocean, past rock that against rock grieves,
> There at the globe's deepest dark and visceral lust,
> Can I hear the *groan-swish* of magma that churns and heaves?

The diction, Breslin states, "is that of an original and gifted poet, but the prosody, taken in isolation, is that of doggerel." In fact, the diction—save for "*groan-swish* of magma," a barbarically magnificent phrase—might be thought curdled (particularly "rock grieves" and "deepest dark and visceral lust"); but the rhythm indeed approaches an automatic churn-and-roll—is far from being Warren at his best. Still, one can read it sympathetically, or not. To see it as "meter" is to condemn it in advance. What Warren often writes, Breslin notes, "is clearly intended as an iambic meter, with frequent anapestic substitutions." But though "strict" or "loose" iambs (in Frost's terms) are bound to come thick and fast from the pen of one gratefully trained in the English tradition, as Warren was, a clear intention to be iambic is debatable. I think that iambs are nothing Warren counts on; the verse tilts whichever way it must. The accents show you the way to go; counting will only trip you up. "But then he starts demoting the stress of heavily-accented syllables," adds Breslin, "in order to fit them into the anapestic rhythm. One quickly becomes uncertain where the accents should be placed." Nonetheless, the first three lines, he says, are pentameter; the fourth may or may not be pentameter (he protests this ambiguity). But, forced to scan the lines, and allowing them their natural accents (and in poetry even rhetorical emphasis is natural), I would mark them all as hexameters: the first and second, for instance,

> Belów / all síl / ken sóil- / slip, all / crín kled / eárth-crust
> Fár déep / er than / ó cean, / pást róck / that agaínst / róck
> griéves

(this last not iambic at all). But, again, with this poetry metrical analysis (at least of the monitoring kind) is mistaken. The rhythms clearly delineate (and regulate) themselves; their motions are all but italicized. As James Wright said when reviewing *Promises*, "We find the poet like the tennis player keeping his balance and not taking a fall, and feel some kind of relief which is at the same time a fulfillment." We find "a skilled performer . . . always daring to expose his balance to chaos and always regaining the balance."*

One can go further and say that meter—in the full sense of regular rhythm plus rhyme—deadens Warren's gift. It distracts him from his

---

* Wright nonetheless determined "a system of five strong stresses" in the lines of "The Child Next Door": "The regularity becomes clear only if the reader is willing to strain his senses a bit—to give his physical response to the rhythm, as it were, a kind of 'body-English.'" But it takes some straining indeed to find a system of five strong stresses in, say, "Took a pill, or did something to herself she thought would not hurt." Perhaps Warren's rhythm is not best described as a "formality which is deliberately driven to test itself." Formality, or a "strong regularity" counterpointing a "strong distortion," may overstate Warren's defense against chaos.

internal pursuit, drawing him toward trivial externals. (This is not a statement against rhyme and meter in general, but a description of what happens in Warren.) Witness the conclusion of "Convergences," a recent poem about a boy's encounter with a feral tramp, who is last seen disappearing into a train tunnel:

> And your heart gives a cry
> For height, for some snow-peak high,
>
> And lighted by one great star.
> Then in dark you ask who you are.
>
> You ask that, but yet undefined,
> See, in the dark of your mind,
>
> As you once saw, long years back,
> The converging gleams of the track
>
> That speared that small dot yonder
> So that it was sucked under
>
> The mountain—into that black hollow
> Which led where you cannot know.

Having clearly intended the couplet form with its convergences, Warren yet does not reduce us to gratitude for what he can do with it. On the one hand, by demand of his temperament, the formality is driven to test itself, and not one of the lines is regular iambic trimeter or tetrameter. On the other hand, the lines seem formally nagged to be of a similar length, with the result that some eke out what they have to say, or say it facilely: "And your heart gives a cry"; "For height, for some snow-peak high": "And lighted by one great star." It cannot help that the rhyme nags too.

By contrast, the two-line stanzas of "Ah, Anima!" are strong and free. There has been a hurricane and

> you have lain down
>
> In the shards of Time and the un-roar of the wind of being,
> And when, in the dark, you wake, with only

The *klang* of distant boulders in your eyes,
You may wish that you, even in the wrack and pelt of gray
    light,

Had run forth, screaming as wind snatched your breath away
Until you were nameless—oh, anima!—and only

Your mouth, rounded, is there, the utterance gone. Perhaps
That is the only purity—to leave

The husk behind, and leap
Into the blind and antiseptic anger of air.

Here the rhyme crucial to closure, "air" with "there," is discretely in-
ternal and long-intervaled. (The rhyme with "anger" is still more sub-
merged.) Nor is any phrase called up merely for metrical duty. What
is there sweeps in, longs to "run forth." A rhythm of breath-snatching
destiny (a destiny missed) governs the whole. The lines are indifferent
to isocolon, and impatient of every limit (none tolerating a terminal
period until the last). The two-line form is less a place for settling than
a conduit to make the motion quicken. What substitutes for tradi-
tional sorts of regularity (the elastic stanza form aside) are a sinewy
dance of phrases within each sentence and a free alternation between
lines roaring unbroken to the end and lines broken before the last two
or three syllables (most of these last collecting in rhyming pairs: "with
only," "and only"; "to leave," "and leap"). In Warren, what elimi-
nates verbal pastiness and waste is not traditional prosody but a pecu-
liarly vivid conception of what free verse can be. It is free verse, not
meter, that chastens his relation to high words; free verse that makes
him attend.

Warren reading: a high-raised sing-song against which the drawled,
almost growled articulations, the speech rhythms, tug in counter-
movement.

A rusty voice as ready to be inflected up or down as the handle of a
water pump and drawing on sources far within.

Unapologetically Southern, scrappy with regionality, homely but not afraid of emotion. Full of the flakes of time and wear. Full, too, of the feeling of the boy who once stood

> drunk with the perfume of hedge blossom
> And massive moonrise . . .
> In a long lane and cried out,
> In a rage of joy, to seize, and squeeze significance
> From whatever life is—whatever.

Sturdy with acquired knowledge and withstood pain. A cracked thing insistently magnificent.

Warren has three bagsful of words: one for the philosopher in him, one for the naturalist, and one for the hero. The contents of the first (*Truth, Time, fate, No-Time,* and so on) have caused some readers to sneeze, or feel fleeced. Almost everyone values the second (with words like *hawk, mountains, red west, moon*). Perhaps a few are a little dubious about the third (the suffocating density of *pain, know, tell me, cry, heart,* and so forth).

What is wonderful is the way these different lexical sets become woven together. Reacting as the English Romantics did against a national shrinkage of inner depth and native experience, Warren writes what Josephine Miles called the Romantic "spirit's narrative," the "individual's lyrical story," in which a "descriptive panorama of heroic proportions, stressing scenes and sublimities," and an intense quest are further enlarged by meditations on time, anger, energy, the past, passion, truth, beauty, an immanence of meaning, or human affections. (These are the elements, as well, of Ishmael's spiritual narrative and lyrical story in *Moby Dick*; on the American side, Warren inherits from Melville as well as Faulkner.)

Warren's stars, streams, eagles, and so on belong first of all to site (they are more image than type, more presence than image). Out of love, this poet summons whole landscapes onto the page. Yet these landscapes are already encoded with passion. Warren is less the scrupulous observer than the painter of his own yearning. Even "Sunset Scrupulously Observed" is notable less for finely etched detail than for a dramatic sense of contrast and scale:

> A flycatcher, small, species not identified, is perched,
> Unmoving but for tiny turn and scanning
> Twist of head, on the topmost twig, dead,
> Of the tall, scant-leafed, and dying poplar. It
> Is a black point against the cloud-curdled drama
> Of sunset over dark heave
> Of the mountain.

The great rise of things—the heave of the mountain, the cloud-curdled drama of sunset—is already implicit in "A flycatcher, small." Warren but starts with the small; he yearns for the large (the grand, the bold).*

Yet the element of the "small" is all-important to the poetry. (Everything in what works is all-important to it.) A list of Warren's capitalized ponderosities leaves one unprepared for both the naturalistic texture and the heroic tenor of his poetry—the charged situations, the vivid settings, the hammering of the reflections, the questions like yelps of pain or like cries of gratitude. In Warren, philosophical inquiry, the grasp of the grand, is almost a physical action. Certainly it involves acute emotional crisis. The resulting vertical chord of experience is satisfyingly rich, profound.

In a thoughtful review of *Being Here*, Charles Molesworth described Warren's manner as "a grand style flecked with regional flavor and theatrical abstractions," explaining these last by remarking that

---

* I am a creature of this world, but I am also a yearner . . . I feel an immanence of meaning in things . . . I think I put it as close as I could in a poem called 'Masts at Dawn'— 'We must try / To love so well the world that we may believe, in the end, in God.' . . . I would rather start with the world." *Robert Penn Warren Talking: Interviews 1950–1978*, ed. Floyd C. Watkins and John T. Hiers (New York: Random House, 1980), p. 234.

Warren writes, after all, at the intersection of the self and a "cosmic" meaning. "Positively eager to invoke . . . grand, capitalized abstractions, usually considered *verboten* by one of the fundamental tenets of modernism," Warren takes poetry "back to its primordial entanglement with religion and philosophy." Molesworth speculates on what lies behind this: a "deliberately archaic Protestant voice . . . trained to bring up the four last things"; the old Agrarian "quarrel with modernism, especially its mistrust of absolutes and its essentially urban consciousness"; and a strong preference in the American lyric for "the rigors of litany and exaltation." What I would note is how troubled this Protestant voice is, how thwarted its rage for sacramental meaning—how the grand abstractions slide in and out of the lines like specimens under a microscope, often inconclusive, even blank. Warren's theatricality (as at the close of "Unless," "Trying to Tell You Something," or "Heart of Autumn") is usually for the sake of a big emotion despite the absence of a big meaning, "cosmic" truth. His is that God-bereft sublime melodrama that, as Peter Brooks said, is a "form of the tragic . . . for a world in which there is no longer a tenable idea of the sacred." Quoting this comment in an article on Clyfford Still, Nancy Marmer adds that melodramatic excess would elicit "from reductive imagery a charge equivalent to the transcendent flash of spiritual meaning available to earlier art." Man's uncertain "situation in the universe," Warren implied in writing about Stephen Crane, prompts a literary "play of contrasts, of reverses." It makes the imagination veer to stark oppositions. It enforces fierce reconciliations.

Certain words impress themselves on Warren as brilliant, felicitous, magical: perhaps redemption is *here*, and not so much in anything signified as in the indefiniteness of the signifier. "In an author's lexicon," remarks Roland Barthes, "will there not always be a word-as-mana, a word whose ardent, complex, ineffable, and somehow sacred signification gives the illusion that by this word one might answer for everything? Such a word is . . . never *pigeonholed*, always atopic (escaping any topic), at once remainder and supplement." In Warren's lexicon the mana words are "Truth" and "glory." Because these stage a potential of richest meaning, they are near-fetishes. Warren struggles to erect them like a tent in a cosmic waste, but for the most part they flap away; as do, at times, even the somewhat more manageable words "Time" and "joy."

What you hear is a demand that such words yield up their precious secrets. You hear them being approached from and by the words "I," "face," "flesh," "blood," "love," "rage," "listen," "stand," and still others. You hear a dialogue between the words of yearning and the words of essences. The former will not back off. The latter will not give in.

Warren's heroic temper requires the prickle and groan of short Anglo-Saxon words. His longing for a pure sublimity, on the other hand, favors the late-lit library windows and the thin starlit clouds of Latin polysyllables.

In "Snowshoeing Back to Camp in Gloaming" the Anglo-Saxon and Latinate words, packed closely, relieve one another like the black and white in a lump of granite. I quote the opening:

> Scraggle and brush broken through, snow-shower jarred loose
> To drape shoulders, dead boughs, snow-sly and trap-laid,
> Snatching thongs of my snowshoes, I
> Stopped. At the edge of the high mountain mowing,
> I stood. Westward stared
> At the half mile of white alabaster unblemished
> To the blackness of spruce forest lifting
> In a long scree-climb to cliff-thrust,
> Where snow, in level striation of ledges, stretched, and the sun,
> Unmoving, hung
> Clear yet of the peak-snagged horizon—
> The sun, by a spectral spectrum belted,
> Pale in its ghost-nimb.

On the one side, scratchy words like "Snatching," "scraggle," and "snagged"—words snarly with consonants; on the other, words like "striation," "spectral," and "nimb," which seem numb and withdrawn. Because the monosyllables predominate you have to break through the lines as through brush. The Latinate words come to announce that the quest has ended in fright and failure, stymied by an anemic ethereality, a pure and castrating cold.

Yet even the Anglo-Saxon lexicon varies self-refreshingly. If all the words possess vigor, some are unfamiliar. "Scraggle," for instance, is in Webster's Third Edition but not the Second. Its unusualness keys us for the risky metaphysical adventure to follow. "Jarred," "drape," "dead," "trap," "snatching," and so on jut their consonants at us till we come to "mowing"—Anglo-Saxon too, but less blemished by use than the common cow-and-deer-trampled "meadow." If Anglo-Saxon "scree" is no more common than the Latinate synonym "talus," which Warren uses elsewhere, it yet sounds more densely physical; its vowel pierces the mountain silence, renders it mountain-harsh and formidable. Thanks to these niceties of diction, the terrain seems the more treacherously material and strange.

The Latinisms are no less skillfully used. After the thrashing Anglo-Saxon, "alabaster unblemished" sounds especially snow-formal. (Formal, too, in its inverted word order, which leaves "unblemished" unqualifiable at the protected end of the line.) In "spectral spectrum" the seeming redundance (an actual one as to sound) causes each word to pale. Here appearance blurs into apparition; "spectrum" is forced to look at its own ghost. As for "striation," its horizontal polysyllabism reinforces "level" and "ledges"; it is a verbal example of "stretched," another word with a fittingly flat *e*. Then, compared to the more familiar "nimbus," the short, motionless "nimb" seems to have sacrificed something, frozen up. It also seems the weaker for being spliced to another word—would seem to be so even if that word were not the weightless, coughing, Anglo-Saxon "ghost."

The yearning of vitality for meaning requires both vocabularies; but since the (Latinate) "glory" Warren is after flares, "of a sudden, up, / In a blinding blaze, from the filth of the world's floor," it must come to terms with (Old English) "Truth" and "Time." ("Fate" may derive from Latin *fari*, "to speak," but seems all jab.) Something of the same mixture shows up even in the strenuously Platonizing "Evening Hawk," with its "Geometries and orchids that the sunset builds." "Orchids," if not Anglo-Saxon, harks back to *orkhis*, the

Greek word for testicle; "Geometries" calls up a word Warren favors even more—namely, "mathematical"—though Greek *geo*, or "earth," is sealed within it. The description would minimize the difference, indeed confuse it. Lucien Goldmann remarks that the tragic man would hold daily life and meaning together for an instant in his agony, his condition discontinuity and crisis, his heroism a healing return to totality.* Warren's language seems instinctively to be thus repairing. In "Acquaintance with Time in Early Autumn" the lovely phrase "Still ravening on the world's provocation and beauty" offers up the Latinate "provocation" as prickly and pagan, leaving the Anglo-Saxon word "beauty" to harbor everything serene. This turnabout is in the same spirit as "Geometries and orchids." Perplex the opposites. Put them in one another's shoes.

Despite a scattering of unusual words, such as the technical and beautiful "astrolabe," and despite some syntactic dislocation, Warren's poetry is a form of plain speech. We find not the "Hunger of the Word" that, in Barthes's exaggerated claim, is "common to the whole of modern poetry," making "poetic speech terrible and inhuman." We find, instead, the hunger of statement. We find, despite and because of "the morality of form," "the social function of language."

In fact, to some, Warren's language is all too common. Reviewing *Rumor Verified*, Donald Hall found "a collage of cliché, mixed metaphor, abstraction and melodrama." Certainly, he notes, Warren "began as a careful [poet], and perhaps his career is a history of throwing off his astutely civilized restraints. Our literature is full of palefaces going redskin; there is something heady about letting go. But . . . Warren goes too far into the wilderness to return bringing us poems. On his way, he may have stumbled on a method—cliché and abstraction salted with violence—to write the poems his literary culture desires." But what is now and again at fault in *Rumor Verified* is not primitivist

---

* Goldmann writes: "The demand of the tragic mind is that the body would put on immortality. The tragic soul is great and immortal only in so far as it seeks union with passion." *The Hidden God: A Study of Tragic Vision in the Pensées of Pascal and the Tragedies of Racine* (New York: Humanities Press, 1964), ch. 4.

gusto but (an old paleface disease, and a familiar antagonist in War-
ren) a word-disparaging cynicism:

> And you,
> Yet yearning, torn between fear
> And hope, yet ignorant, will, into
> The black conduit of Nature's Repackaging System, be
>   sucked.
> But that possibility is simply too distressing
> To—even—be considered.

This language is not unrestrained; it is only unloved.

Just as poets may be either palefaces or redskins (in a famous but
notably reductive scheme), so they may be either hierarchs or repre-
sentative men (in a scheme hardly less reductive). Hall opens Warren
and finds the "commonplace" question, "Have you ever seen your
own child, that first morning, wait / For the school bus?" Is this an
objection to the commonplace or to the common place of life? He
finds that "orgy of sanguinary commonplace," the close of "Going
West," a poem about the crash of a pheasant against the windshield of
a speeding car:

> I have seen blood explode, blotting out sun, blotting
> Out land, white ribbon of road, the imagined
> Vision of snowcaps.

These lines from "Going West" had not been among those of War-
ren's I prized; but Hall has roused me to find some virtue in them. Far
from being an orgy, they delicately structure what they have to say,
and climax in moving *disappointment*, "imagined" adding an "astute"
complication. Withal, they say their piece firmly, in vigorous accents;
they say it out. They sum up a common experience with a sorrowing
visionary vehemence. We could find a worse epitaph for the century.
In one sense their eloquence is indeed "redskin"—is like that of the
great orator Indian chiefs, the eloquence of the morally appalled.

The *too often* in Warren: snow peaks; dawn; wing-glint; single leaves falling; something reminding you of something; the interruptive use of "again" ("it will, again, come"); the compound "knife-edge"; God's name taken in vain; the word "trying" ("trying to remember"); the word "mission"; the word "glory"; the word "grinds"; questions beginning "Have you"; the expression "no doubt"; the word "joy"; crows calling; the phrase "in anguish" ("and in anguish / Flee"); the anxious imperative "you must"; the know-it-well "of course"; listening to your own heartbeat; the word "heart"; the word "yes"; the word "little"; the word "scream"; the expression "the old" ("the old guaranteed rhythm"); the assurance "you know"; the word "Platonic"; things not knowing their own name; references to roars; explicitness; discursiveness; the word "mathematical"; the word "truth"; poems about something stalking you.

The *too much*: unasked-for advice delivered unsympathetically; facile references to God's mercy and other characteristics; the words "mystic" and "darkling"; neurasthenic commands ("Be careful!"); long titles.

The *too little*: quietness; weeding out in the *Selected Poems*.

Extensively revised in 1979, *Brother to Dragons* was brought closer to being "recent"—mature Warren. But great improvement though it is, it is only the 1953 version pruned. Playing surgeon to his own work, Warren has spotted and removed numerous verbal tumors. But the piece remains overlong. Something of the problem Robert Lowell noted in reviewing the original version still lingers: "As for the characters, nothing limits the length of their speeches except the not very importunate necessity of eventually completing the story." The situation is all-too-posthumous. As Delmore Schwartz said, the question is: "once one has faced the actuality of human evil, how is it possible to believe truly in any human ideal and aspiration?" Thomas Jefferson, his nephew Lilburne (who murdered a slave), other members of the family, and "R.P.W." (as Lowell said, "Pilgrim, Everyman, Chorus and Warren, the real person") "exist within the disillusion and despair of this question, striving and failing to answer it." They suffer the melancholy of feeling morally lost. The few approaches to hope and faith are like sickening lurches. Gathered somewhere beyond the grave (or only on the page) these characters cannot redeem what has happened; they can only talk.

In the revised version, the verse has its moments. To be sure, bloated rhetoric from 1953 still floats by—Warren dropped "the day's finicking shamelessnesses" but kept "The impudent daylight's velleities, and errors"; and so on. But the writing is never quite so bad as Leslie Fiedler praised it for being. "Bombast," he said it was—"bombast . . . in the technical sense of the word: bombast as in Seneca or the Jacobean dramatists, a straining of language and tone toward a scream which can no longer be heard, the absolute cry of bafflement and pain." But though *Brother to Dragons* is the most despairingly melodramatic of Warren's works, it is too morally earnest to suggest a scream. In fact, its vice of tone is a certain pompousness that wears no clothes, a straining for *virtuous wisdom* in the incertitude of the void.

What saves the work (and for a very long modern poem it reads wondrously well) is, in Louise Bogan's words, its "virtuoso use of folk speech" and its workhorse narrative and descriptive middle style. "It's just his blues come on. He loves you still" is monosyllabic folk poetry—has learned from Robert Frost. And folk speech becomes subtle and strenuous with reflection in

> And I wanted to yell "Stop!" But couldn't
> For if a thing is like an awful remembering
> That comes from you deep inside, then you can't say "Stop."
> For it's already happened, it's you.

As for the middle style, it is easy to go along with: antimelodramatic, mimetic, ready to hand, and frequently better than workaday: "And blackberry, man-high, dry-snagging for your blood."

Yet there are few clean long runs. The problem is hinted at in R.P.W.'s self-description as

> A fellow of forty, a stranger, and a fool,
> Red-headed, freckled, lean, a little stooped,
> Who yearned to be understood, to make communication,

To touch the ironic immensity of afternoon with meaning,
While the sun insanely screamed out all it knew,
Its one wild word:
Light, light, light!
And all identity tottered to that remorseless vibration.

It is the stilted making of communication that adds pomp to the otherwise arresting

> We must remember that always the destroyer
> It is who has most need of love: therefore destroys.
> And in the unity of life remember
> That destruction's but creation gone astray

A touch too much of didacticism makes overprecise the accents of

> every act to become an act must resolve
> The essential polarity of possibility,
> Yet in the act polarity will lurk,
> Like the apple blossom ghostly in the full-grown fruit.
> Yet all we yearn for is the dear redemption of
> Simplicity.

A wish to touch ironic immensity with dignified meaning turns to frost the formality of

> When ice breaks, the rivers flood effortlessly,
> And the dog-fox, stranded on the lost hillock,
> Barks in hysteria among the hazel stems.
> . . . . .
> The rigid
> Muzzle triangulates the imperial moon.

This last is beautiful, but as verse it seems to be lifting its skirts up out of the mud.

How good is the writing in Warren's other book-length poem, *Chief Joseph of the Nez Perce, Who Called Themselves the Nimipu—"the Real People"* (1983), which is also in freed-up blank verse? It is more carefully consistent than that of *Brother to Dragons* but less excited and exciting. Its beautiful thin piercing note comes to us as from far away mountains. Heartbreaking as Chief Joseph's betrayal by the Washington government is, the language has already mostly given up the fight. Where the earlier work strains for sacramental monumentality, *Chief Joseph* is elegiacally mild. The writing lacks the "ontological" amassings that can make literature seem denser and richer than life. The words flow with a lovely accomplishment, then are gone. Pristine images of blue mountains, shag of conifer, "stream-yelping canyons," dust "swelling slow in the pale pink of dawn-shine," "plains of great grass curried / By wind-comb or lying gray-green in its slickness" seem already traces of themselves as you read. Warren's line is too little knotted against dispersals. Should we not feel grateful for this unexpected chasteness of style? Yes, and yet without his gnarled magnificence Warren is strangely subdued. Something, you feel, is wrong.

Except for several documentary prose inserts, *Chief Joseph* is a weave of two voices: the poet's, discursive, and the chief's, *faux naif*. Joseph sounds more "Indian" here than in the white transcription of his rebuke to the government, which is quoted by Warren in *American Literature: The Makers and the Making*:

> "Into a dark place my father had gone.
> You know how the hunter, at dawn, waits,
> String notched, where the buck comes to drink. Waits,
> While first light brightens highest spruce bough, eyes slitted
> Like knife wounds, breath with no motion. My father
> Waits thus in his dark place. Waiting, sees all.
> Sees the green worm on green leaf stir. Sees
> The apsen leaf turn though no wind, sees
> The shadow of thought in my heart—the lie
> The heel must crush. Before action, sees
> The deed of my hand. My hope is his Wisdom.
>
> "Oh, open, Great Spirit, my ears, my heart,
> To his sky-cry as though from a snow-peak of distance!"

If the heroic Warren had been a man of the people, all burden of re-
sponsibility, all conscience, all love, this is how he might have sound-
ed. (The Indian in Warren has always been not a lawless "redskin,"
but a great chief.) Still, the impersonation does not quite work; it re-
mains a paleface's ventriloquism. It's a touch studied, self-conscious.
Besides, nineteenth-century Indian oratory was sterner than this, its
earnestness more athletic, with less vibrato.

Since Joseph's voice is cut from the curt-vital side of Warren's own
typical style, we must not wonder that the poet sometimes sounds as
Indian as his hero:

> Their ponies, crossed
> With the strong blood of horses, well-bred, graze
> Richly the green blade. Boys, bareback, ride naked,
> Leap on, shout "Ai-yah!" Shout "Ai-yee!"—
> In unbridled glory. Eagle wing catches sun.
> Gleams white . . .

Yet his impulse to elaborate, now bookish, now cinematic, is no less
in evidence. The history and geography of the struggle are fuel to its
flame. The wide view, the disabused view, inspires it. Thus on page
32, at the top, a sentence rises that sweeps over the Little Bear Paw
Mountains, the coulees and canyons southward, the grass plains and
alkali flats and stands of dead poplars farther on, past still more can-
yons and coulees, then the Little Rockies, then the glittering Missou-
ri, and so on till (a third of the way down page 33) it resumes (what
had been lurking all along) the chronicle of the bluecoats' chase of the
Indians: "And there, / Two hundred miles off, slow, slow, in distance,
. . . the advancing / Riffle of dust. They come." The sublime expanse
of the land is suggested by a panoramic sentence assuming a privi-
leged, inhuman perspective: "If you were the eyes of the Eagles of
eagles."

In part, the Southern respect for forebears speeds Warren into
sympathy with Joseph—turns him against the hypocritical Christian
bluecoats, whose spring of action is really the vanity of personal glory.
Nostalgic for what in *Democracy and Poetry* he names "a sense of vital
relations among individuals," "a community as distinguished from a

mere society," he honors in the Nez Perce that "Spirit" of a people that, in Hegel's words, enables the individual "to have a definite place in the world—to be *something*. For [the individual] finds the being of the people to which he belongs an already established, firm world—objectively present to him—with which he has to incorporate himself." In contrast to the white man, each of whom is still "alone with America," for the Indian there was (as Chief Seattle put it) no place in this country where a man could be alone: "The ground where you stand," he explained, "responds more lovingly to our feet than yours, because it is the ashes of our grandfathers. Our bare feet know the kindred touch."

From his isolation in corporate America, Warren turns as if for an herb-cure to a people who together formed a *Being* for each and all, till driven to the desolate make-town of Nespelem in Washington State, where today the hastily carpentered shacks stand in bare disbelief on the patchy lots, none wanting to be recognized by the neighbors. But the facts turn the poem into still another elegy for noble manhood and love of the birthplace. Hence the fleeing bowstring tingle and whirr of Warren's valedictory words. The "Mother," our earth, has become an old tale. The definite, sovereign presences are gone.

THREE

Sunny Particulars

"*In reading,*" Vladimir Nabokov said, "one should notice and fondle details. There is nothing wrong about the moonshine of generalization when it comes *after* the sunny trifles of the book have been lovingly collected." It is not the most natural thing to read, or to write about, Warren in this way; for, as Stanley Plumly notes, "the broad, sometimes sweeping nature of his poems tends to obscure the smaller, brilliant moments." To dwell, then, on some of Warren's "sunny" moments may serve a useful purpose, that of refining an appreciation of his poetry.

1.   *Where eye-into-eye mountains see sun come.*
     (*Chief Joseph of the Nez Perce*, p. 28.)

The chief as poetic first-man, mirror-seeing a seeing, multiplying his faculties and his courage (eye to eye). (Compare "The sun, / Man to man, stares you straight in the eye" in "Going West," *Rumor Verified*.) "Metaphysical claustrophobia" (a modern paleface pathology, according to *Democracy and Poetry*) steams off like morning mist.

The deadlock hyphens of "eye-into-eye" impale each eye by the arrowing force of the other.

A touch of cartoon Indian talk: "see sun come." (Fee, fie, foe, fum.)

2. *But dimmer by distance, almost transparent / In late light, un-formed as a thumb-smear, blue blur / On the sky's autumnal yel-lowness: Howard.*
    (*Chief Joseph of the Nez Perce*, p. 33.)

The images, the syntax, the periodic construction all say, "We do not want General Howard to come"; yet, inexorably, the brute negative at the outset already sealing his advent, he comes.

Even so late as the colon—that cleft stick—the sentence is still try-ing to pin him to distance. (The next lines tell of how this general, "Old One-Arm," knows "Himself snared in God's cleft stick of jus-tice"; but that is of no help to Chief Joseph.)

No verb, as if that would stop Howard cold in his tracks. But the spying of him, his very appearance, is a verb. If he appears, it is in or-der to advance; he follows but to pursue; he is Howard, dread name, name with a host of faces, an action.

"Dimmer by distance" would diminish him by a fastidious exacti-tude and a guttering short *i*. The *d*'s also rally against him. "Almost transparent" feels eager to decorporealize him; the stress on "almost" sounds keen. "Unformed as a thumb-smear, blue blur" grants him only a begrudged visibility, here correlative with a blurred series of sounds. It hints at the white man's disfiguring effect on the land, his botched and botching spirituality, his confusion.*

The day is late, the season late, but still Howard comes.

3. *Snow red, then redder, / And reddening more, as snow falls / From the unperturbed gray purity of sky.*
    (*Chief Joseph of the Nez Perce*, p. 41.)

A fragment orientally complete. Yet it recalls those not-right, spell-binding full-page art reproductions that resolvingly read at the bot-tom: "Detail from—." It is as stylized and snappy as a corner from an Uccello.

---

*   Commenting on Stephen Crane's *Red Badge of Courage* in *American Literature: The Makers and the Making*, Warren said: "Blue is the color of man outside nature." *American Lit-erature: The Makers and the Making*, vol. 2 (New York: St. Martin's, 1973), p. 1643.

The unpleasant *e* in "red, then redder" momentarily and deceptively turns to something warmer in "And," only to assert itself again, sickeningly, in "reddening." When "snow" reappears it is indifferently and incongruously not the same snow, but an expression of the unperturbed sky. The *ur* (twice) in "unperturbed" and again in "purity" is further back in the mouth than the "e" of "red," and seals the phrase off in essential remoteness.

As "Snow red" gives way to "then redder," the rhythm quickens; it further quickens with "And reddening more." This syncopation seems as heartless as the unperturbed gray purity of sky, which also comes to us in syncopation. Not so, cries the imagination, stricken by the dreadful unrelentingness of the focus: its transfixion. The one care is to avoid trauma, play dumb: speak of the color red, not of blood. Isolate the sensory. The sensory, as in "gray purity," is innocent.

All human madness, folly, violence lies in the incremental paradigm "red, then redder, / And reddening more." Is rampant there; horror added to horror and unable to stop horror. As for time, it is helplessly divided between the part of it that has already fallen—catching blood in its makeshift basin of ice-crystals, only to wash it away unredeemed—and what has yet to fall, is even now falling. Of course its sky would be gray. And of course this gray means nothing at all.

4.   *And feet / Find the rustle and kitten-tongue kiss of the foam creeping in.*
      ("Chthonian Revelation: A Myth," *Rumor Verified*, p. 4.)

Feet so generalized that for the moment, out of pity, you adopt them. And now your feet have ears, the whole body listens through them, concentrating its sentience there, to find the rustle. This last, true to its nature, attempts to withhold itself in its elusive syllables and through eluding the lock-in alliteration of "feet / Find"; but is found.

Then, with a tactile shock, the feet cease to hear and become whole body, wholly body, tightening deliciously at the ocean-endearing, body-invading foam. The lion ocean with kitten tongue.

The sounded vowel of "rustle" reappears in the more compressed word "tongue" and in an obvious but satisfying way the *k*'s in "kiss" and "kitten" kiss. Fate winks in the inexorable alliteration of "feet / Find . . . foam," but this fate has been sought out, is a storied bully-roar like (here it is again) fee, fie, foe . . . feet find foam tongue. "Creeping" also harks back to "feet," as if rushing to meet it in an aural destiny.

5.   *Finally, comes first dawn-streak, sallow / Or slow glow from one small cinder of red / Beyond black trees.*
      ("After Restless Night," *Rumor Verified*, p. 55.)

The inversion in "comes first dawn-streak" complains as much as impatient "Finally" does against the slow coming: unceremoniously, it shoves the arrival into first position, a tactic that loses as much as it gains, since it further delays the grateful naming of the dawn-streak. After a sleepless night the temper is frayed, even desperate. Everything irritates and disappoints. "First" is half a gripe (no all-at-once?) and "-streak" gnashes "dawn" with its hyphen. Then, compounding the aggravation, the *ow* in "sallow / Or slow glow" drips thick as tallow and congeals three times.

What was wanted, then? An eager new start? But this new day, "one small cinder," seems only a feeble flare-up of burnt-out days gone before. And the trees intervene like the black bars of a fire grate . . . trees blackened as if by a previously exhausted blaze.

Description? Rather, experience, interior as a headache or despair.

6.   *Dividing fields, long hedges, in white / Bloom powdered, gently slope to the / Blue of sea that glitters in joy of its being.*
      ("Another Dimension," *Rumor Verified*, p. 70.)

Mere existence is marked by division and long reaches (time, effort); its beauty and joy are a superficial powdering. Being, by contrast, is as free of straining and number as "Blue of the sea that glitters in joy of its being" is free of caesura. The sea coincides with itself, and that is the profoundest joy. The prepositions "of," "in," "of" ("of sea that glitters in joy of") are like the lights on its surface that twinkle now here, now there, as the sea signals to itself its pleasure in its own illimitable expanse.

"Gently slope": living life naturally if yearningly and attentively through to the end is the only path to redemptive ecstasy. The joy of life is its final self-completion, the moment when destiny rocks in the cradle of fate.

7.   *Gasp-glory of gold light of dawn on gold maple.*
      ("Gasp-Glory of Gold Light," *Rumor Verified*, p. 72.)

To enforce its claim, the line is literally breathtaking. The monosyllables "of gold light of dawn on gold" hoard the little breath left over after "Gasp-glory," so that "maple" faints with more than its usual dying fall.

"Gold light of dawn on gold": spying the gold tree nimbed in its own mellow fulfillment and self-farewell, the gold light of dawn, in its eternal beginning, discovers what most resembles it at the opposite end of time, and rushing to meet it gasps in delight, in the sweetness of a fugitive reconciliation. (It is anyway in the nature of light, which has no inner bounds, to refer to other things, in a physics of adoration—to gasp.) Does this union occur in "no-Time," or "Time fulfilled"? The absence of tense is unable to decide. Between diurnal arrival and a seasonal leavetaking, the line is all delicious distraction. Certainly the moment dissolves the division Warren is often conscious of, which elsewhere he puts as follows: "Here . . . the . . . shadow, there, of the wide world, the flame."

"Gasp-glory" is a startled union, even for a compound. It works the intellect as hard as it does the mouth. A glory sudden as a gasp. A glory like astonishment. An astonishing glory that makes the poet, even his compound, gasp.

The line is full of echoing and re-echoing doubles: not only the alliterating compound but the duo stress of *gold light*, the rhyme of "dawn on," the repetition of "gold," the similar fall of "glory" and "maple," and the doubling of *of*. This last is generously periphrastic—

"of gold light of dawn"; it follows the flinging of the self-forgetting (if mirror-finding) light. Yet the exclusion of articles pulls everything together in a sharp-drawn gasp. The line concentrates a specific glory as a virtual node of Being, an unexpected quick blaze at the end of a far journeying.

8. *Where now boughs hung heavy, white only, no crimson / Of maple, no willow by destiny yellow.*
   ("Snow out of Season," *Rumor Verified*, p. 73.)

The two *no*'s negatively invert this lament for the loss of life-establishing distinctions. At least they try. The first flaunts a crimson maple, the second a yellow willow. Together they hinge a panel of fall to one of winter, so that both the autumnal maple and willow, with blank snow for foil, suddenly flame with life. In this context, "crimson" startles, like the sight of blood. And a "willow by destiny yellow" is—sounds—mellowly organic: a perfection meant to be. The close of this lovely phrase harmonizes with its beginning: ripeness is all.

As for the snow, it can move boughs only from outside—is pure burden, inert. This the doublings of rhyme and accent in "now boughs" and "hung heavy" attest. Then, too, "Where" adds its weight to "white," the cold winds of winter blowing in the initial consonants. "White only," "no crimson," and "no willow" all droop, "hung heavy." Even as it enacts this absence of expression, of anything to express, poetry must protest it, and does. But the vivid images of maple and willow are resisted by the rhythm. "Of maple" sounds limp after "no crimson," one stress to two; and the liquid and fleeting "by destiny yellow" is not so firm as the severe "no willow." The cheerful foliage is no longer actually in view, and the rhythm declares it gone. The boughs hang heavy "now." Fate has overtaken destiny, the colorful, even-to-the-end-benign pattern of life.

9.   *And hear, somewhere, a summer-thinned brook descending, / Past*
      stone, and stone, its musical stair.
      ("Have You Ever Eaten Stars?" *Rumor Verified*, p. 88.)

The sound of "hear" feels closer to the ears than that of "where": it
feels "here." "And hear, somewhere" is first near, then distant, the lat-
ter effect enhanced by the parenthesis.

Hear "a summer-thinned brook descending": the declaration be-
comes an unwitting directive by its vivid illustration of what was
heard. "Summer-thinned" is hard-stressed and raised like a brook bot-
tom pressing close to the water surface. "Thinned" is self-illustrating,
the more so after the deeper resonance of "summer." It rhymes, in a
thin continuity, with "descending," the tail of which obligingly drops
down.

Hear the brook descending "Past stone, and stone, its musical
stair." This is even more delicately and self-delightingly enactive. The
brook begins to seem debonair. Rid of its former, its youthful, turbu-
lence, the brook takes to maturity like a seasoned dancer, with a heart
made light by wisdom. The graceful sway of "Past stone, and stone"
gentles motion with duration. After these monosyllabic iambs, the lit-
tle spill of syllables in "musical" is a refreshing quickening. The word
all but tinkles. Then "stair," echoing "somewhere" and even "hear,"
and balancing "stone," connects these several things, as stairways do.
(Throughout there is a measured stepping of rhyme, from "hear" to
"-where," from "some-" to "sum-," and so on.) A resonant hum bal-
ances the sibilant slide and keeps the little brook from running too
shallow.

Poetry, language in a self-extending, self-remembering, and self-
refreshing mood, meets in the changing, continuous, and musical
brook its contenting paradigm.

10.   *There, by a deer trail, by deer dung nourished, / Burst the gleam,
      rain-summoned, / Of bright golden chanterelles.*
      ("Have You Ever Eaten Stars?" *Rumor Verified,* p. 89.)

"Chanterelles" is finally borne to us, rhythm-summoned, at the
breaking end of a chant disguised as a declaration. First a ritual of ex-
cited pointing ("There"). Then teasing asides, the fond sashay of "by a
deer trail, by deer dung nourished." Then the calmest, most elabo-
rate, most delayed of bursts.

Here the interruptive "rain-summoned" harks back, pace slow-
ingly, to its co-agent in nurturing, the dung, a drumming resonance
answering to the duffy one. The feeling for organic process is strong
("deer dung nourished," a phrase gradual-growth-slow) but no less
strong the elation over the transcendence of dung and darkness in the
bright chanterelles.

The whispery syllables of "chanterelles" insinuate the word into
our deepest favor. There they are, an inexplicable richness produced
by wholly natural, even insignificant means. And that is how glory ar-
rives in our quarter—from out of "sky-darkness" and dung, doubtless
undeserved, always expected.

11.   *Beyond the black lace of low bough-droop / Sky shows, and stars
      sown random and rabble and white.*
      ("Recollection in Upper Ontario, from Long Before," *Being Here,*
      p. 13.)

A barbarous lace, this, of dropping boughs: the figure forces delicacy
onto roughness, smallness onto largeness, pattern onto accident, man-
ufacture onto nature, and vice versa. In the peek-a-boo fashion of
lace, this liberating mutual transgression hides another: nature, if thus
domesticated, is at the same time sexualized. A "show" of lawless
white beyond black lace . . . a lace, however, instinct with mourning,
the sex already exhausted by guilt, low and drooping.

The close-packed similar-sounding monosyllables in "the black lace
of low bough-droop" seem trapped in a net. Meanwhile something

behind the black lace runs riot (with the help of polysyndeton and the disyllabic "random" and "rabble"). This celestial sowing of white oats suggests a nightscape, a wild escape, an escapade, of sperm.

In their quickened anapestic rhythm ("-dom and rabble and white"), the stars lead on like the wild crowd in Warren's novel *Wilderness*—they're as dense and disorderly, and who can say what mischief they may be up to, who can stop their alarming profanation of space? The nihilistic "language of sexuality," notes Michael Foucault, "has lifted us into the night where God is absent, and where all of our actions are addressed to this absence in a profanation which at once identifies it, dissipates it, exhausts itself in it."

12. *By what star-tumbling stream, or through / What soundless snow which wipers groan / To cope with.*
    ("Part of What Might Have Been a Short Story, Almost Forgotten," *Being Here*, p. 53.)

The poignantly ambivalent Warren universe: intimate, adverse. Companionable "by" gives way to heavygoing "through" and antagonistic "with."

"Star-tumbling stream" casually, indeed all but negligibly, compresses Shelley's blithe and sublime "Worlds on worlds are rolling ever, / From creation to decay, / Like the bubbles on a river / Sparkling, bursting, borne away." Does the stream bring the stars to grief or polish them like a rock-hound's tumbler? The image is too insouciant to say. No matter, for the stream is beside you, time befriends you, is your spectacle, star-laced, ever-flowing.

Till time explodes into terror, discloses itself as a flurrying dispersal, snowflake-tumbling. The adjective "soundless" is an unbearable withholding (the stream begins to sound in its vacuum, as pure loss). Dead-mute evidence of entropic randomness, the snow is abstracted from all expression—against this the wipers groan as they must, in the midst of a Miltonic series of moaning *o*'s, laboring to give man a view of the road ahead.

The concluding "with" ("To cope with") is too weak to buttress the long second phrase, and leaves us in mid-contest, with nothing concluded. How lovely by contrast, how much more to be preferred, the balance of "*star*" and "*stream*" and the reluctant-to-let-go *m* in "star-tumbling stream."

13. *The first .44 explosion, cottony / In distance, but solid too, as though at the snatch / Of a ripe boll you'd found the hot slug inside, blood-wet.*
("Deep—Deeper Down," *Being Here,* p. 55.)

The muffled deep-throated "un" sound, heard first in "explosion," returns almost at once in "cottony," miming and intensifying the quality observed. "Snatch" is wonderfully vivid even in sound ("distance" is cottony by comparison); and "ripe boll," amplified by "though," stands out ripely against the earlier "solid." The zinging monosyllables multiply: "snatch," "ripe," "boll," "you'd," "found," "hot," "slug." These are the sounds of action, of excitement, of something hot and ripe and up close.

A stunning descriptive precision is infiltrated and overtaken by a curious wild element of transgression. Something distant, a sound, turns, in the chrysalis of the "as though," into something close, if conditional: a sound and more, a physical tearing and a visual spying. Violence has multiplied, from sense to sense to sense (for "hot" and "wet" figure in too). We cannot miss, besides, a crude sexual overtone in "snatch" and "hot," or the disturbing quality of "blood-wet." In their warp of suggestion the lines register the intuition that to fire a rifle, snatch off a boll, and make a sexual assault are alike rages against being kept out by appearances, even if what is inside is bloody, anomalous, the "rich slime of being." Behind the ripe boll lies what was not meant to be uncovered, seen. The sanctity of appearance has been violated. In *The Life of the Mind* Hannah Arendt repeats Adolf Portmann's distinction between authentic and inauthentic appearances. The first come to light of their own accord, the second (plant roots, inner animal organs) are "visible only through interference with and violation of the 'authentic' appearance . . . . Inside organs . . . are never pleasing to the eye. Once forced into view, they look as though they had been thrown together piecemeal, and . . . they appear alike." The exposed boneless slug is an obscenity in the realm of appearance. But the boll had to be snatched away. Guns must be fired. Women penetrated. For appearance is an intolerable barrier to the something inside, behind, unseen. Appearance is the ripeness between us and the mystery of origin and death.

14. *The hollow is Danae's lap lavished with gold by the god.*
     ("No Bird Does Call," *Being Here*, p. 66.)

A polygamous, made-on-Parnassus marriage of "hollow," "god," and "gold," as also of "Danae," "lap," and "lavished." The latter group lies in the center of the line, compact as a lap; "gold" and "god" spill back all the way to "hollow." Yet no spoiling effect of a mechanical arrangement or the squinting jeweler's art. Instead, strong-limbed motion, big-limbed beauty.

But can the gorgeous and glittering legend of Danae still be "hit" for poetic delight, even if, as here, subvertingly applied to passive and voluptuous but infertile autumn? An eccentric talent, like Ashbery's, could bring it off, but by skewing the "classic" feel of the image. Not unhonorably, Warren attempts it straight. And indeed, in context, the ball goes beautifully into the pocket. But that is where you find it upon returning—already sunken, experienced, exhausted.

15. *The bubble, / Enormous, red, molten, of sun, above the horizon, / Apparently motionless, hangs.*
     ("Prairie Harvest," *Being Here*, p. 74.)

The writing minces, but in order to swell and slow the passing parts, as if to give them ontogenic loom, and to protract the act of writing itself. And all because the sun is about to (you'd think for the very first time) go down.

In their vehemence and number, the adjectives—"Enormous, red,

molten"—overwhelm the fragile "bubble," like so many garish, pos-
turing semblances to which the disabused noun gives the lie. Yet
"bubble" is the lie (the hysterical figure), and the adjectives are fact, or
close enough. The description is divided against itself: part immedi-
ate, part prophetic; part excited, part chagrined.

In repeating (if garbling) "molten," "motionless" reenforces itself,
braving "Apparently." On the other hand, the *uh* sound in "horizon,"
repeating the ones in "The," "bubble," "Enormous," "molten," "of,"
"sun," "above," and "the," firmly glues this word to the others, set-
ting no store by "above" and sealing the fate of the sun.

Strip the sentence of its suspensions and it reads "The bubble of
sun hangs." The three interrupting phrases—"Enormous, red, mol-
ten," "above the horizon," "Apparently motionless"—concentrate
both the syntactic and the semantic resistance to the imminent disap-
pearance. Yet "the bubble of sun hangs" is less disturbing than the sen-
tence in its resistances and delays. The first betrays no fear; the second
is all alarm. When "hangs" finally falls into position, it whangs like a
dropping blade.

Characteristically, the writing deliberately flouts a limit—in this
case, time. Engorged with what it wants to detain, it struggles against
the unfelt, general, detached character of language. This alone is writ-
ing. To write is to oppose death.

16.   *The eagle rides air currents, switch and swell.*
       ("Eagle Descending," *Being Here*, p. 77.)

A syntactic switch-maneuver, unusual in Warren but dictated here by
his pervasive principle of enactment.

You want first to read "switch" as what the eagle does, parallel with
"rides," despite its disagreement in number. But "swell" makes you
switch "switch" over to "currents," from verb to noun.

"Switch and swell" swells the meaning of "currents."

If the mind had a stomach that fluttered and floated as direction
switched . . .

17.   *Late August star-fall, / When the first crickets crinkled the dark.*
("Amazing Grace in the Back Country," *Now and Then*, p. 8.)

Usually no sharp particularizer in observation, even here Warren merely gestures in homage to late August star-fall, though attentively enough to make the *a* vowel sink at length into the soft *l*'s, and the acute terminal *t*'s give way to quieter *r* and *l*. Yet he comes up with the delightful discovery and invention—perhaps the happiest moments of poetry involve both—that crickets crinkle the dark.

Eyes fixed on the remembered star-fall, the ears hear a counterpoint in the rapid curl-up of the cricket's song, one that draws the surface of the darkness with it into shrills. Or have they simply harkened to the word "crickets," in which "crinkled" already lies crinkled up?

18.   *Uttering, "Lust—lust—lust," / Like an invocation, out loud—and the word / So lovely, fresh-minted.*
("Amazing Grace in the Back Country," *Now and Then*, p. 9.)

The erotic and the aesthetic are born in the same instant, intertwined inside a fuzzed word. A twelve-year-old boy's profane counterpart, a poet's counterpart, to "amazing grace."

The word "lust" rubs against the night like a velvet file. Already a "focal word" in Coleridge's sense, it has "acquired a *feeling of reality* . . . If we do not grasp it, it seems to grasp us, as with a hand of flesh and blood, and completely counterfeits an immediate presence." Yet the repetition "lust—lust—lust" foretells the something-not-yielded-up by lust, the "Pain of fulfillment-that-is-not-fulfillment": a panting cycle.

Though "minted" seems to come cool and firm out of "fresh," the word can do little to still the intestinal urging, the *uh* of "Uttering," "lust," and lovely": the hint that this word is in the bowels of speech, energy, and beauty. "Minted" needs all its strength to keep from drowning in the echo of "invocation." Magic, not fabrication, rules the night.

In any case, what is fresh-minted is to be appreciated; held up to the light, before it is spent. The word "lust," however, is more like a punctured balloon than a coin—despite its dental *t*, a bag of wet escaping air.

19.   *Time / Is only a shade on the underside of the beach-leaf / Which,*
       upward, reflects a tiny refulgence of stars.
       ("Dream," *Now and Then*, p. 29.)

Time is shade; eternity, light. These opposites, which can never meet, yet lie as close as the two sides of a coin. This estranged proximity is eerie. Life, if in-between, is far closer to the shade than to the light. It is *in* the shade, the shade is on it. It merely "reflects" the light, the light reaching it is "tiny."

Yet you want to see this leaf with its tiny refulgence of stars. You think of the little treasure chest of weak, concentrated starlight; you'd almost sooner see this than eternity direct. You feel the romance of dimness and unimaginable distance and of far, but strangely transmissible, light.

"Tiny" seems the more to be valued for not being qualified by niggling "only," as Time is ("Time is only a shade"); a fairy miniaturization of the glory of innumerable vast stars. And "refulgence" sounds like an elation of light because of the way it reflects the *ub* in "upward" but spreads it tensely up and back in the mouth. "-gence" is juicy. The word is full to the mouth, unusual, somewhat elusive—a glamor.

20.   *To leave / The husk behind, and leap / Into the blind and antiseptic*
       anger of air.
       ("Ah, Anima!" *Now and Then*, p. 34.)

The straining iambs offer hope of a successful leap; then again they seem to mire the effort: to *leave* the *husk* be*hind*, and *leap*—this is discouraging. Even apart from the rhythm, the ear hears several of the same things being taken up again: *lea* in "leave" and "leap," the whining close of "behind" and "blind," the article "the," the conjunction "and."

Then polysyllabic "antiseptic" wriggles like a cat before making a jump, quickening anticipation, and the first syllable of "anger" almost whangs past itself. "Anger" then contracts, fiercely, into "air." The ear is finally convinced of a Dionysian shedding of heavy, self-repeating form, despite the sharp wistfulness of the infinitive, "to leave."

21.   *Clumps of horses, fog-colored in sea fog, rumps / To the sea wind, standing like stone primitively hewn, / While the fields, gray, stretch beyond them, and distance dies.*
("The Mission," *Now and Then,* p. 42.)

"Clumps": five consonants swallow the sole vowel, just as, in the scene described, the inanimate attempts to take over the animate, gray-whiting it, rendering it indistinctly elemental, forcing it to turn lookalike rumps toward the sea fog and sea wind. Quick molds of life appear to be insensate shapes hacked from stone. The horses are distinguishable from the gray fields only in seeming to be heavy dead matter in the foreground, whereas the fields extend without mission in the distance, which by definition emerges but to die.

The sound-patterning of "clumps . . . fog . . . fog, rumps" whispers "enclosedness . . . sameness." "Standing . . . stone" confirms itself through its rigidifying repetition. When it comes to the fields, the only epithet for which the syntax pauses is "gray," which is ironically separated off as if it were a special feature instead of what it is: the common lot under the all-demoting fog. Distance dies in your very ears as the disyllable "distance" contracts, the vowel gaping open like a mouth, into "dies." The period knows when to fall.

22.   *While heart of the backlog / Of oak simmers red in the living pulse*
       of its own / Decay.
       ("Heart of the Backlog," *Now and Then*, p. 63.)

A text full of twists. "Heart" is surprised by "backlog," which de-
centers it, yet "backlog / Of oak" looks and sounds tidy, intended:
the log is where someone wants it, its red heart warming as if being
appreciated. A "simmering" heart might be in a cooking pan; this one
is in the fire, *is* the fire, and pulses—or rather its decay does. It lives
and dies in the same motion and moment.

An instinctual utopia, perhaps. The rage for life and the desire for
death swooning into each other, till uncertain which is which. Fatigue
and freshness instantaneous in a radiant node.

The Dionysian tamed and backlogged into the Apollonian but
mutteringly remembering its rages, still blind except to its own red
heat.

A fable of destruction as the costly, flamboyant condition of life.

23.   *The night pants hot like a dog, it breathes / Off the blossoming bay-*
       ou like the expensive whiff / Of floral tributes at a gangster's funeral
       in N.O., / It breathes the smell love makes in darkness.
       ("Old Nigger on One-Mule Cart Encountered Late at Night When
       Driving Home from Party in the Back Country," *Can I See Arcturus
       from Where I Stand?*, in *Selected Poems*, p. 14.)

What is missing in this night that *pants hot*—a night of the body, un-
sanctified, breathing, giving off smells, smelling—is the achieved dura-
tion of spirit. Conscience is as suspect in it as "sincere" mourning at a
gangster's funeral. Everything is given over to the body and its death.
What love "makes" is a smell: a rich funereal smell. (The cut floral tri-
butes trail the "little death" that is accompanied by pantings and the
smell love makes in darkness) In this poem, love-making is as deper-
sonalized and abbreviated as the initials N.O. Later there is "sweat-
grapple, in darkness, then / Sleep." Then the "hour / When joy-
sweat, or night-sweat"—the difference appears minimal—"has dried
to a microscopic / Crust on the skin."

Three speech-breaths, the middle one expensive/expansive. Each statement has its own distinctive rhythm—the first short of breath, the second a flowery expenditure of the same, full of the *overthereness* and overpowering *arrival here* of the blossoming bayou, the third breathing more easily, and in wonder; but they come—and go—thick and fast, like pants. It is not breath that lasts but—the close of the poem will intimate it—written poetry, a "name."

24. *And that thought is not words, but a roar like a wind, or / The roar of the night-freight beating the rails of the trestle, / And you under the trestle, and the roar / Is nothing but darkness alive.*
("I am Dreaming of a White Christmas: The Natural History of a Vision," *Or Else,* in *Selected Poems,* p. 31.)

The specific thought in question—that the chairs in the old family home are *"empty, they're empty, but me—oh, I'm here!"*—is experience, even an experience in words, but not, as in poetry, an experience *of* words, for grief, panic, guilt, and terror shut their eyes to the precise words, deafened as they are by the meaning. The thought is a roar, and the roar itself nothing but darkness, darkness "alive"—a hair-raising abstraction from the peculiar organic *nihil* that forms in Warren a primal terror.

The poet himself is, however, word-precise. Poetry, he says in *Robert Penn Warren Talking* (p. 203), "offers an inner landscape . . . it offers a sense of what man is like inside. What experience is like." The lines are analytical by way of description, evocative by way of analysis. Suppressing "like," they insist on the crunch, the claustrophobic sensation of metaphor: "And that thought is . . . a roar."

A roar like wind—but this is too diffuse to convey the physical palpitation and is revised to what can leave no doubt of it, the roar of the night-freight beating the rails of the trestle. This is perfect in its loud, thumpety-thump duration ("night-freight beat-" is sharply percussive, "rails" blurs with "trestle," as it ought). But, with torture-chamber inspiration, it must then be placed over the self, the better to dominate and terrify.

"Roar" shifts from the middle of one line, to the beginning of the next, to the end of the third, proving inescapable and unremitting. And "trestle" lurches from the distant, indifferent end of one line to the hovering-overhead middle of the next.

All this exactitude, which is as fine as the touch of Audubon's brush, does not prevent the passage from roaring, its greatest precision its seeming runaway rush and rumble.

25.   *The saw, for a moment, ceases, and under / Arm-pits of the blue-shirted sawyer sweat / Beads cold, and / In the obscene silence of the saw's cessation, / A crow, somewhere, calls.*
("Chain Saw at Dawn in Vermont in Time of Drouth," *Or Else*, in *Selected Poems*, p. 39.)

The sibilance of the saw's sound seeps into the silence, as if washing back from the lovely extended hush of "cessation"—back through "saw's" and "silence" and "obscene." The sibilance ceases, more or less, with this softly flickering polysyllable; the comma and the line-end enhance its meaning.

At this cessation—of labor and of sound—arise two pressings-out: cold sweat-beads and a crow's call. How cold those beads are: the shock and tickle of the contiguous stresses (*sweat / Beads cold*) and the confirming off-rhyme of "Beads" and "cold"—both words compact and beadlike—render the writing shiveringly and deliciously tactile. But these beads are merely the incongruously cold exudings of a heated body; they fall from it as exhaustedly as silence from the obscene saw.

By contrast, the crow's call, farther off, sends us at large into the world. It frees us from the murderous concentration of the saw and the dumb, opaque operations of the body. We may miss the enhancingly definite figure of the "blue-shirted sawyer," but "somewhere," delicately set apart by the commas, is liberty itself compared to "under / Arm-pits," with its crooked line-break, which is part of the image ("for a moment" had also been protectively set apart.) Moreover, this call arguably lies in the joyous category of "expression," as against the physical pressing out of the sweat. It enters the silence as the pert, protesting voice of living nature, or so it seems; is naturalness itself, the antithesis of obscenity. Where the saw, pure destruction, was anti-place, antitime, the call is perhaps territorial, an affirmation of things as they are. In Warren, a crow call is a reminder that "the world is real. It is there." The silence should be cheered . . . But it belongs to the saw, it waits upon the saw's resumption—upon its "Lash and blood-lust of an eternal present," its mechanical dismemberment of the past.

26.   *And the wax-wing's beak slices the blue cedar-berry, / Which is as blue as distance.*
   ("Small White House," *Or Else*, in *Selected Poems*, p. 41.)

For a moment you would almost think the wing was beaked. "Wing's beak" edges us into seeing how like a wing is to a slicer. But it is a blue cedar-berry that is sliced, not blue air, albeit a berry "blue as distance." In the tranquilizing shade of blue, the coupling *as*'s in "as blue as distance" bridge foreground and background. This egress into distance is a welcome way out from the hard density of particulars in the first line: the two compounds, the tight mouth-twisting phrase "wax-wing's beak," the slicing contiguous stresses of "wax-wing's beak slices," and the cedar-berry-firm "blue cedar-berry."

   Characteristic of Warren's rhythm is this tense knotting up, followed by a slackening and release—a muscular contraction and relaxation. Here the beauty of the rhythmic letting-off lies in the protracted yet soft second-syllable of "distance." This syllable wants almost as much stress and has the length, and more, of the first syllable; the word enacts itself, is self-extending.

27. *Arid that country and high, anger of sun on the mountains, but /*
     One little patch of cool lawn:
     ("Rattlesnake Country," *Or Else,* in *Selected Poems,* p. 45.)

"Arid" is thrust at us in pitiless priority and immediacy, and with ty-
rannical capitalization. Time's yes/no in physical, malignant, insur-
mountable, overbearing form.

The far-gesturing "that" is thus deprived of its relief. And syntax
makes impotent the potentially redeeming, if disdainful, "high."

*Ar*id that *coun*try and *high*—the bang of this insufferable rhythm is
repeated with oppressive, monotonous symmetry in *an*ger of *sun* on
the *mount.* On both "Arid" and "anger" a tomahawking accent. Small
surprise to learn later that one of the mountains is named Mount Ti-
Po-Ki or that the lake below it stretches "Tight as a mystic drum-
head."

In this poem, nature plays red Indian to the paleface soul—the hu-
man need for creating a little Eden in an arid hell. In keeping with this
need, the second line tames the adjectival function back to its usual
fertilizing subordination: "*One little* patch of *cool* lawn." Here the
word order is expectable ("orderly"); the accents softer, more equable
and social; the rhythm free of compulsory repetition ("One little" is
almost tripping). And the *l*'s hint of liquidity. Between their drawn-
out resonances, "One" and "lawn" gamely if briefly prolong the cool
patch—this after the vowel-rhyme of "but / One" insists across the
line-break that this one patch, at least, is really there, has a real exten-
sion.

The colon at the end hinges this introductory symbolic gate to the
rest of the ranchy text, which elaborates its hot/cool opposition, the
discrepancy between the denials of reality and a pleasure principle
that remains convinced of its innocence and good deserts.

28. *All day, / The sky shivers white with heat, the lake, / For its fifteen miles of distance, stretches / Tight under the white sky. It is stretched / Tight as a mystic drumhead. It glitters like neurosis.*
("Rattlesnake Country," *Or Else*, in *Selected Poems*, p. 45.)

As above, so below: a demonic tension, a neurotic concentration of causality: gravity, time, contingency. The formula applies even in the positioning of certain repeated thumb-screw words:

> The sky shivers *white* with heat, the lake
> ... *stretches*
> *Tight* under the *white* sky. *It* is *stretched*
> *Tight* as a mystic drumhead. *It*

The vertical alignments: bars to the spirit, which is change, a liquid mobility outside causality.

Short *i*, in "shivers," "its," "fifteen," "distance," and so on, has the tightness of shiver and glitter. The something ungracious, ungenerous in the sound is plucked like a nerve-jarringly loose string throughout parts 1 and 2 of the poem. Short *e* is also worked—here in "stretches," "stretched," and "drumhead"—for a repugnant tension. (Later, in "flesh, in that sweat-drench, / Slides on flesh slicker than grease," it becomes the *eh*! of disgust.)

"Glitter": light grown reckless and dangerous from rejection and over-crowding. Light shaking on the water with an almost audible rattle.

29. *Rode hard at / the Sphinx, at the "Father of Terrors," which / in that perspective and distance, lifted slow from / the desert, like a great ship from hull-down. / At its height, / it swung. His cry burst forth.*
("Flaubert in Egypt," *Or Else*, in *Selected Poems*, p. 55.)

Nominally Flaubert in Egypt, this charger is an image of the tragic poet who rides hard at the truth till "all is redeemed / In knowledge."

(As Cleanth Brooks noted, Yeats and Warren are alike in their pil-
grimage to philosophical terror, their "fierce refusal to shield [their]
eyes from what is there.")

The tragic poet begins in ignorance—a far perspective—and an in-
cautious desire to know the truth. He ends in a breathtakingly close
knowledge of necessity, a knowledge that is—miraculously—joy:
"His cry burst forth." An early poem of Warren's, "Dragon Coun-
try," states the paradox: "Necessity of truth had trodden the land, and
heart, to pain, / And left, in darkness, the fearful glimmer of joy, like
a spoor."

"It swung" is confirmingly preceded by a literal visual shift. A sub-
lime surprise of the heat-wavering desert. And, another surprise, it
seems to be Warren's own invention. So does the thrilling image and
fine phrase "like a great ship from hull down." Flaubert himself
wrote: "I can contain myself no longer, and dig in my spurs; my horse
bursts into a gallop, splashing through the swamp . . . I begin to shout
in spite of myself; we climb rapidly up to the Sphinx, clouds of sand
swirling about us . . . It grew larger and larger, and rose out of the
ground like a dog lifting itself up." It should be no offense to Flaubert
and his travel-note to acknowledge that Warren's version is in every
way superior—is poetry.

Implicit in the ship image is the advent of mysterious other regions,
other cultures, other mental climates—an exotic bill of lading. More,
a happy, heroic surmounting of the destructive element (sand, sea).
Keeping one's head above the waves. Indeed, holding the head high.

30. *Thus I, / Riding the spume-flash, by gull cries ringed, / Came.*
     ("The True Nature of Time," *Or Else*, in *Selected Poems*, p. 58.)

The verse-line intervening between "I" and "Came" is the dimension
of the heroic, the space of courage—the area that, for this poet, gives
life its thrill.

What back-tossing explosive power the destructive element dis-
played in its "spume-flash," how everything conspired to keep the
seafarer inside the screaming circle of his own thoughts and desires

("by gull cries ringed"), far from love, from "you" ("And you, at the pier edge").

"Came" cuts through all this, the reward for all his "Riding," itself a word valiantly and flexibly opposed to the stiff but similar "ringed," as well as rousingly supportive of the "I." This coming draws in its wake flashing ejaculation and elemental cry. It is triumphant but already anticlimactic, a retirement.

The heart struggles for arrival and, learning to love the struggle, leaves itself behind in it when it arrives.

31.   *Night of the falling mercury, and ice-glitter. / Drought-night of August and the horned insect booming / At the window-screen. / Ice-field, dusty road: distance flees.*
      ("Reading Late at Night, Thermometer Falling," *Or Else*, in *Selected Poems*, p. 69.)

Distinct opposites on the remembered wheel of the seasons, the night of the falling mercury and the drought-night of August nonetheless blur together to a mind musingly abstracted from time, time which has left it so little. Their contents merge: "Ice-field, dusty road." Space itself catches the contagion and flees.

If Warren Joyced, he might have written "Icefieldustyroad." His way of saying it stops the wheel first here, then, after a rapid half-turn, there. The lines are like a pinned paper disk, half August half February, and it is left to the reader to spin it all into singular "time," field-roaddistancedroughtice, till all is a furious passing, a metaphysical famine.

Prickingly vivid, that prehistoric, minatory "horned insect" booming at the window screen—a true Southern insect-monster. And inside the house the poet's father, his mind elsewhere, himself horned ("glasses / Low on big nose"), reads, he too seeking entry into something: "and I think I hear / The faint click and grind of the brain as / It translates the perception of black marks on white paper into / Truth." Such is his own "indecipherable passion and compulsion."

32. *And at night nuzzle / The hazlenut-shaped sweet tits of Lucy.*
(*Audubon*, IV, in *Selected Poems*, p. 95.)

Audubon could "keep store, dandle babies," and "nuzzle" Lucy, but, a fool of wilderness beauty, of fate, a divine innocent, he chooses otherwise, or has no choice. The luscious rhyme of "nuzzle" and "hazlenut," the cozy alliteration of "night nuzzle" and "shaped sweet," the erect, titillated *t*'s, tell how much he is missing.

Yet this imagined nuzzling is opposite the heroic, at the soft edge of the comic. It would make of our hero a bit of a calf. Lucy, like a clever temptress, and knowing her man, has transformed herself into mother nature, but her hazlenut-shaped tits only betray the true object of Audubon's passion. "Sweet tits" is at once mouth-wateringly sensual and "placing." Shades of standard lust and standard pleasure, no high calling.

Is Audubon not more distinguished because, "After sunset, / Alone, he played his flute in the forest," a celibate Pan with autoerotic—but artistic—reed?

33. *You saw, from the forest pond, already dark, the great trumpeter swan / Rise, in clangor, and fight up the steep air where, / At the height of last light, it glimmered, like white flame.*
(*Audubon*, IV, in *Selected Poems*, p. 95.)

"You saw": this Audubon's fate is less to paint than to see, like that child who "went forth every day, / And the first object he looked upon and received with wonder or pity or love or dread, that object he became." What Audubon sees, within the rapt distinctions of appearance, is his own half-known passion at large in the world, unconsciously acting out its fierce freedoms and hard necessities. How the language participates in the clangorous rise of the great tumpeter swan, delighting in its self-delighting energy and aspiration to an ecstatic redundancy of self-presence, pure being. The stages of this ascendance are marked by incremental levels of rhyme: "pond . . . swan"; "air where"; "height . . . light . . . white." "Fight" lies to the other side of "steep air," which must be surmounted before it gains its aural crown in "height," "light," and "like white flame."

Last light, for as in Warren's own career the greatest hunger for being, for its glory, is reserved till the end. Let the soul at the last dare the white heat, "the light / Of unanointed Blaze," until it achieves "the Designated Light." Is this not the "last wish" of the artist—to leave the land of dead weight and become, through the force of his own pulsations, that purest of impure things, an angel of desire, all ardor?

34. *Listen! Stand very still and, / Far off, where shadow / Is undappled, you may hear / The tusked boar grumble in his ivy-slick.*
   (*Audubon*, IV, in *Selected Poems*, p. 95.)

In Warren, to "be" is to be in the world and alongside it, a privileged spatial "Being-in" (in Heidegger's phrase) that allows adventure, context, truth, beauty, pleasure, as well as "that in the face of which one has anxiety." Here the potential anxiety of hearing a grumbling wild boar is eased by "Far," which forms a gentle word-family with "hear" and "boar," structuring a distance that is at the same time a closure.

Deep in shade and low on the rich overgrown floor of the earth, the boar is both alien to the listener and a dusky dream of his own "hidden" animal nature. A not-uncomforting grumble, picked up by pricked animal ears.*

If Audubon stands in the firing line of the commands to "Listen!" and "Stand very still," so does the reader, who is thereby corporealized "within" the world of the poem, transformed into a listener deep in the unspoiled American wilderness. "And . . . you may hear" converts the commands to promises. You are already convinced you want to hear this as yet unspecified sound—convinced of the joy of being worlded.

---

* In 1847 a reviewer said that Audubon's birds represent "the imagination or the soul," and his quadrupeds man's appetitive instincts: "It is as brave of us, and as necessary, that we should be true animals, as that we should be true angels." See James R. Justus, *The Achievement of Robert Penn Warren* (Baton Rouge: Louisiana State University Press, 1968), p. 93.

"Slick"—creepily tactile, next thing to the primordial slime of being—unobtrusively closes the passage back on the first syllable of "Listen," sealing it off as a single aural spell.

35.   *The world declares itself. That voice / Is vaulted in—oh, arch on arch—redundancy of joy, its end / Is its beginning, necessity / Blooms like a rose.*
       (*Audubon*, IV, in *Selected Poems*, p. 95.)

In *Audubon*, joy thrives on sublimation—on keeping the tusked boar far off and grumbling. When conscience itself is satisfied, forgiving and forgetting its wounds, when remorse is cast out, then (as Yeats said) "We are blest by everything, / Everything we look upon is blest."

Not heroic but ejaculative, a vital surprise and overflow, a manic release of guilt-freed energy, this vaulting "voice" (like the wrangler's *"I-yee!"* in "Rattlesnake Country") declares a sudden indomitableness of living energy, its expansion as at the summons of a Vital God. "Vault" and "arch on arch" evoke a cathedral of joy, an aural cathedral within the visual cathedral of space.

A horizontal echo folds a poem over on itself; arches it back; is aural redundancy; a vertical deepening. It is notable in

> That voice Is
>   vaulted in—oh, arch
>   on arch—redun
>   dancy
>   of
>   joy, its end
>   Is
>   its begin   ning

"Joy" returns the ear to "voice," identifying its great quality and illustrating the nature of joy itself (redundancy). "Its begin-" relates to "its end" in a similar way, the circularity now specified by the semantic content. In two successive lines, "Is" is lined up with "Is" in triumphant first position, suggesting a surplus of being and presentness—the gift of a miraculous coincidence of fixed universal law and sportive, indeed sacral, organic impulse.

FOUR

His
Varying
Stance

*I*f *there were* an "exact spot" in Warren, a point where the reader could press his or her nose and make all the lines converge to form a portrait of the poet, the outline of his stance, what would it be? Has it perhaps already been quoted? Is it the need "Of seeing life as glory"? The urgent, "Oh, tell me the nature of passion and the fruit thereof"? The defiant "Passion is all"? Or Audubon's "What has been denied me? . . . There is never an answer . . . The question is the only answer"? His yearning nonetheless to "frame a definition of joy"?

Surely it is all these things, which are really a single demand that life have a meaning commensurate with the human yearning for meaning—the body's yearning, and the mind's. They are all one fear, too: that passion may have to be its own paradise as well as its own earth and hell. The will to power and glory, the will to truth and glory, to a beatitude of meaning, alternately rasps and rejoices.

Passion is what *must be*, for, whatever its confusions and disingenuousness, it is authentic, it is of the bone and blood, compared to the conventionalities of what it will perhaps suffice to call (after Heidegger) the "they," the collective identity. More, primordial as its appetency may seem, it is human, full of hope and grandeur-in-the-making, compared to the radical moment when the heart, in brute nakedness and blind terror, simply *beats*, an organic X, an active something/nothingness. It is this primordial moment from which all the others in Warren are in flight, though an ambiguous flight, one that keeps pausing and harking back to the hypnotic beat that could possibly be the answer to everything or, conversely, the evidence that an answer will be denied.

The Heartbeat

The sense of the "heart" as less a haven of holy affections than an elemental creature in "a dark cave of / No-Time" isolates Warren even from the Romantic poets he most resembles. The bony finger of nothingness was never laid so nakedly, so probingly, so provokingly, on the "heart" of Wordsworth or Keats as on his, and if Shelley asked "And what were . . . earth, and stars, and sea, / If to the human mind's imaginings / Silence and solitude were vacancy?" it was from the self-affrighting edge of his belief in "the secret Strength of things / Which governs thought, and to the infinite dome / Of Heaven is as a law."

But it will not do to enter here into the various vacillations of these poets or the shadows of the void in the last poems of Shelley and Keats. Keats in "To Autumn" might be said to gaze "into nullity," to find "a lovely nothing," as James Joyce said he himself had done for over half a century; he might be thought as tragically earthbound as Warren, as prepared (and ill-prepared) to worship fallen Beauty and the Vital God. But a signal difference remains: the complete absence in Warren of the soft-breathing romantic bloom, of the warmth and glow that, save for the most extreme griefs, suffuses even the sorrowing Romantic. When Warren recasts the famous funereal motto "Beauty is Truth,—Truth Beauty,—that is all / Ye know on earth, and all ye need to know," it is with a cold-snap severity: the wind-plucked cables grinding against an immense old oak in sub-zero weather sing "Of truth, and its beauty" under the "crackling absoluteness of the sky." In Warren the atmosphere is more shivering, the godless sky colder, clearer. Much as he may be our Keats, raw-boned and awkward as our Keats would be, much as he himself began, in "first dark," with an expectation of sublimity ("Tell me a story. . . Make it a story of great distances, and starlight"), he has perceived, with Ahab, that "There can be no hearts above the snow-line." He has found himself in the "dark cave" where the "human breast" used to be; he has seen with Sylvia Plath how it is the frost that makes the flower, with Yeats how it is the resin of man's own heart that flames upon the night.

Warren's work throws the label "existentialism" off like a wet blanket. He begins with his rage to discover an "immanence of meaning," "destiny," the "peace of definition." At the same time he senses that the only meaning, and a harsh one, lies in the rage.* To the equivocal Yes/No of the physical (the reactive) heart, what might be called the imaginative heart says (with a grandeur-remembering defiance) "No!" ("no" to the "no," and to the equivocation); or, when it is more honest, "If": *if* you could eat glorious stars, *if* there were a Platonic ice-land of lethal purity, if we could leap from our husks and be swept along by a ferocious world-Anima, *then* where would night and ripped time be, who would need to turn into marble to withstand pain? But in Warren's truest and most shuddering moments, the "if" recedes, the beauty of the irremediable shocks him into an unexpected joy. The heart has its "place," after all: precisely the devouring world. Its happiness is one with its *fate*, its song of limitation. In its "last" kingdom, the heart finds itself willing to settle for nothing less than this chill sublimity. Besides, its former kingdoms having receded together with history into delusion, it must be this kingdom, or none.

Yet if the alarmed heart alarmingly hints at nothingness, its very persistence, its parrying beats amid terror, constitute an "ontological" stand. Walter J. Ong notes that all hearing places us "at a . . . core of sensation and existence"; hearing one's own heart puts one peculiarly at the edge of one's own being—the heart suddenly becomes "ontic,"

---

   * In Warren's late years (as, sporadically, in the early work, most notably in "The Ballad of Billie Potts"), Thanatos steps forward to whisper the low and delicious word "death," which has the meaning of mystery, of a profundity beyond or beneath the senses, beyond yearning.

   As for the Warren of world enough and time (almost world enough, almost enough time), his empathy with hawks, brooks, stars is more than equaled, *Audubon* excepted, by his fear of the unknown in himself, of death, of forgotten important truths, of folly and weakness. Hence his stress on "fate," as against "God"; on the ambiguousness of "Truth," as against illumination. Except in passing he is not a "mystic," even of the pagan or vitalist kind. Victor Strandberg makes much of Warren's phrase "osmosis of being" and little of his need to stand apart, where he cannot be further injured by fathers, mothers, townships, or what Emily Dickinson called "overtakelessness," including "God." See Victor Strandberg, *A Colder Fire: The Poetry of Robert Penn Warren* (Lexington: University of Kentucky Press, 1965) and *The Poetic Vision of Robert Penn Warren* (Lexington: University of Kentucky Press, 1977).

and ontology (the "I am") is a flutter of apprehension around this violent "core." Yet hearing one's own heart is also proof, of a sort, that one is still "on." You shake the battered watch and it still goes:

> Why did I stand with no motion under
> The spilt-ink darkness of spruces and try to hear,
> In the soundlessness of falling snow,
> The heartbeat I know as the only self
> I know that I know, while History
> Trails its meaning like old cobwebs
> Caught in a cellar broom?

Compared to history, at least, the heart *is*. Compared to the world (with its "soundlessness," its "spilt-ink darkness") the heart speaks. It says "self," or rather "itself," which lies outside intelligence; at least it is never tired of saying this.

But it might also be saying, "I'm trapped"; it might be tapping out a plan for rescue. Or is it only a mechanical pump hooked to an alarm system? In its fits of saliency, it proves at once loud and unforthcoming. All mystery could be in it, or a famine of meaning. "On into the Night" concedes the ambiguity, yet yearns to believe that something is being signaled from in there. The poem reaches back and almost touches fingertips with Romantic poetry, in which nature is all analogy with the human. But here there is nothing magical in the analogy; no Presence in nature makes the comparison exalting. On the contrary, nature is as prey to night and silence as human beings are. The still-fresh silence of its evening notably does not betray an inaudible World Soul: "And taciturn, / The owl's adrowse in the depth of a cedar"; "The thrush-throat only in silence throbs now." Nature is merely nature and the heart's blood sinks:

> Shadow and shade of cliff sift down
> To darken the dimmest under-leaf,
> And in the secret conduits
> Of flesh I feel blood darker flow.

Then comes a still more unmistakable portent of mortality:

> Bulbat and bat will soon scribble
> Their lethal script on a golden sky.

Analogy brightens a little in

> From the apple orchard, a century ruined,
> The he-bear will utter his sexual hoot,
> Deer will come forth for autumn forage

but, colored by the "paradigm of the seasons" as it is, it still precludes eternity.

Discouraged by all it has thus deciphered in nature, the heart shakes off analogy and suddenly becomes aware of its own message, its "undecipherable metaphor":

> Later, the last of night's voices is heard—
> The owl's mystic question that follows his glut.
>
> Then silence again. You sleep. Moonlight
> Bathes the world in white silence. No, no!—there's one sound
> Defined now by silence. The pump in your breast,
> In merciless repetition, declares
>
> Its task in undecipherable metaphor.

In that "undecipherable" and redundantly again in "metaphor," what might not lie hidden? Nature or metanature, both are possible; what is plain is the will to meaning. "Undecipherable" is tendentious, and an unintelligible "metaphor" is a contradiction in terms. Although "pump" implies a functionality uncomprehended by itself, it may yet serve some intelligent design. And "task" is prickly with mission and destiny.

But the perturbation—that "merciless"! The stasis of "repetition" is intolerable. It matters that meaning is baffled, and in so unremitting a manner. It matters that the "white silence"—that nihilistic parody of Shelley's white radiance stained by the material dome of many-colored glass—startles the heart into sounding out its code, as if sending for help. "Task" defends against this insight, this terror that only the negative of the sublime is now sublime.

The heart "appears" only when least sure of itself. *Is* most securely when not manifest. This gives appearance a bad name. Perhaps Gorgias was right? "Appearing is weak, since it does not succeed in being"? Poetry is called in to dispute this: all that does not appear, it says, is weak. "Since we live in an *appearing* world," argues Hannah Arendt, "is it not . . . plausible that the relevant and meaningful in this world of ours should be located precisely on the surface?" Do not Being and Appearance (in this world of ours) coincide?

Poetry sets its imprimatur upon appearance in the very process of becoming an appearance. Its sincerest flattery is its emulation. Yeats broke through his antiseptic Platonism to the same conclusion: "What theme had Homer but original sin?" The poet's tongue is else "a stone." Warren's struggle with a dissociate Being and Appearance is less marked than Yeats's, but not his effort to make Appearance displace Nothingness. For him, too, "profound philosophy" begins in "terror"; for him, too, "the last kiss is given to the void."

"In the star-pale field, the propped pitchfork lifts / Its burden, hung black, to the white star": these early lines stunningly, if studiedly, convey Warren's tragic sense of appearance. Lifting its burden, it is an offering—but to what? Is it sufficiently noticed by any but a tragic, a human, attention? Warren's black and white landscapes dramatize (melodramatize) the evident injustice—the *dim* support for appearances. So this poet adopts appearance as his own, and with "A heart-stab blessed past joy or despair" sees, "in the mind's dark, once more, / That field, pale, under starlit air." If not apologetic, his love of the world is irremediably shadowed, daunted, injured. He sees it not with a sunny eye and not as a connoisseur, but in the stricken way one looks at a beautiful invalid, half glancing aside, overcome with the *drama* of appearance. His gratitude struggles with his dismay: so much beauty and yet something somehow scanted, something essential. (It is this metaphysical distraction that keeps Warren's descriptions more dramatic than detailed, more rapid than caressive.) To speak of the stars as an "eczema" of glory, as Warren once with sublime absurdity does, is not to dismiss them but to imply that the whole visible universe seems as arbitrary and unintended as a rash (seems rash).

Like Dickinson's or Yeats's, Warren's consciousness is modern, restive, uncertain, except in its most tragic deepenings; and like theirs haunted by scarcely believable celestial conceptions of old. It is not without its polarity (the sort his chosen adversary, Emerson, said "we can only obey"). His collected poems will be an ivy-riot of twistings this way and that. (His intimations that certain of his partial collections might be thought single poems are wishful thinking, resulting from a desire for the "dear redemption of / Simplicity" and an ambition for a large, whole achievement.) A Christianized Platonism (very vague in detail as in its largest terms) is in tow to his sense of guilt, one that half seems adopted as "representative," a Southern grimness. It must be this that swerves *Or Else* (despite the strong patient earthly witness of "Rattlesnake Country," "Sunset Walk in Thaw-Time in Vermont," and other poems) back to "Platonism" at the close. "A Problem in Spatial Composition" notes how "The hawk, in an eye-blink, is gone"; how the heart is confirmed in its knowledge that "*beyond is forever*." This "knowledge" has, however, only a sentimental weight. By contrast, the conclusion of "Loss, of Perhaps Love, in Our World of Contingency" in the next volume, "We must learn to live in the world," is painfully earned. Page by page and volume by volume, in any case, the impulse to abandon the earth is flouted by the impulse to affirm it, or at least to bear with it.

Such resolution as there is lies in the semi-darkness of tragic joy, where the face lifted to the acid starlight is "stripped to white bone" and "This is happiness." To be alive yet turned toward death and able to bear it and all the more alive because of it is to mix elation with gravity in the most prodigious way. Appearance is satisfied; it is in *this* world that, in Dickinson's words, "To be alive—is Power." The absolute, too, is satisfied: nothing more utter, for the living, than the contemplative knowledge of the murderous indifference of the stars. Even the harsh demands of purity are reduced to a merely murmur-

ous protest by this compromise between defiance of death and ac-
knowledgment of fate. The tragic hero is a marked man, and knows
it. His punishment for existing at all is already secure—indeed it began
at birth. But precisely this frees him for the criminal joy of Will, the
joy of existing anyway.

Warren's best tragic poems are *Audubon*, "Trying to Tell You
Something," "Loss, of Perhaps Love, in Our World of Contingency,"
and "Unless."

On the potent side of tragedy lies an illicit blood-excitement, a Di-
onysian ecstasy that would play hawk to all existence, or at its lowest
ebb be blood-brother to every beautiful, masterful, and suffering
thing. This is to treat the primal "heartbeat" as a drumlike incitement
to sensations of joyous power. It can lead to a wish "to leave / The
husk behind, and leap / Into the blind and antiseptic anger of air"
("Ah, Anima!").

Warren's best Dionysian poems are "Red-Tail Hawk and Pyre of
Youth," "Sila," and "Preternaturally Early Snowfall."

The opposite response to the brutal heartbeat, the "Platonic" reac-
tion, registers a repugnance to power, a yearning for the "lethal" glory
of frozen impulse, suddenly pure, suddenly God's.

Apart from the sublime passage in *Brother to Dragons* on the "land
of Platonic ice," Warren has but one considerable "Platonic" state-
ment, "Evening Hawk."

At moments, transcendence closes, the blood-drums grow quiet,
and even the tragic alternative, the sharpened sense of the self as the
starlight whittles at it, lacks heart. Life seems too antimetaphysical,
too saturninely material, to admit of any joy. The "cost of experi-
ence" begins to mount, the account books darken. All the poet can do
is offer his testimony. Life has become pathetic: transitory, passive.

The strong pathetic poems are "Rattlesnake Country" and "Folly
on Royal Street before the Raw Face of God."

On the other hand, if the stars shut man out, and if his body feels
uncomfortably bestial and alien, doesn't he have his own kind to
comfort him? Can't he turn, as Virginia Woolf supposed, to the gen-
eral stream of human existence and so escape Heraclitean flux, Empe-

doclean discord? True, history is the midnight attack of bootheels on cobblestones. But to the side of history there are wives, daughters, sons—sons in particular, inheritors of the masculine passion-quest.

Warren's notable poems of family and brotherhood are "Sunset Walk in Thaw-Time in Vermont," "Snowshoeing Back to Camp in Gloaming," "Waking to Tap of Hammer," and "Night Walking." The mighty (even as to title) "Old Nigger on One-Mule Cart Encountered Late at Night When Driving Home from Party in the Back Country" cultivates brotherhood but swerves away from it at the last.

Finally, almost by way of postscript, for so it has proved in the poet's own career, there is the strange post-tragic crossing into the mysterious realms of death, or the post-tragic acceptance of the benign cycles of process. Transition, or metamorphosis, replaces the strong tragic stance. To stand off from death is no longer noble; it grows mean. "Acquaintance with Time in Early Autumn" sounds death for the possibility of "gratitude"—it forms a transition to still later poems in which death forms a pure enchantment.

These are "Heart of Autumn," "Caribou near Arctic," "Paradox of Time," and "Dead Horse in Field."

Even at best, such categories are, if conveniences, divisions for the reader to stub his toes against. Ignorant of the categories to which they might be subjected, the poems break them freely and in advance. The notable instance is the long and flexible *Audubon*, which (1) first introduces the tragic and (2) then matures it into a marvelous transitive moment of consummated fate ("This is not a dimension of time"); (3) glances at the Platonic in its spectacle of the "footless dance" of birds that "cry / In a tongue multitudinous, often like music" ("They do not know / Compassion, and if they did, / We should not be worthy of it"); (4) offers a pathetic elegy on American passion (the adventure of love knowledge) as "the wreck of a great tree, left / By flood, . . . the root-system and now-stubbed boughs / Lifting in darkness"; and (5) inscribes the line of passion-descent from Audubon to Warren, their transhistorical brotherhood. Again, with Janus face, "Acquaintance with Time in Early Autumn" yearns back toward Dionysian summer and forward to posthumous autumn, and in "Heart of Autumn" the speaker seems never so blood-alive and Dionysian as when he elects (is finally elected for) a rapturous crossing to the other side.

To echo one of Warren's resolved-and-resigned *We must's*, we must take the poems as they come.

Eating—Our First Aggression

In "Sila" a boy's great husky eviscerates a doe and, fearing that the animal may still be alive, the boy slits its throat before burying it in a snow-grave. The curious moment occurs when he tastes the doe's blood on his knife.

The poem may be taken as the poet's belated recognition (or imagining) of his baptism in blood, without which he would not have become a poet (he might have become, instead, a historian, a philosopher, a theologian).

From the slit throat, blood-petals drip onto the snow, a great rose blooms where the boy stands, and the sky bleeds in sympathy its own massive rose:

> but petals paler as higher—
> The rose of the blood of the day. Still as stone,
> So he stood. Then slowly—so slowly—
> He raised the blade of the knife he loved honing, and wiped
> The sweet warmness and wetness across his own mouth,
> And set tongue to the edge of the silk-whetted steel.

> He knew he knew something at last
> That he'd never before known.
> No name for it—no!

Later he cries out "into vastness / Of silence: 'Oh, world!' "—a protest torn between wonder and deprecation.

What is it that he knows at last, what refuses to be either named or denied? Something that can only be tasted? What is the meaning of the taste, or the tasting, of blood?

"Man eats of the fruit of the tree of knowledge, and falls," Warren writes in "Knowledge and the Image of Man." "But if he takes another bite, he may get at least a sort of redemption. His unity with nature will . . . be that of . . . the unity of the lover with the beloved." Eating is our first aggression against the world, the prototype of all the others. It not only keeps us alive; it administers to our illusion of power, deals out sensations of increase, and temporarily stills the fear that we ourselves shall be eaten. The boy's killing and tasting of the doe is Adam's first bite, self-augmenting; but, simultaneously, for his sorrow of "knowledge" is instantaneous, the incorporation of the doe's substance with his own furthers a pathetic unity (with the doe, the day), in part as "of the lover with the beloved."

The actual throat-slashing is surgical ("set / The knife's needle point where acuteness / Would enter without prick of pain"). Yet this knife is a fetish to the boy, who loves honing it, loves not less the "silk-whetted," that is, bloodied, "steel." To him it represents an indefinite if "acute" extension of himself (both tooth and penis); there is a physiological unconsciousness in his relation to it, as when "his free hand, as though unaware, / Slides slow back / To grope for the knife-sheath." The knife focuses what the rough character in "Two Studies in Idealism" calls the "two things a man's built for, killing and you-know-what":

> And a man needs something to take with him when he dies.
> Ain't much worth taking, but what happens under the cover
> Or at the steel-point—yeah, that look in their eyes.
>
> . . . Yeah, Christ, then you know who you are—
> And will maybe remember that much even after you've died.

As the boy "cuddles the doe's head," he "longs for connection" and feels "Twin eyes / Hold his own entrapped in their depth." And after slitting the throat he lets "down the head, / Aware even yet of the last embracement of gaze." The experience has been made momentous for him by the ontological charge ("then you know who you are") in both the aggressive and the phallic modes of power.

If the boy not only takes the animal's life but tastes her life-and-death, has it inside him, what will he not be able to know? She becomes something of a totem animal, killable only in the presence of the god and only for the sacred purpose of a consanguinity between the god, the animal, and the worshipper: one potency, one profundity. Those who eat the same substance become the same substance. What would the boy become? The common life of everything? The interchangeable vitality in the world? For whom would he gather the bouquet of blood-roses, those in the snow and the sky?

His Lawrentian blood-knowledge is inarticulate but keen: it is power knowing itself. For the Eskimos, so the epigraph relates, "Sila" means "the very breath of life, but not physical life; . . . clear-sighted energy." But this screens the boy's discovery that to lose life is pitiably to lose power, as women seem to when penetrated and "covered" by the male. Hence the "Alas, poor Yorick" beginning, the reference to an early settler's skull, which by now "must be pulping to earth, and . . . grinless." Against this the boy's "own muscles [pulse] in joy, just as when / Hands clasp for the lift of the beauty of butt-swell." Life is power; what is no longer alive is female, drooping, injured, pitiful.

The boy performs a mercy killing on the female weakness in himself. His desire to "give explanation" to the doe is a doomed need to account for—to explain, to explain away—vulnerability, pain, defeat, death. All may be all, as "Red-Tail Hawk and Pyre of Youth" would have it, but at the same time is, quakingly, "part of all," embattled, ultimately subject. The boy's sense of this duality is overwhelming. He all but perceives—"Oh, world!"—how power is only weakness at the other extreme. The thrill of killing is half terror; power is double-edged, self-threatening. If Dionysian power is lined with Dionysian pathos, the maenad tearing live flesh with her teeth and weeping, it is because power can never be all-powerful, absolute, safe from itself.

For Warren, all is to begin with and repeatedly thereafter a violence. Simply to be here is to be subject to stabs of "instancy." It is to find oneself, besides, at the buffeted center of "the poor world's abstract storm," a world darkly given over to a "mission of mythic and beautiful rage." Here, space crouches like a great cat—"distance drowses and blinks and broods its enormous fiat"—and time itself is "fanged." The "sun's heel does violence in the corn-balk," and we must mind even the "Slick . . . blood of shadow." Silence, too, "Rages, it ranges the world, it will / Devour us."

And all the while we are driven by "garbled" compulsions.

> We are the blade,
> But not the hand
> By which the blade is swayed.

Yet cursed, not excused, by the unshakable "paradox of fate and will," our will is ferociously "living," it pants and clanks, and our history bangs "Bootheels on cobbles." Then sex is "one death in two," and even our "dream" must be grappled with, as cunning Odysseus leapt on "mountainous Ajax," till the great head bounced on hard ground and "blood filled / That mouth from its tongue, like a grape-cluster, crushed."

In much of this there may be a familiar male paranoia, but it has its honorable heritage. Back beyond Yeats, for instance, stands Schopenhauer, blaming the universe for its irrational violence ("the worst of all possible worlds"); expostulating with life ("must be some kind of mistake"); noting how, as in "Sila," will and conflict flare up everywhere, and pity is the one universal bond; observing that, as in "Rattlesnake Country," his daily savaging by the scheme of things makes the human "beast" the more savage.

Warren's is the Schopenhauerian violence fallen from a manageable unifying theory into the cloud-scut of intuition, into plurality and incertitude—Schopenhauerian virga.

Yet his greatness lies in fighting the hasty and simplifying conclusion that human life must be some kind of mistake. He breaks open the carcass of the lion to get at the virulent sweet hive. At the least he would say with Audubon, "a world which though wicked enough in all conscience is *perhaps* as good as worlds unknown."

Still, Warren's mainstay, passion, is voracity turned half outward, half inward, self-quickened by this potentially all-unifying and all-devouring division. It remains primed with what he called "the crime of self." Any guilty thing may float belly up within it, including "the dream of the eating of human flesh." The "labor of grinding [jaws] by which life is" figures its law, identifies its lust. Passion *is* the eating in life—of memory, of thought, of ears that yawn open like eaglets in a nest, and of what (after Saint Augustine) Warren calls the "lust of the eye." And all life long there is "our werewolf thirst to drink the blood of glory." Then comes the time to be eaten by death—whereupon passion is annealed back to its etymological base, which is "to suffer, to endure, to be patient," and which is near allied to "punishment."

The story of both the joyful aggression and the joyful submission of passion is best told in *Audubon: A Vision*. I shall focus on the first two of its seven parts, for it is here that most of the passion, most of the conflict, is concentrated. Here passion is celebrated and deplored (but more celebrated than deplored) as a primal yearning for the "all," though a particular object—a white heron, a gleaming gold watch, a story—may prove at any moment the magical focus, the burning glass turned on the dry thirst inside a man or woman. Here passion, though never innocent, is uncovered as a fierce appreciation, its covetousness metaphysical, the rage of a spiritual privation and a spiritual hope. Here, too, passion already begins to sense the humility that must someday crown its pride, perfect its nobility. Already it begins to hunger for an ultimate retributive fate.

But first it should be noted how much this poem about passion is itself the work of passion. *"A Vision"*: the poet's seeing of Audubon would suck the marrow from the documentary record—the autobiographies, nature writings, letters, any delectable scrap. The poem appropriates Audubon's enthusiasm for beauty and uses it as the seedbed of its own much greater passion. It is almost frank about this: the second of the two epigraphs, a fragment from Elizabeth Bishop's translation of Charles Drummond de Andrade's "Travelling in the Family" (as a translation, itself a loving piece of acquisition) reads as follows: *"I caught at his strict shadow and the shadow released itself with neither haste nor anger. But he remained silent."* Silence may or may not be sympathy. Would the historical Audubon like what Warren has made of him? This horrific, sublime substitution? Warren visits on him a violent love, a still more violent need. He stuffs Audubon's eyes with sights, fills his mind with thoughts, his sensibility with nuances and raptures, his psyche with nightmares, whose origin and stamp are unmistakably those of Robert Penn Warren, lost dauphin of the imagination's former grandeurs.

This reconstituted and remolded Audubon has more of the Old Adam in him than the actual Audubon chose to reveal. His guilt is like a lump in his throat, if not a mote in his eye. He has the deserved bad conscience of passion. It tinges some of his perceptions a frightful blood color or a reductive black and white. But before Warren enacts Audubon's seeing—that is, his essential nature, his passion—he makes short shift of biographical legend and (even) fact:

> Was not the lost dauphin, though handsome was only
> Base-born and not even able
> To make a decent living, was only
> Himself, Jean Jacques, and his passion—what
> Is man but his passion?

Not who, but what a man is, his inner pitch, is the question passion must raise. So, through the eye of this needling first question— "what / Is man but his passion?"—we pass at once to a privileged if fictitious intimacy with Audubon's seeing, his peculiar way of being in the world. What we long for when we open any biography, the idiosyncratic quick of the subject, is with faked fact and true authority instantly evoked:

>   Saw,
> Eastward and over the cypress swamp, the dawn,
> Redder than meat, break;
> And the large bird,
> Long neck outthrust, wings crooked to scull air, moved
> In a slow calligraphy, crank, flat, and black against
> The color of God's blood spilt, as though
> Pulled by a string.

Saw,
It proceed across the inflamed distance.
Moccasins set in hoar frost, eyes fixed on the bird,
Thought: "On that sky it is black."
Thought: "In my mind it is white."
Thinking: "*Ardea occidentalis*, heron, the great one."

Dawn: his heart shook in the tension of the world.

Dawn: and what is your passion?

Already with "Saw," momentarily abuzz with potential destruction, seeing is a doing, if virtually autonomous and blind. The whole man is focused there—his name, or a pronoun, dispensable. To this stylish copier of natural appearances, seeing was primary, painting all but a transparent activity. But even Audubon's seeing bends back on the seer like a mountain train. The perception in the comparison "Redder than meat" is hysterical. Over the sweep of the interruptive phrase "Eastward and over the cypress swamp," seeing connects up with an object that, though named the dawn, reeks of violation. For this passion-seeing, the "break" of light is haunted by the Passion, the divine pierced by the hardness of the world. This seeing discloses a divided sphere where power and sacrifice, beauty and violation, love and suffering, mingle terribly, like a sky of blended light and blood. The dawn thus perceived is a portent of passion's transgressions, oblation, and pain. Yet the fullest revelation of its wrongs and torments would not deter it, for without it there would be no light in matter, no light that matters. The world would keep, in Martin Buber's words, "a total stranger"; it would "not give itself to you," and "should you die in it, your grave would be in nothingness."

Oedipal guilt (for which in Freud's view the Christian Passion sought to atone) would account not only for the impression "The color of God's blood spilt" but the skulking phallic imagery of the heron's "Long neck outthrust," the "wings crooked," and even the puppet string, which suggests the twitch and compulsion of sexuality. Married but celibate, Audubon would seem to have renounced enough, but his seeing is nonetheless (and in both senses) charged with guilt. The dawn runs the murdered father's blood together with the crucified son's.

All active passion is phallic aggression against the sacral integrity of the Whole, even if fixed on some "part." To Audubon's passionate eyes, the heron is char-black against an inflamed sky, the immolative flames of his seeing seconding those of the holy and aggrieved distance. The heron is a figure all "fallenness": a winged but mechanical phallus; a crank and offensive writing, or drawing, against the flamy purity of Being. Accordingly, Audubon's vision burns it on the stake of the dawn.

Seeing that reduces the great heron from its mysterious creatureliness to "flat" signs, that injects the white bird with "crank" black intimations, is, to transfer Susan Sontag's phrase for camera shots, "sublimated murder—a soft murder." The hunter's eye takes a bead on the bird and, being a writer's eye as well, devitalizes its black motions into script. Appearance becomes seeing's calligraphy, just as writing is seeing's darkness. Audubon's eyes are "fixed" on the bird, much as his moccasins are set in the hoarfrost. He imposes himself, he rivets the world to his dominant, doubtful presence. As a painter he is given to flagging down, to freezing, appearances. He paints by first shooting a bird, then painting a "shot" of it, just as Warren, in order to write *Audubon*, had to abandon his original narrative project and make "each element in the poem . . . a 'shot.'"

Thought pegs the heron, too. The rigid structuration of

> Thought: "On that sky it is black."
> Thought: "In my mind it is white"

gives us one slow, thick, dull explosion after another. It recalls Bergson's characterization of the intellect as a box, a freeze-frame resisting the living current of reality. After its fashion, the intellect is struggling to adjust—intelligently—to a contradiction between two orders of data. But without care, mechanical, it merely compares (white versus black) and classifies (*Ardea occidentalis*). The violations it practices are systematic, made for the dusty shelves of order.

The second half of part 1 effects a remission. Here, seeing is soothed into a surcease from guilty aggression by the melting light, the honied stupor, of autumn. Its sudden gentleness is the sweetness in death's cup:

> October: and the bear,
> Daft in the honey-light, yawns.
>
> The bear's tongue, pink as a baby's, out-crisps to the curled
>   tip,
> It bleeds the black blood of the blueberry.
>
> The teeth are more importantly white
> Than has ever been imagined.
>
> The bear feels his own fat
> Sweeten, like a drowse, deep to the bone.
>
> Bemused, above the fume of ruined blueberries,
> The last bee hums.
>
> The wings, like mica, glint
> In the sunlight.
>
> He leans on his gun. Thinks
> How thin is the membrane between himself and the world.

Eating has—importantly—been put by. It is a period of post-repletion, for sleep after a heavy meal. The bear and the bees, though heavy with fat or fume, are blessedly dissociated from the horror of God's spilt blood, all tearing and grinding of passion. With envy, with secret gratitude, Audubon observes the spotless, unused teeth of the drowsy bear. You feel the comic relief as its yawn opens on a curled tongue pink as a baby's and out-crisping to the tip like an innocuous paper party-whistle and stained only with the black blood of already ruined blueberries. "Honey-light," with its dreamy, delicious narcosis and golden diffusion, makes the very atmosphere lickingly sweet and forms with the fumes of the ruined blueberries (fumes exuded by the oozy *u*'s) an infant's paradisiac environment-as-food. Food that, still more paradisiacally, is no longer wanted, comforting as are its winy waftings.

Temporarily, teeth, sting, gun are all rendered inert; the flesh of things is safe from rending. The sting of passion itself has been drawn. Where earlier lines had twice been held up by colons as heralds and daysprings of passion ("Dawn: his heart shook in the tension of the world. / Dawn: and what is your passion?"), "October" is stopped by a colon only to be put at ease by the clownish bear, victim and benefactor of the annual breaking up of "the tension of the world." Far to the other side of the tension, "Yawns" blearily echoes "Dawn." "Bear" forms a no less soporific rhyme with "October." And the syntax itself, with the interruptive "Daft in the honey-light," seems to yawn. The association of "Daft" and "yawn" brings to mind Elias Canetti's dazzling analysis of comedy—in particular, laughter, when "the mouth is opened wide and the teeth are shown"—as a sublimation of eating, a harmless symbolic act, the teeth (though hardly kind) refraining. Throughout, the accents are deliciously distinct, as physically enjoyable as the full extension of a stretch, while the slacks are heavy as honey-drips (*sweet*en, like a *drowse, deep* to the *bone*).

Toward the bear, the bees, the blueberries, the light, Audubon leans in a slow regard. If anything in him still ravens, it is his conscience, which culls every sign of truce and innocence, down to the bemused hum and mica glint of the last bee. But what he experiences is less appetite than feeling, less feeling than transparency, less transparency than love. In one of the agrapha in Hastings' *Dictionary of the Bible*, the disciples, passing the carrion of a dog, say "What a stench!" "How white the teeth are," Jesus replies. A saintlike capacity for seeing without defenses, with appreciation, descends on Audubon as a blessing of the season—a season in which the teeth of things are pulled.

Then thought enters this Eden, like a serpent that says "Take and eat." Covetousness dimly lurks in "Thinks / How thin is the membrane between himself and the world." "Membrane" is provokingly sexual. Audubon is back where rage begins, afraid of his solitude, ashamed of its insignificance. From here the desire rises (in the words of another poem) to fling "blood / And the blind, egotistical, self-defining / Sperm" into a tormenting otherness. Although Audubon's thought is nearly a joyful exclamation, it pits something over against him. The concept "the world" describes the "all" of which he is a very little "part." In truth, he has degrees more of autumnal softening to undergo before his deep knowledge of his own fate redirects his aggression and he will want to lift his rifle only against himself (and against the penalty of his fate).

Part 2 is decisive in ensuring this further ripening. In a cabin where Audubon has sought shelter for the night, a frontier woman tries to kill him. He survives, safe but scathed. Having descended into a nightmare-pit of terror and guilt and discovered there his own part in the human rage to eat and be eaten, he is more than ever resigned to being "denied" and to die. Fanged himself, he will surrender to the nibbling teeth of time. He is weaker than before, and stronger, chastened but tempered. He is John James Aubudon, whose destiny it is to immortalize "the original state of the country,"* but a man, and a guilty one. His upper, conscious life, his romance with "the beauties of that nature, from which I have certainly derived my greatest pleasures," is henceforth an all but conscious anodyne to the inner nightmare: "Continue to walk in the world. Yes, love it!" He enters upon a new romance—the chill, terminal romance of fate.†

Warren takes John James Audubon's brisk anecdote and makes it gravitate hugely within. The simple, alert, good-natured John James is crossed by the debilitating psychological shadows of a Kafka or Hawthorne. This Audubon *wants* his throat cut. He discovers in himself a guilt-wish to be unmanned.

Brushing aside as a pipe dream the actual Audubon's prefatory Arcadian "brilliance of . . . flowers, . . . fawns gamboling around their

---

*   Quoted in Robert Penn Warren, Cleanth Brooks, and R. W. B. Lewis, comps., *American Literature: The Makers and the Making* (New York: St. Martin's, 1973), p. 1063. Also quoted there is Audubon's account of the attempt on his life, taken from John James Audubon, *Ornithological Biography* (1839).

†   Warren stretches the word "fate" to cover both (1) a distinguished personal destiny, as when he says that "Audubon resisted his fate and thought it was evil," and (2) death as the crowning/uncrowning of a life, a completed destiny. *See Robert Penn Warren Talking: Interviews 1950–1978*, ed. Floyd C. Watkins and John T. Hiers (New York: Random House, 1980), p. 235.

dams," and so on, Warren emphasizes, straight off, the revolting evidence that, where man is, there also is oral crime, oral filth:

> Shank-end of day, spit of snow, the call,
> A crow, sweet in distance, then sudden
> The clearing: among stumps, ruined cornstalks yet standing,
>   the spot
> Like a wound rubbed raw in the vast pelt of the forest. There
> Is the cabin, a huddle of logs with no calculation or craft:
> The human filth, the human hope.
>
>   Smoke,
> From the mud-and-stick chimney, in that air, greasily
> Brims, cannot lift, bellies the ridgepole, ravels
> White, thin, down the shakes, like sputum.
>
>   He stands,
> Leans on his gun, stares at the smoke, thinks: "Punk-wood."
> Thinks: "Dead-fall half-rotten." Too sloven,
> That is, to even set axe to clean wood.

Against the day that began redder than meat is now set the "Shank-end" of another, as if to say that time itself is but a devouring. And the throat-sweetness of the crow is merely a romantic deception of distance. In the clearing, with its stumps and ruined cornstalks, spat snow, greasy sputum of smoke, smoke bellying the ridgepole, Audubon finds the dregs of both oral and phallic nightmare. .

With a foreboding that approaches self-knowledge, Audubon anticipates more than "the stench of that lair":

> What should he recognize? The nameless face
> In the dream of some pre-dawn cock-crow—about to say
>   what,
> Do what? The dregs
> Of all nightmare are the same

When the door opens upon a face "Raw-hewn, strong-beaked," a "tumble and tangle / Of dark hair," dark eyes glinting "as from the unspecifiable / Darkness of a cave," an "It" that is astonishingly also a woman ("It is a woman"), the dregs disclose themselves as the Terrible Mother who, instead of docilely offering herself up as food, incarnates all bestial rapacity. Audubon has knocked for admittance at a "strong-beaked" womb. But he wants to be admitted. A man, therefore a son, phallic and guilty, he has always wanted (though till now only in "the dream") to be at once devoured and unmanned, his phallic crimes indistinguishable from his oral ones.

Entering this fearful female space, Audubon finds another guest, an Indian who that very day had accidentally put out his own eye with an arrow. This self-mutilated presence (straight from the original account) acts like a comic-grotesque sign of the psychic events already beginning to take place in Audubon, an only half-blind Oedipus seeking punishment.

Almost at once the woman wants to pluck from Audubon the body-warmed time-piece he draws out suggestively from under his hunter's frock (on a "thong-loop," it parallels the string-pulled heron on which with somewhat less rapacity he had "fixed" his own eyes). Audubon is moved by this mirror image of his own intolerable passion for what is winged:

> Takes his watch out.
> Draws it bright, on the thong-loop, from under his hunter's-
> frock.
> It is gold, it lives in his hand in the firelight, and the woman's
> Hand reaches out. She wants it. She hangs it about her neck.
>
> And near it the great hands hover delicately
> As though it might fall, they quiver like moth-wings, her eyes
> Are fixed downward, as though in shyness, on that gleam, and
> her face
> Is sweet in an outrage of sweetness, so that
> His gut twists cold. He cannot bear what he sees.

By means of this magical object—a key to the passion-world of time—the woman seems to recapture the fullness of her own promised time: "Her body sways like a willow in spring wind. Like a girl." She becomes original, fearful, with desire, her hands like Shelleyan moths fluttering for a star. From the midst of her squalid life she spies something even she cannot bear to see fall. So it is that Warren irradiates with the light of his creative attention, and through his deep complicity with every passion, John James's efficient "She was all ecstasy, praised its beauty, asked its value."

Soon Audubon's watch is back where it belongs and the woman sullenly prepares the food. This is perhaps the place to note that she has a split nightmare identity. On the one hand she is the Eaten Mother (she has been worn down, in part, by caring for two now-grown sons); on the other, she is the Mother of Eating—is not only strong-beaked, and not only prepares Audubon a meal, but later drinks from a jug and hones a knife; and when her two grown sons "come in from the night" they prove "The sons she would have": they "Hunker down by the fire, block the firelight, cram food / Into their large mouths, where teeth / Grind in the hot darkness" (a sibling's nightmare). "A mother," notes Canetti,

> is one who gives her own body to be eaten. She first nourishes the child in her womb and then gives it her milk . . . Her passion is to give food, to watch the child eating and profiting by the food it eats . . . Her behavior appears selfless . . . But what has really happened is that she now has two stomachs instead of one, and keeps control of both . . . The concept . . . of digestion as a central process of power holds for the mother too . . . The mother's power over a young child is absolute . . . There is no intenser form of power.

Audubon's unconscious mind agrees. This woman who envies him his watch is nonetheless a presence of frightening magical power, and soon he will be reduced to a state of sweet lassitude before the approach of her spit-wet knife.

As the woman prepares the food, the Indian, in a signal to Audubon, "Draws a finger, in delicious retardation, across his own throat." ("Delicious" is perverse and clairvoyant.) Audubon beds down on "bearskins which are not well cured, / And stink." His gun is by his side, "primed and cocked." He pretends to sleep. Against the background of her son's grinding jaws, the woman grinds the knife, wetting it from lips pursed "sweet as to bestow a kiss." Audubon thinks "Now"

> And knows
> He has entered the tale, knows
> He has entered the dark hovel
> In the forest where trees have eyes . . .

He knows, too, that the tale is to end with a "scream," but what is its meaning? He can only enact the meaning:

> Does not understand why now a lassitude
> Sweetens his limbs, or why, even this moment
> Of fear—or is it fear?—the saliva
> In his mouth tastes sweet.

> 'Now, now' the voice in his head cries out, but
> Everything seems far away, and small.
> He cannot think what guilt unmans him, or
> Why he should find the punishment so precious.

> It is too late. Oh, oh, the world!

In the next instant Audubon is saved, but not through any manly effort of his own. "The door bursts open, and the travelers enter: / Three men, alert, strong, armed"—a phallic police.

What is thus thwarted, the "end of the dream," is a fantasied eye-for-eye system of justice. He who would eat of the woman would have his throat cut by her (the knife a metallic tooth); he who would penetrate her would be passively pricked and bled by her blade.

Taller than he is, androgynous, this woman is desexed by her desire to have the timepiece. With knife in hand, she incorporates the phallic authority and aggression of the (absent) father. In sum, she is Audubon's bad conscience.

Apprehended, the woman suffers in his place—dies by a rope-grip around her neck. No wonder Audubon cannot eat the next morning before the hanging: "The cold corn pone grinds in his throat, like sand. It sticks there." That he is still one of the eaters, not the eaten (he foresees that a crow will alight on the hanged woman's shoulder) is owing to no merit or even to any wish of his own. Besides, he is still near his own nightmare, and if the guilty melancholiac does not want to eat, as Canetti observes, "the real reason is that he sees himself as being eaten and, if forced to eat, is reminded of this."

At the hanging, Audubon is struck by her stonelike beauty and "becomes aware that he is in the manly state." T. R. Hummer says of this extraordinary moment that the hero is thus "reborn to love of the world." He finds in Audubon the hero with a thousand faces. This hero, encountering the goddess who embodies "the life of everything that lives" but "also the death of everything that dies," is killed and "put together in a new way." The paradigm fits, but as externally as a slipcover, a general thing that fails to distinguish Warren's text from others. In any case, instead of being put together in a new way, Audubon learns that it is better not to come apart. To think that he had wished to! His erection is a survivor's shout, a flourish of the ransomed blood. He stands before appearances excited once again. He now understands the inner "tale" well enough to know that it is best left in the unconscious dark. He might now repeat after Schelling, "The emotions are glorious [only] when they stay in the depths."

As Warren put it elsewhere, "Man lives by images. They / Lean at us from the world's wall, and Time's." Audubon is "reborn" when his body reaffirms the radiant world of semblances. His eyes "lust" again, his flesh conforming. No doubt his erection is in part a response to the gruesome parody of female surrender; but even with a noose around her neck this hag is formidable and rebellious.* What she symbolizes is not so much the sexual victim as, precisely, a stony courage before the chisel of fate—a triumph of both will and appearance:

> And in the gray light of morning, he sees her face. Under
> The tumbled darkness of hair, the face
> Is white. Out of that whiteness

---

* Audubon's own text is most ambiguous as to whether a hanging had taken place. It was, however, to Warren's purpose to assume that one had.

> The dark eyes stare at nothing, or at
> The nothingness that the gray sky, like Time, is, for
> There is no Time, and the face
> Is, he suddenly sees, beautiful as stone . . .

In the dim Godless light of morning she stands forth not only in legalistic, transgression-baiting black and white but with the black and white melodramatic vividness of a figure in the old cinema. Fate, moreover, has divided her with a white and black severity, her blanching horror contrasting with her dark defiance. She is the hypnotic focus of all appearance—a heroine of a spirited being-as-appearance. (She trusts in no other world: "If'n it's God made folks, then who's to pray to?") So it is that she puts life back into Audubon. Willing herself to *be*, even at the terrible end of her own "dream," she represents phallic rage, an unapologetic will to power despite the cruelest outward defeat:

> The affair was not quick: both sons long jerking and farting,
>   but she,
> From the first, without motion, frozen
> In a rage of will, an ecstacy of iron, as though
> This was the dream that, lifelong, she had dreamed toward.
>   The face,
> Eyes a-glare, jaws clinched, now glowing black with
>   congestion
> Like a plum, had achieved,
> It seemed to him, a new dimension of beauty.

This original, disturbing episode pushes to a tragic extreme the credo stated by Hannah Arendt: "In this world which we enter by appearing from a nowhere, and from which we disappear into a nowhere, *Being and Appearing coincide*." Phallic exuberance underlies appearance, and passion supports it; or else passion, unmanned, lets the world die into gray "nothingness."

Being denied "the end of the dream" becomes part, perhaps the chief part, of a "definition of joy," though one that Audubon senses rather than frames:

> He thinks: "What has been denied me?"
> Thinks: "There is never an answer."
>
> Thinks: "The question is the only answer."
>
> He yearns to be able to frame a definition of joy.

Joy lies in being spared the ugly "end" of psychic regression. It lies in a felicitous ignorance of the dregs of nightmare. Joy: the benign romance of appearances, family romance disguised in the fruitful mating of mother nature and father time, the son at liberty to "walk in the world," his timepiece a reminder of both opportunity and mortality.

Art, moreover—though this the text illustrates more than intimates—is an adjunct to such joy, since it multiplies appearance in the image of passion. "Perhaps the superior work of the imagination," wrote Philip Rieff, "is self-concealment, keeping us at a safe distance from ourselves and from each other." As Helen Vendler saw (referring to the passage "And knows that the dregs of all life are nightmare. / Unless. / Unless what?"), "Audubon's work and equanimity answer the 'unless.' To terror and nightmare he answers with vision by night ('In my sleep I continually dream of birds') and drawing by day." The aggression in his seeing, painting, and writing (and even in his shooting: "Over a body held in his hand, his head was bowed low, but not in grief") has been put in its proper perspective, as relatively benign, since it proliferates and enhances rather than conceals and destroys appearances; without a too cruel irony it can be called reverence, or "love knowledge."

Audubon is now prepared to see--to revere--fate itself under the hallowing and beautifying aspect of appearance. In the opening section of part 4, grown older, he imagines his own end as a nobly achieved appearance of which he is at once the subject (the "quarry") and the spectator, indeed the executor (the hunter). Though I quoted most of the lines earlier, they bear repeating:

<blockquote>

The blessedness!—

To wake in some dawn and see,
As though down a rifle barrel, lined up
Like sights, the self that was, the self that is, and there,
Far off but in range, completing that alignment, your fate.

Hold your breath, let the trigger-squeeze be slow and steady.

The quarry lifts, in the halo of gold leaves, its noble head.

This is not a dimension of Time.

</blockquote>

At the end, then, a life justified by its pride, maturity, and harmony with the natural scene. Because of the primacy that appearance has for him, Audubon conceives his death not as a disappearance, or even as consequent on his decline (the halo of gold leaves displaces decay from the noble "quarry"), but as the last and most climactic of his appearances. (Because reality is "first of all of a phenomenal nature," notes Arendt, our sense of "what a living thing is essentially" is "determined by the relatively short time span of its full appearance, its epiphany.") Even his death is to be of the world as well as in it, regardless of its ambiguous relation to "the dimension of Time."

Concurrently, his end is to mark the last and most decisive of his self-activations. In a consummate, ruinous act of realizing concentration, his eye will "shoot," will tot up, all the appearances he has been, while his finger lovingly maneuvers for the "trigger-squeeze." He will accede to death only by clutching it as his own last phallic decision. His authoring and acquiring will, his will not to be unmanned, plots to transcend time by closing it up.*

---

* Perhaps latent here is the fantasy expressed in Emily Dickinson's poem "My Life had stood a Loaded Gun"—that the poet's ability to "speak" so that "The Mountains straight reply" will live longer than its "Owner" will. See *The Complete Poems of Emily Dickinson*, ed. Thomas H. Johnson (Boston: Little, Brown, n.d.), p. 369.

If even at the end appearance is everything, so is will. The heart-shaking "tension of the world" lies in the contradiction. Even the crack of doom will not resolve the give and take between them. Part pole and part silken tent, the world will still stand by their differences.

Only conscience will be resolved on the day Audubon wakes to blessedness; not too soon, but inevitably, retribution will be exacted. *Ornithological Biography* tells of how the hag's two sons, "athletic youths," enter the shack "with a dead stag on a pole between them." Warren suppresses this Oedipally troublous detail only to secrete and transpose it to part 4, where Audubon reserves to himself the pleasure of bringing down his own proud potency: "The quarry lifts, in the halo of gold leaves, its noble head." Of course a still greater sacrifice could be made: the "emphatic," executory thumb could be another's. But a tragic conscience does not require this total death of self-definition. It knows too well the justifications of will, of all the lusts, in a world in which appearance is the fruit of the vine of death, of which we must take and eat, or be nothing. At best, Audubon's bloody sense of his own identity will rise like a large red moon through the kicked-up dust of the prairies till, white, free, diminished, but even then hard in its own radiance, it escapes "the dimension of Time."

The Thirst for Vision

Passion wants appearances not only to be but to mean, wants them to say *You*! or *We*! as a mother might, or a mistress, or a father womanly with love, or God in his mercy.

Tragic joy is possible only when this childish insistence ceases. Or so "Loss, of Perhaps Love, in Our World of Contingency" intimates. That vague sense of loss? It may derive from what you felt as, sunlight dappling the bathroom floor, "your mother / Bathed you." Or from the idiot narcissism that once expected the violets "buried now under dead leaves (later snowdrifts)" to dream how they "will see / You again pass, cleaving the blue air." Whatever its cause, renounce it. For only then will you know the stabbing joy of unmeaning, uncaring contingency, the dragon that will rescue you from the maidens of your sentimentality. Blessed accident, light-thewed angel of reality, the thunderclap can startle you into rising made all anew, and with powers to glorify what has been merciful. "We must learn to live in the world."

But it is not in the nature of passion to abide in chaste preparedness. It wants all, and wants it now. Passion that should know "we never seek things for themselves, but for the search" (Pascal). *As if* it would do more than merely haunt the past, it engages in darting bat-flights of memory and nostalgia. As if it could bear the revelation of its own innate primitivism, it engages in "the dream of the eating of human flesh." It is the dilettante of its own hungers.

And yet its sorrows are real, for some basic deprivation we have indeed suffered. Psychoanalysis can but offer metaphors for a loss too profound to be understood, and perhaps even prior to the psyche. If memory itself makes the truth lyrical, by obscuring it ("What is it you cannot remember that is so true?") this *ur*-memory makes it metaphysical. An antilife, it blows from a land of lost content like Housman's "air that kills." The dunes in the body might be irritated by a sense of the waves they once were. Or, to the moist protoplasm of the blood, the Sahara of abstract "energy" might seem more kindly than the glistening foliage of Eden.

Whatever the reasons, grief is native to passion. Like "Rattlesnake Country," "Folly on Royal Street before the Raw Face of God" (in the same strong volume, *Or Else*) hints this with a telling persuasion. Unusual in the way it dwindles, grows almost mum, it protests the raw face of God—the hot New Orleans sun—but with a passion that suggests nostalgia for the absent refined face of the mother, and perhaps beyond that for a face too star-dim even to be raw, a primal excuse from pain.

Here nature itself, with its gaudy cosmetic camellias and bougainvilleas, its sperm and fish-smells, quite defeats nostalgia. A gull, "Whiteness ablaze in dazzle and frazzle of light like / A match flame in noon-glare," screams "for justice against the face of God," venting the complaint of everything within the Gulf-city scene. What exists, here, lacks charm and fullness of existence. Something in the scheme of things, and not merely the vastness of that scheme, diminishes and desiccates everything. The "hurricane" of spring is one name for it, the "blaze of noon" another; something elemental is inimical to individual existence, reducing it to shabby compulsions.

The poem begins by reeling with and away from the recognition that man is condemned to nonfulfillment. Here actual drunkenness strives to be a "total eclipse" of a fundamental thirst, but is only a sleazy, wishful "almost":

> Drunk, drunk, drunk, amid the blaze of noon,
> Irrevocably drunk, total eclipse or,
> At least, almost, and in New Orleans once,
> In French Town, spring,
> Off the Gulf, without storm warnings out,
> Burst, like a hurricane of
> Camellias, sperm, cat-squalls, fish-smells, and the old
> Pain of fulfillment-that-is-not-fulfillment, so
> Down Royal Street—Sunday and the street
> Blank as my bank account
> With two checks bounced—we—
> C. and M. and I, every
> Man-jack skunk-drunk—
> Came.

The roisterous thump and hopeful absolute construction of "Drunk, drunk, drunk," the swaggering rhythm of "Irrevocably drunk," the jittery gaiety in the sound of "At least, almost, and in New Orleans once, / In French town," and so on—all this fails to disguise, it rather betrays, an undertone of nausea. The nausea is concentrated in the catalogue of what spring has tossed up like so much debris of its own blind making, a list that exudes a powerful sexual disgust. In part, the various jammed-together compounds in the passage intimate the bitter enforced condition, the inner hurricane, of existing as what Schopenhauer called "concrete sexual desire" ("The sexual passion is the kernel of the [involuntary] will to live, and consequently the concentration of all desire. Indeed, one may say man is concrete sexual desire.") More strictly, "fulfillment-that-is-not-fulfillment" betrays the sickness of passion itself, of which sexuality is merely a burning-glass focus, passion brought to the smoking point and to spasm.

An "old" pain indeed, and perhaps not only because, in Norman O. Brown's words, "man has been subjected to a systematic effort to transform him into an ascetic animal. He remains a pleasure-seeking animal. Parental discipline, religious denunciation of bodily pleasure, and philosophic exaltation of the life of reason have all left man overtly docile, but secretly in his unconscious unconvinced, and therefore neurotic. Man remains unconvinced because in infancy he tasted the fruit of the tree of life, and knows that it is good, and never forgets." Certainly the pain Warren tells of is reinforced by this "systematic effort" to transform man into an ascetic animal—and so fierce a denial as this noontime blaze must be fatherly, male. It is pertinent that the day is Sunday. But perhaps the troubles of our proud and angry dust (it is pertinent, too, that the street is Royal) are from eternity, and shall not fail. Oral famine, oral rage—these may be the mere physical expression of what Jacques Lacan calls "demand," an already irremediably alienated hollow within the infant, an unreasonable insistence on untellable extents of love.

Yet of course, as a man gradually learns not to put everything into his mouth, even his oral pleasure diminishes, he fills his mouth with drink or words instead—perhaps he mouths "out . . . Milton for magnificence." But before Warren intimates as much, he introduces two other oral comedians, a cat and a cop:

> A cat,
> Gray from the purple shadow of bougainvillaea,
> Fish-head in dainty jaw-clench,
> Flowed fluid as thought, secret as sin, across
> The street. Was gone. We,
> In the shock of that sudden and glittering vacancy, rocked
> On our heels.
>
> A cop,
> Of brachycephalic head and garlic breath,

Toothpick from side of mouth and pants ass-bagged and
   holster low,
From eyes the color of old coffee grounds,
Regarded with imperfect sympathy
La condition humaine—
Which is sure-God what we were.

We rocked on our heels.

However dainty the cat's jaw-clench on the fish-head, however royal the purple shadow of the bougainvillea, the scene glares with the meaninglessness of the world, its very light like bounced checks. To the inner mouth the world is food, or nothing. This scene is charged with naughtening—nausea over the scraps, the wrong food, littering the world. With his primeval head, garlic breath, toothpick, and coffee-colored eyes, the cop sardonically confirms the thesis that man is a (poor) "pleasure-seeking animal," even while, as an unsympathetic gun-toting authority, he represents the patriarchal attempt to make the human animal ascetic. Plainly the three roisterers remain "unconvinced" by his standing nix to the oral extravagances of infancy. "Sure-God" freely takes the name of the Father in vain on this Sunday in vacant Royal Street, in which only the cat, lawless, unpoliced, flows out of the glittering void—that compound of "civilized" denial and glaring demand.

    Another concrete naughtening presence, compared to which even the cop is human and sympathetic, is the sun, the "raw face" of God:

               At sky-height—
Whiteness ablaze in dazzle and frazzle of light, like
A match flame in noon-glare—a gull
Kept screaming above the doomed city.
It screamed for justice against the face of God.

Raw-ringed with glory like an ulcer, God's
Raw face stared down.

             And winked.

> We
> Mouthed out our Milton magnificence.
>
> For what is man without magnificence?
>
> Delusion, delusion!
>
> But let
> Bells ring in all the churches.
> Let likker, like philosophy, roar
> In the skull. Passion
> Is all. Even.
> The sleaziest.

God fails to exist except as the sickness of the world (of "demand"). That he shows only a "raw" face indistinguishable from an ulcerous inner organ confesses that he cannot appear.*

Milton contradicts this sense of him, and at least the three young men can mouth out Milton for magnificence; but it is Milton, not God, who is "ours." Spirit is nothing other than relation, and this God without countenance, worried out of countenance, cannot relate. "The freedom of [man's] being and of Being," wrote Martin Buber in *I and Thou* (from which Warren quotes respectfully in *Democracy and Poetry*), "consists wholly in the truth of relation between *I* and *Thou*," a relation like "the air in which you breathe." Buber adds that when a culture (and every great culture "rests on an original relational incident") hardens into the world of *It*, causality "rises up till it is an oppressive, stifling fate." Stifling, an *It*, is this Sunday "blaze of noon"—Destiny transformed "into a demonic spirit adverse to meaning." Here the "fiery stuff" of will creates a world of death, of "fate

---

* At best, Warren's is the "hidden God" of tragic man. The latter, in Lucien Goldmann's words, suffers "the disorder and confusion" of being "placed between the vanity and presence of the world and the reality and absence of God." He "rejects compromise and relative values in the name of a demand for absolute justice and truth"—as here the gull screams for justice against the face of God. But where the tragic man limned by Goldmann—for example, Pascal—nonetheless places himself "entirely in God's hand," Warren's lacks "tragic faith" in God, is unable to carry on a "solitary dialogue" with Him—and this seems to me the more truly tragic position. See Goldmann, *The Hidden God: A Study of Tragic Vision in the Pensées of Pascal and the Tragedies of Racine* (New York: Humanities Press, 1964), ch. 4.

that does not know spirit." But whereas Buber believes in fresh original relational incidents, the image of the ulcer-faced God hints at a psychosomatic disorder for which there may be no (earthly or heavenly) cure.

The strategy and therapy of mouthing out Milton strikes at both the metaphysical claustrophobia and the drying mouth of infancy. However borrowed the words, however sublimated the oral gratification, however self-conscious the echoing syllables, the recitation (as we can gauge from the line itself) is orally vigorous: "We / Mouthed out our Milton for magnificence." After each of the three lip-gluing *m*'s, the other sounds force the mouth open: the infant in a man is not to be denied everything. Milton's words posit a realm, that of art, which simulates the outer glories of the physical and the inner unity of the metaphysical. Poetry is relational and sensual at the same time—sensual without being demonic. The three young men turn to Milton as to a linguistic counterpart of the gorgeous bougainvillea and its shade, but also as to a sympathetic face, to a voice and comprehending eyes. "Our Milton" makes him a source of general human pride, a humanistic possession—proof of what the human mouth, however deprived, can do: how much absorb, and what pleasure give.

Implicit in the poem, not least in its very existence, is the way out and way back of poetry. Yet "Delusion, delusion!" warns against all illusory magnificence. Although bitter and gestic, the outburst is more than self-abuse. The deeply sobering outcome of the poem honorably attempts to create a chastened poetry of dignity without magnificence. We have a youthful moment, as if the last, for extravagant gestures. There is another in the comically magisterial "But let / Bells ring . . . / Let likker . . . roar," and in "Passion is all," which only wishes it were so. On Royal Street, of a Sunday, passion doesn't count for much of anything.

Now the reenactment of passion gives way to a sober summary, a weighing of the damage, of the subsequent years. What is henceforth enacted is the death of passion. Disconsolately, the poem alludes to the demonic causality of modern history as another vacancy, another stifling fate.

The three friends went their separate ways toward desolation. One, the speaker, may have saved himself by stepping onto the shaky suspension bridge of art:

War
Came. Among the bed-sheet Arabs, C.
Sported his gold oak leaf. Survived.
Got back. Back to the bank. But
One morning was not there. His books,
However, were in apple-pie order. His suits,
All dark, hung in the dark closet. Drawn up
In military precision, his black shoes,
Though highly polished, gave forth
No gleam in that darkness. In Mexico,
He died.

For M.,
Twenty years in the Navy. Retired,
He fishes. Long before dawn, the launch slides out.
Land lost, he cuts the engine. The launch
Lifts, falls, in the time of the sea's slow breath.
Eastward, first light is like
A knife-edge honed to steel-brightness
And laid to the horizon. Sometimes,
He comes back in with no line wet.

As for the third, the tale
Is short. But long,
How long the art, and wisdom slow!—for him who
Once rocked on his heels, hearing the gull scream,
And quoted Milton amid the blaze of noon.

As it addresses the historical dimension of naughtening, as well as the universal phenomenon known as maturing, the poem turns white-lipped indeed. The likkered pseudo-bouyancy gives way to a numb notation that moves one to say: "But this is awfully grim; this is hardly even poetry." Nothing here to mouth out until the youth-remembering close. The mouth, like the syntax, is now vestigial. There is no heart left for performance. Instead, the poem records, the poet *writes*.

"War / Came" is at once a minuscule and a titanic sentence. It remorselessly contracts the opening clause of the poem, "we . . . / Came," as if cutting a camellia back to its trunk. Once it was "we," however shakily, who acted; now, more ruthlessly than ever, "we" are acted upon.

Where the early use of the initials "C." and "M." connoted privacy, here it figures the loss of identity, total eclipse for C. and, for M., almost. That "something a man is" that, so Whitman thought, stands "apart from all else, divine in [its] own right," sending sunrise out of itself to withstand the "dazzling and tremendous" sun of reality—this had already been rocked back on its heels in their youth, and is subsequently dark and closeted or shut off like a launch drifting in an open sea. Passion may not be "all," but without it there is only an "it," no man at all. Military efficiency. A "not there." Catatonia. Nothing coming off the Gulf. An *X* with his back to the reader and staring on the empty face of the sea, where dawn strikes like a castrating god.

As for the third: in "wisdom slow," wisdom is perhaps that autumnal Yeatsian kind into which one withers—nondelusion. Even this third, who doesn't denominate himself, is largely a self-absence; he is known to himself most vividly as he who once rocked back on his heels, hearing the gull scream, and quoted Milton amid the blaze of noon. He is the has-been of the would-be of passion he once was. Then the noon hour was long; now the tale itself is short.

Yet he is a poet, and all, and the little, that may imply. Mouthing out Milton was one thing, creating original poetry another: how long the art. Whatever he may have gained in creative pride, this third seems to have paid for in costly toil. An ascetic animal laboring to produce pleasure, master of interior realms, why doesn't he come right out and say what his slow-won wisdom knows: that interiority (passion, demand) grieves in the grave of this world? Isn't this the not-said of the poem, mutely swelling like a lump in its throat?

Yet the poem itself, as a particular kind of saying, contradicts it. Even as it recognizes necessity, the poem belongs, qua poem, to freedom. Its austere compassion, generously offered, protests to the end a world where, in Milton's words, "all life dies, death lives, and nature breeds." It laughs at folly, but mourns magnificence. The poem has not merely wet its line; it has deliberately displaced reality with its own hard-as-crystal feeling about it. It thus gains and asserts its power. It liberates its content from the account books and closets of obscure actuality and transposes it into luminous form, of which every part is permeated by and radiates into the whole.

The poet, at least, has kept passion alive, and writes from it. This, equally, is the not-said of the poem. It agrees with the knowledge of how ill passion fares in this world only in its enforced shuttering against the remembered blaze of noon. It has not abdicated, but it has adjusted. In a last reversal, the poet leads us to see that, especially there in its self-imposed gloom, pasison really is all.

Warren seldom writes even indirectly about art; given the times, he's mulish that way, a holdout for four-square representation—his mind realist, universal, manly. Yet tacitly, his passion (that is, his theme) saves itself, knows itself, increases itself through the transposing activity of his poems, with their sunset and sunrise intensities, their concern not with man but with the image of man. ("In art," Pasternak noted, "the man is silent and the image speaks.") In their urgency and gravity, in the direct purposefulness of their language, the poems are passion-speech. A portion of what passion wants—an "immanence of meaning" in things, a sacramental interchangeability of "part" with "all," or "part" with "part"—is satisfied by the made replica (half substitute, half stopover) of the work of art.

With its narrative extensiveness, "story" in particular evokes the mystery of the whole, in which the parts crowd and press for meaning. It restrains the brusque leaps of metaphor, the impatience of metaphor with time and space. What Roman Jakobson called "the metonymical texture of realistic prose"—though not impatient enough—better meets Warren's needs. In his novel *Band of Angels* the heroine, Amantha Starr, suggests the appeal, the potential healing totality, of story:

> You do not live your life, but somehow, your life lives you, and you are, therefore, only what history does to you.

This is what I have heard said, but we have to try to make sense of what we have lived, or what has lived us, and there are so many questions that cry for an answer . . . it is like children gathering about your knee to cry for a story, a bedtime story, and if you can tell the right story, then these children, then these questions, will sleep, and you can, too.

You feel that if you can answer the questions, you might be free.

Audubon, as noted, ends profoundly and originally with the anti-resolution of a renewed demand for metonymic art of the kind it has just brilliantly exemplified—as if enough were never enough:

Tell me a story.

In this century, and moment, of mania,
Tell me a story.

Make it a story of great distances, and starlight.

The name of the story will be Time.
But you must not pronounce its name.

Tell me a story of deep delight.

That the composition of *Audubon* has not stilled the poet's passion for story has little to do with its substitution of a metonymic sequence of "shots" for traditional narrative continuity, and everything to do with our insatiable human need for our own self-presencing. The skip-and-dart, concentrative, sequential method expresses this need (only, of course, to exacerbate it).

The childlike urging "Tell me a story" is almost physically prodded into vocalization by the remembered hootings of the great geese flying northward in first dark over Kentucky—the child Warren, as Audubon's avatar, avidly listening as he stood, prefiguratively alone, by a dirt road. These hootings, all "destiny," form the fate-germ of his poetic vocation—the cries of harsh, plangent path-longing that he will emulate in his more doubting and even-more-wandering human voice. His ambition has been to write a poetry in which "great distances, and starlight" are reconciled with living creatures in their cries, mostly against the background of "this century, and moment, of mania." To get the vital geese to cluster so close to the clustering stars that it might be the stars themselves that were hooting and the geese that, constellated and "Star-triumphing," bestrode "the icy altitudes"—that would be to evoke the interchangeability of all things in the eyes and ears of passion. It would be to consecrate the intuition of a destiny in which the concrete immensity of the universe is obscurely but poignantly involved.

More than any of his other poems, "Folly on Royal Street before the Raw Face of God" dashes this hope of passion-fulfillment, of destiny-striding. Here the world is not matched to passion—ill enough matched to provoke it, but too ill-matched to give it heart. Nor can the romance of the prelife, the "circuit hope," thrive where the soil is so parched. The poverty of the present is too much with the soul.

Yet it must be observed that the great majority of Warren's poems are passion's complainings. All his yearning but returns him to his deprivations. Yearning, yearning, yearning—will there never be an end to it? Always the question of innate meaning and the question as to why this question exists, why so little comes of it: "Why, all the years, and places, and nights, have I / Wandered and not known the question I carried? / And carry?" A tormented ignorance, a conscious falling short of vision, stalks the poems:

> Where is the Truth—oh, unambiguous—
> Thereof?
>
> .
>
> And whatever
> Vision or anguish
> Swelled in the heart to be uttered was
> By wind crammed in the throat back
>
> .
>
> Man's mind, his heart, live only by piecemeal.
>
> .

Moon-walking on sea-cliffs, once I
Had dreamed to a wisdom I almost could name.
But could not. I waited.
But heard no voice in the heart.

Images of straining effort—of reaching, grappling, leaning, climbing, running—figure the frustrated need for more truth, more "vital contact," more peace of definition:

> Have you ever
> Had the impulse to stretch forth your hand over
> The bulge of forest and seize trees like the hair
> Of a head you would master? Well,
> We are entitled to our fantasies, for life
> Is only the fantasy that has happened to us
>
> .
>
> A man and a woman, perhaps they lean
> Into cold dimness of gauge-lights
>
> .
>
> The body,
> With the towel now trailing loose from one hand, is
> A white stalk from which the face flowers gravely toward the
> high sky.
>
> .
>
> Running, feet bare on
> Sand wet-packed and star stung. Phlegm in lungs loose.
> . . . . .
> To understand
> Is impossible now. Flight from what? To what? And alone.

The dream is to "embrace / The world in its fullness and threat, and feel, like Jacob, at last / The merciless grasp of unwordable grace / Which has no truth to tell of future or past— / But only life's instancy, by daylight or night."

When this dream grows feeble or bitter the note becomes

> Why should the heart leap? We
> Are old enough to know that the world
> Is only the world
> . . . . .
> But we often forget.

Again: "What tongue knows the name of Truth? Or Truth to come? / All we can do is strive to learn the cost of experience." And, more grimly:

> If I set muzzle to forehead
> And pull the trigger, I'll see
> The world in a last flood of vital red—
>
> Not gray—that cataracts down.
> No, I go to the windowpane
> That rain's blurring tracery claims as its own.

After all, one may well end (as the recent "Paradigm of Seasons" intimates) with

> The painful bellows of the lungs of an aging man
> Who follows, with a burden of supplies on his back,
> A snow-choked trail.

For all that, Warren cannot bring himself to abandon passion—to die in advance of actual death. And perhaps nothing could be better calculated to prolong life, to constitute and swell it, than this yearning for an impossible totalization of all feeling; of all glimpses of beauty and all hints of truth; of all sensations of power; of all yearning to be taken up, like a babe, into the arms of the world.

Passion may not be able to lift itself by its own bootstraps into vision, but would vision keep it? Vision, in consummating it, would end it, convert it to the "gravity of stone." Not for passion "The Moments of Dominion / That happen on the Soul"—the "White," the too white, "Election!" These are too little of the world; it is possession of the world that passion asks.

Passion lacks the self-purgations of mysticism. Oedipus is in it; Adam and Eve are in it. There is more thrill at the prospect and power of being glorified within and by the all than of being dissolved from the tension of identity, though this last may harbor its own possessive intent. Passion needs the ache of division and the elation of trespass. It is happiest in supposing that its "mission is to try to understand / The possibility of joy in the world's tangled and hieroglyphic beauty."

Warren lacks a metaphysical eye for reading brute signs. His sight is Nietzschean—aesthetic, tragic. The signs remain gloriously brute, decipherable only as indecipherable passion. Warren's "image of man" is of tragic man denied explanation and totality, yet wresting nobility from this denial. This poet remains as secular yet stirred up as Melville's "Catskill eagle in some souls that can alike dive down into the blackest gorges, and soar out of them again and become invisible in the sunny spaces, . . . his lowest swoop . . . still higher than other birds upon the plain, even though they soar." Aside from a few recent poems on the metaphysics of death (of which more later), passion has found in Warren its greatest dignity by turning its vision-starved eyes back on its own mortal limits. Then its sight grows clear, its fervor is steadied by courage.

The Void and the Smile

"Metaphysical"—is there any saving this word from folly, pomposity, lies? Met-a-phys-i-cal, a balancing act of five spindly syllables. Long, jutting skyward from the upraised face, is it a magical horn or a pole thumbing a nose?

Warren uses it chiefly to back and beef up the mystery of time. In "Part of What Might Have Been a Short Story, Almost Forgotten," time looks on with "gaze of blaze" like a cougar's picked out by headlights, only "More metaphysical." "On into the Night" tells of a stream sliding "like an image of Time's metaphysic." For Warren, what makes time metaphysical is its proximity to no-time; somehow it is in on the secret. A "feather-fine brush of Grace"—say, a "lynx-scream"—can turn it around. "Little Black Heart of the Telephone" offers a hysterical variant on a famous Pascal *pensée:* "You've looked up at stars lost in blankness that bleeds / Its metaphysical blood, but not of redemption." If God is "Non-Life," then "we would worship Death, the Father," or so observes Jack Burden in *All the King's Men.*

If you take time itself apart, you find no-time. Saint Augustine pondered the matter, noting that the smallest particles of moments . . . [fly] with such speed from future to past, as not to be lengthened out with the least stay." "Too mighty for me," "way out of my ken," this great intellect concluded. "But is there a now or a then?" Warren echoes. "What, ah, is Time!" Like space, it is one of "our arbitrary illusions." Because of it, life is "only the fantasy that has happened to us"—a "bright emptiness" like a snakeskin found in the garden in autumn and held up "in the mellow light."*

The most paradoxical of Warren's pagan goals has been to know timelessness despite time—to seek "The absolute that Time would, I thought, have prepared, / But has not yet." "In *Audubon* (part 5) the poet dreams of a season "past all seasons," where the wild-grape cluster, "Unripening, ripens" and Audubon's stained lip, "undrying," gleams in the bright wind. But the poet hardly dared lay personal claim to so fanciful a dream: "there is a dream." It was in part 4 of the poem that he opened a way out of time ("This is not a dimension of Time"); but this was a tragic exit indeed: one clear paradoxical instant of no-time to make up for a lifetime of time-smeared incertitudes.

Other potential releases from time are taken up, turned over, put back. The notorious sexual promise of transcendence is one of these. *A Place to Come to* speaks of the "blind, blunt thrust toward eternity" of the "prod of erectile tissue." To leap into the "life-beyond-Time without which life-in-Time might not be endurable, or even possi-

---

* Certainly Warren warms up some old chestnuts; but, as Richard Jackson has shown, his philosophical cogitations about time nonetheless rival in depth and many-facetedness a combination of taxing passages culled from Hegel, Kant, Husserl, Heidegger, Derrida, and still other anatomists of time. See Jackson, "The Generous Time: Robert Penn Warren and the Phenomenology of the Moment," *Boundary 29* (Winter 1981): 1–30.

ble"—this eschatological view of orgasm, with its absurd overreaching, is demoted in "Tires on Wet Asphalt at Night" to "the old / Mechanic hope of finding identity in / The very moment of paradox when / There is always none." Not to mention the fear of that plunge "Into the black center of things," where "nothing equalled nothing" (*Flood*). Before copulating with a blind woman from his town, Brad Tolliver digs his fingers and thumb "cruelly" into her belly. He is offended by her appendectomy scar. Sex itself is an inflammation, a surgery, a removal. It is vehement against male independence.

The categories of the sexual climax? First, the Dionysian: the sense of creative rage mingling suicidally with the devastating experience of a self-dispersal. Second, the tragic, which as Lukács says "begins at the moment when enigmatic forces have distilled the essence from a man, have forced him to become essential." (The orgasm is the body's share in tragic joy.) Third, the comic: ever the same joke, dousing the flash of tragic illumination too quickly, with slapstick violence. Finally, the melodramatic:

> Then heels stopping
> In shudder and sprawl, only whites
>
> Of eyes showing, like death. What all the tension,
> The tingle, twist, tangle, the panting and pain,
>
> What all eploitation of orifices and bruised flesh but
> The striving for one death in two? I remember
> . . . . .
> The glutted, slack look on the face once
> And the faintest blood-smear at the mouth's left corner,
>
> And not till next day did I notice the two
> Symmetrical half-moons of blue marks tattooed
>
> On my shoulder, not remembering, even then, the sensation
> Of the event.

The sexual angel-of-mud reduces those who wrestle with it to grotesque simulations of death throes. Two symmetrical half-moons, blue: a small return for the investment of metaphysical (or, for that matter, physical) ardor.

If the flesh deceives or falters or obstructs, one may disdain it altogether; but for Warren, whose imagination is both muscular and sensual, the senses persist as the arena of joy. His "Platonism" is likely to seem deliciously fallen, as in "Platonic Drowse":

> But your body began to flow
> On every side into distance,
> Unrippling, silent, silver,
>
> Leaving only the steady but pulsing
> Germ-flame of your Being, that throbbed
> In Platonic joy for the world.
>
> The world, in Platonic drowse, lay.

But this is a republicanism of the senses, not a Platonic aristocracy of the soul; a melt-out, not an ascesis. It is not mysticism but a rumor of it, caught on the edge of a sleep induced by repeated hot licks of the sun.

Warren's most strenuous "Platonic" poem, "Evening Hawk," is torn between image and idea. As image, the hawk enshrines the poet's Nietzschean love of heroism; as idea, it is the Platonic Good, the Platonic True. The poem attempts to break into allegory with

> Look! look! he is climbing the last light
> Who knows neither Time nor Error, and under
> Whose eye, unforgiving, the world, unforgiven, swings
> Into shadow.

The poet cannot know all this except by wanting to believe it; here his mind ceases to be wholly realist, universal, and manly and becomes sharply, universally judgmental.

With its rhythmic loveliness—an evening lull quickened by hawk-motions—and its unrepentent sensory vividness, which triumphs to the end, and most of all the hawk's animal vigor, the poem stays alive, however fought over from inside. The emotion remains true and intact, because the poet is not contemptuous of vitality per se, but only of vitality that fails. Here, vitality in its full power is consonant with Platonic freedom from death and error.

With his Augustinian disdain of garbled compulsions, Warren never escapes the conflict that, as Unamuno regards it, is "the basis of the tragic sense of life": the conflict between the vital, which is antirational, and the rational, which is antivital. At his strongest—as in his best poem of hard-knocks realism, "American Portrait: Old Style," he loves the world even in his anger, "And love is a hard thing to outgrow." But the costs tell; the impulse to strike out at the feebleness of life (as if there were something better) mounts and mounts. But "Evening Hawk" creates the myth of an earthly vitality which is *as good as* Platonic impregnability. The image of vitality is the phallus, here winged and climbing and surviving avalanches of light. The hawk's wing is a scythe, time collapses but the hawk himself remains a force unspent. History may "Drip in darkness like a leaking pipe in the cellar," but the hawk and the bat with its "ancient" wisdom and "The star, . . . steady, like Plato, over the mountain" soar and last.

Triumph and failure are both male. To stand up in the light is male; to fall and drip is male. To judge man as unworthy is male and to defy the judgment no less male. The hawk is both father and son, in a crackling synthesis. Higher than poetry (it rises free of "the guttural gorge"), this evening hawk is yet nothing other than poetry as it outsoars "time and error." It is poetry as the son, seeking to be consubstantial with truth and glory, the father.

The father? "Dead," said Freud. Reified into principle beyond error. Steady as a star over the mountain. Ancient wisdom. As such, he is cold; he pinches the vital nerve till it goes to sleep. The contrary principle of the son is to seize eagerly on what will afford him power and glory. So, though this hawk may be "like philosophy" (like the one in "The Mad Druggist"), he is even more like the hawk in "The Leaf"—a hawk that shudders "to hold position in the blazing wind" while catching, "white, the flicker of hare-scut, the movement of vole." He is like the eagle in "Fall Comes in Back-Country Vermont" that "Shoulders like spray the last light." He is a Napoleon of the thermals, a vital god, a master of the golden, sustaining air—a node of time-fever, a speck of flesh-glory. If he is also implicitly a tearer of flesh, his particular potency lies in exploiting the last light, light now cruelly remote from the earth-heavy beings below—his taking it, like an *über*-creature, as his due element. You would not think to find him, wings folded, plunged again in the mountain's shade.

The "true" father is deathless, the "false" one dies. "The truth always kills the father," Jack Burden notes, after digging up dirt about his own. Nothing so unforgivable as the father who fails of power and glory (which, in the vital zone, are one). When "the testicles of the fathers hang down like old lace" it is time to light out for new or transcendent territory. Disappointed in his own father, Jed Tewksbury in *A Place to Come to* settles for the storyteller's revenge. (The burden of every story is, Roland Barthes remarked, the Oedipal pleasure of unveiling the truth, staging the "absent, hidden, or hypostatized" father.) Asked by the fellows to tell a story, Jed hems and haws then relates how "pap . . . got kilt." Kilt despite possessing, and proudly as well as ruefully displaying before his son and the stars, "the biggest dong in Claxford County." The father's first fall is to complain before his boy, "and what the hell good does it do me!" His second, unfortunately literal, is to lose his balance while urinating on the hindquarters of the mule pulling his wagon. He tumbles and two of the star-glinting wheels, one in front, one in back, run over his neck with "perfect precision," Platonic dispatch. How forgive the "father who had . . . left me defenseless. I shook with the discovery of hate."

The rule that the truth always kills the father, that the only perfect father is in heaven, terrifies the son, for the son is "the father / Of [his] father's father's father": he has inherited the male principle. His one hope—mythic—is to become himself a hawk, or a sort of hawk-star, faultlessly chaste in unexhausted potency. Those who discipline desire, Socrates said, emancipate the virture in themselves, and "when the end comes, they are light and winged for flight . . . Those who have once begun the heavenward pilgrimage may not go down again to darkness . . . they live in light always." This is the fantasy of "Evening Hawk," but arrested in the avalanche—the rude physical glory—of light. The female earth, female space, the consuming red sun of sunset must be mastered or withstood by the hawk-son, or hawk-poet, until the moment for the final phallic plunge into death, as in "Heart of Autumn," where the metamorphosis of the speaker resembles an erection: "and I stand, my face lifted now skyward, / Hearing the high beat, my arms outstretched in the tingling / Process of transformation, and soon tough legs / With folded feet, trail in the sounding vacuum of passage." Death alone is the time for a fierce coming.

In "Evening Hawk" the poet himself remains a less localized presence within the poem than the hawk does—he might be the generosity of the earth to all that exceeds it. But by remaining general he is everything he voices, including the behavior of the hawk; and when he says, "If there were no wind we might, we think, hear / The earth grind on its axis, or history / Drip in darkness like a leaking pipe in the cellar," the plural pronoun remains open to the hawk as well as to unspecified human companions. In "Preternaturally Early Snowfall in Mating Season," by contrast, the animal figures, a buck and doe, are decidedly all the parental glory and perfect presence there is; the speaker remains lower than they are, a learner, admiring and envious. A celibate camper, he is wakened in the night by a "blast, wheeze, snort, bleat / And beat and crash of dead boughs." In the morning, he sees "marks / Of plunge, stamp, trample, heave, and ecstasy of storm." Disturbed snow like rumpled sheets; metonymic traces of an incomprehensible, deadwood-destroying energy; the debris of a transgressive knowledge. The animals are Rilkean; their beings flow into eternity; and as the poet wanders the suddenly white world, he becomes almost pure enough to guess at their "glory." The inside of his head is scrubbed as "with ammonia" till there is only "the simple awareness of Being."

How he wishes he himself could burst into life-beyond-time through the physical storm of passion. Well, he wishes this and not. His celibacy must be a standing doubt as to the wisdom of recklessly abandoning identity; his poetry his preferred noise of glory. Besides, the preternaturally early snowfall suggests a deep prohibition; the glo-

ry may be "guessed at" only in its chill. Even his witness of the primal
scene was but an alarm in the ears, with nothing of the seductive
about it. After the white landscape scrapes his mind, it is "hard to get
a fire going." He is still a cold exile outside the bedroom door of the
gods.

Frequent in Warren is an approach to the preternatural or tran-
scendental, followed by a return. The latter may be simply a rhythmic
turning back, a natural contraction after a dilatation, as in "Antin-
omy: Time and Identity." Here "The canoe / On blackness floats"
and "High, Stars stare down, and . . . I wonder / If they see me,"
and "Timelessness" spreads "on the time that seems past and the time
that may come"; then "Dawn bursts like the birth pangs of your, and
the world's, existence, and "One crow, caw lost in the sky-peak's lu-
cent trance, / Will gleam, sun-purpled, in its magnificence." The re-
turn to light and time is willing and without sorrow; it even looks for-
ward. Elsewhere, dismay or terror may be sickeningly mixed with an
interrupted, still hungry sense of the absolute, turning the route back
into a reluctant retreat. So it is (again) in "Speleology," where the boy,
lulled by cave-darkness and stream-song, lapses from identity, only to
wake with a scream:

> Had light—
> And once more looked down the deep slicing and sluicing
> Of limestone where water winked, bubbles like fish-eyes, a
>   song like terror.

His humanness is, after all, his safe, known world; and the "all" is not
God-bright but fish-primitive. *"Is this all? What is all?"* Still, he wakes
years later wondering "What would it be like to be, in the end, part of
all."

Again, in "Snowshoeing Back to Camp in Gloaming," the poet
turns with both regret and relief from his pilgrimage into a "land of
Platonic ice," one that has frozen his loins and opened up voids where
God himself fears to go. He is not quite ready again for the common
necessity that on occasion blooms like a rose. There was something
up there, in the mountains, that a braver man might have found:

So starward I stared
To the unnamed void where Space and God
Flinch to come, and where
Un-Time roars like a wind that only
The dead, unweeping, hear.

Oh, Pascal!
What does a man need to forget?

Still, he went far up toward the mystery and it is as a metaphysical beast "fur-prickled with frost" that he returns toward his warm home:

But moved on, however, remembering
That somewhere—somewhere, it seemed—
Beautiful faces above a hearthstone bent
Their inward to an outward glow.

Remembering, too, that when a door upon dark
Opens, and I, fur-prickled with frost,
Against the dark stand, one gaze
Will lift and smile with sudden sheen
Of a source far other than firelight—or even

Imagined star-glint.

A: The mystery is what stopped him, paralyzed, at the edge of a high mountain mowing:

So I stood on that knife-edge frontier
Of Timelessness, knowing that yonder
Ahead was the life I might live
Could I but move
Into the terror of unmarred whiteness under
The be-nimbed and frozen sun.

The life he "might live" would be timeless, in fact free of distinction, "unmarred." But this would mean both psychic and physical castration—hence the terror of that knife-edge frontier.

B: A terror more psychological, perhaps, than metaphysical. The supine white female space of the mowing transforms him into a frozen son—the more so for being backed by the threatening father-vertical, "the blackness of spruce forest lifting / In a long scree-climb to cliff-thrust." The inhibition of a primal desire is death—negative no-time. Yet the return of time, through a symbolic sexual transgression (the sun making contact with jag-heave of mountain), spreads the gradual death of real time:

> Magenta lapped suddenly gray at my feet,
> With pink, farther up,
> Going gray.
>
> Hillward and sky-thrust, behind me,
> Leafless and distanced to eastward, a huge
> Beech clung to its last lone twinge
> Of pink on the elephant-gray—far under
> One star.
>
> Now the track, gone pale in tree-night,
> Downward floated before me, to darkness

Neither alternative is happy, but only one is sufferable: the heroic loneliness of the vertical beech, pink in last light, its vigor unspent even if the light is graying.

A: Yet the death before birth, not after it, may be the terrible draw of the mowing. Mother particle, father energy. This mowing is a preface to "the unnamed void where Space and God / Flinch to come." The abysmal appeal and pall of the inanimate—of which Freud himself was one of the great poets—is presented in the black and white terms of the old cinema, but minus the fascination of (living) evanescent flickerings. It is merely static; chill; a screen in an empty theater, white from abandonment. Beside this cosmic screen, Plato himself looks like a child playing with a palette of gaudy hues.

Asceticism is passion turned toward death. The image of the void takes asceticism to its logical limit, but passion can't follow it all the way; something blood-warm in it baulks.

B: Asceticism is the white of Oedipus' eyeball.

A: Oedipus himself may be thought an impure imagining of a metaphysical hunger (Dickinson's "Tooth / That nibbles at the soul"). Heidegger is never more tantalizing than when he says: "We cannot regard Oedipus only as the man who meets his downfall; we must see him as the embodiment of Greek being-there, who most radically and wildly asserts its fundamental passion, the passion for disclosure of being, i.e., the struggle for being itself." Of course, Heidegger did not have in mind the disclosure of a metabeing, one as annihilative to passion itself as a blank movie screen to the figures that flared on it. But what else is being that it should require passion to disclose it? What is utter, if not an unimaginable pre- or postbeing, an antibeing, such as that sublimely alluded to in "The Ballad of Billie Potts"?

> The salmon heaves at the fall, and, wanderer, you
> Heave at the great fall of Time, and gorgeous, gleam
> In the powerful arc, and anger and outrage like dew,
> In your plunge, fling, and plunge to the thunderous stream:
> Back to the silence, back to the pool

Life is "the long compulsion and the circuit hope."

But to picture the heart as a fish heaving "in the ribs' dark basket borne / West from the great water's depth whence it was torn" is one, one very beautiful, thing; to image the "all" as a cosmic windstorm of energy another. The cry, "Oh, Pascal! / What does a man need to forget?" may mean a man has everything to forget if he's to go on with the warming illusion of his individual life. Referring to the "infinite immensity of spaces of which I am ignorant," Pascal said, "I am frightened and am astonished at being here rather than there." Something of the same metaphysical vertigo afflicts the speaker as he moves on, recalling "That somewhere—somewhere it seemed . . ." He has understood down to his quick that his being alive and being here are not privileged but absurd. He now gropes for the living and loving as if they were remnants of a dream. He will need to be taken in like some stray alien inhuman thing and thawed at the several fires before being set to rights again. Not set to rights, but brought back to the vague anguish that made him strap on the snowshoes in the first place. He cannot at once fall back into forgetting. Time itself must tinkle thinly after the strict silence of that frozen stretch.

B: All this—the shock, the vertigo—applies to the Oedipal adventurer rejecting the temptations of unconscious fantasy, turning tail as one become a beast, and urgently requiring to be made human again, received back into the bosom of common family romance, the family album once more open to his smiling face. Only one thing will save him from both frozen impulse and lawless fire: the humanizing gaze in which the mother's eyes burn like a deep, shaded, and redeeming source. Nostalgia, said Bachelard, "is the memory of the warmth of the nest," "of man made warm by man." The fire the poet anticipates is a contrary double sign—at once the gentle heat at the base of the consciousness of happiness, and the flashingly tempting and prohibited (don't touch!).

A: The firelight will blindly if cheerfully finger the walls, as if apprehending a calming meaning. I foresee in it the return of the masculine "vital spark" and a mind once more free to play over the familiar surfaces of things.

As for the saving gaze, the poem makes this seem not merely grateful in the existential night of things, but as inexplicable as the metaphysical enigma, deeper than firelight or starglint. Rilke's words in the third Duino elegy might have been addressed specifically to this Penelope stayathome: "Oh gently, gently, / let him see you performing, with love, some confident daily task,—lead him out close to the garden, give him what outweighs / the heaviest night . . . / Restrain him . . . "

B: A taint of masculine self-aggrandizement enters vis-à-vis this Penelope, a melodrama of metaphysical heroism while the little woman waits faithfully at home. But in fact the poet is rather quick to delude himself with thoughts of fires and sheens and smiles and gazes, with their unfortunate reminders of full-color liquor ads featuring after-skiers. "But moved on, however, remembering / That somewhere—somewhere, it seemed": this does not carry conviction.

A: He turns from the metaphysical to the ethical dimension as a second best. Even with its "No!" of unmarred whiteness, the void means more to him than the hearth. But he can only inhabit the inhabitable. The case requires sympathy. Mountain cabins have fires. Wives smile.

In "Sunset Walk in Thaw-Time in Vermont" Warren approaches the ethical realm from the other side, the physical one, in a complementary either/or. Here, the darkening wooded landscape does not suggest a void, but instead is heroic, rawly physical; and the human protagonist represents not civilization but a rugged nobility, precisely the courage of and for the physical. His aim is not to discover the absolute but merely to take a stand in the relative—be a standing-place. The choice, here, is not between timelessness and time but between time as flight and time as duration—again, no real choice at all. There is no inner division, only a man-to-world conflict, as the poet is first shattered by an instance of the passing, then put on his mettle to spin, as if from out his own bowels, a tenuous new psychic home for himself within the physical. This results in his climactic vision of a human cycle of vigilance against death.

B: A vigilante posse, in effect. And all male. Extraordinary how this poet writes about others with eager and prehensile passion only when his subjects are male authors, or his father, or, most especially, most gobblingly, his son. A blazing ego affinity heats "Waking to Tap of Hammer" and "Night Walking" far beyond the gentle warmth imparted by what might be called the poems of "the smile."

Of these last, the most passionate is the barbarously beautiful "Youth Stares at Minoan Sunset." Here a youth, perhaps the poet's son, is first a black silhouette against the melting sunset, then turns and sees "us with a slow / And pitying happiness of recognition born of / A knowledge we do not yet have"—the male, again, as a metaphysical brave.

What gives the end of "Sunset Walk" its great conviction is a passionate, if temporally far-flung, male bonding:

> When my son is an old man, and I have not,
> For some fifty years, seen his face, and, if seeing it,
> Would not even be able to guess what name it wore, what
> Blessing should I ask for him?

That some time, in thaw-season, at dusk, standing
At woodside and staring
Red-westward, with the sound of moving water
In his ears, he,
Should thus, in that future moment, bless,
Forward into that future's future,
An old man who, as he is mine, had once
Been his small son.

For what blessing may a man hope for but
An immortality in
The loving vigilance of death?

Here the bushwhacker in the poet—the loner, the rebellious son of all fathers—turns, in reconciled vision, in heartfelt sincerity, into a father who blesses a son who in turn is to bless his own son. Nowhere else in Warren is Oedipal bitterness so morally and magnificently forgotten.

Up to this point in the poem, the speaker might have been the last of his species. But here he willingly fathers, and grandfathers, a community of successive well-wishers. He draws others "in" to strengthen his "stand" in a scene where the snow-covered ground melts from under him. The melt-stream itself becomes his moral muse. It continues only by adding to itself. What passes down the gorge is replaced by more of the same.

A: The stream both attracts and frightens the poet—frightens more than attracts. On the one hand, it is still thaw-thin; it has no reassuring fullness, as yet; it conveys absence as much as presence (the absence of the remembered fullness of summer). It is still part death, too recently snow. On the other hand, it gives itself in an inhuman recklessness to the future. How it rushes into time. He is unable to follow its example, to be himself a stream; he remains a bank from which he sees his aged son as another bank, and so on.

The impetus of his ethical vision is less love for others than a fear of standing alone—he musters a group against the anonymous and transitory stream of time: a bud form of the crowd, with a crowd's urge for growth, and its lifting of the burden of distance from others, a distance that throws the individual back on himself and shuts him in.

The crowd-unit "wants what is happening to him to happen to others too; and he expects it to happen to them" (Canetti).

What explains this need to be a crowd is the sudden unpleasant news that the individual perishes. The physical startle that occasions the poem—the *rip, whoosh, wing-whistle* of the flushed partridge cock—is underlined by a metaphysical terror, after all: *Angst*, the divination of nothingness. The void at hand or just at the edge is, of course, likely to be one with the void *out there*. But, again, this poem is concerned only with the immediately present and absent: not what the stars flee but what flees from the black spruce trees before one's face. An at first unnameable something vehemently explodes into nothing, with a backlash of silence. This is a physical demonstration of the nothingness of which physics is just a dream. But a vivid, startling dream.

There are two ways to live with this dream: to expand in it, and to huddle at its edge. The stream presents a model of extension, necessarily tragic because wholly surrendered to time:

> The boulder
> Groans in the stream, the stream heaves
> In the deep certainty of its joy, like
> Doom, and I,
> Eyes fixed yet on the red west, begin to hear—though
> Slow and numb as upon waking—
> The sound of water that moves in darkness.

The tragic pathos, as Nietzsche said, is "the *affirmative* pathos *par excellence*." It cannot say yes to joy without saying yes to woe. Almost it ceases to distinguish between them, the entanglement itself becoming (to the earthward) a joy. Without being a full-fledged symbol of Dionysian insouciance, the just-fledged stream nonetheless suggests the "formula of *supreme affirmation* born out of fullness, of superfluity, an affirmation without reservation even of suffering." Though its surface is "foam- / Slashed and white tettered," and picked out by "the cold, self-generating light of snow / Strong yet in the darkness of rock-banks," it remains indomitable—"it / Moves," moves with "bulge and slick twining of muscular water." In his last definition of "Dionysian," Nietzsche wrote: "The word *'Dionysian'* means: an urge to unity, a reaching out . . . across the abyss of transitoriness: a passionate-painful overflowing into darker, fuller, more floating states; an ecstatic affirmation of the total character of life as that which remains the same, just as powerful, just as blissful, through all change; . . . the feeling of the necessary unity of creation and destruction." Just so, with a seeming carefree confidence, the stream heaves itself down the gorge, its brutal and necessary "in." Its relation to "the abyss of transitoriness" is trusting-heroic. By contrast, traumatized as he was by the *whoosh* of the escaping partridge cock, the poet resists transitoriness with all his might. He cannot bear, even, to look at the passing stream. Instead, he sees (once he regains his self-possession) only his seeing of it. He secures for himself that much indemnity from the flow:

> I stand, and in my imagination see
> The slick heave of water, blacker than basalt, and on it
> The stern glint, like steel, of snow-darkness.

He has made his mind a basin to hold the slick heave of the water. It is his own pouring away he shuns. But the no-time of imagination or memory is itself next to nothingness; the snow-glint of a snow-glint; the picture, not the thing. A flimsy enough dodge when,

> On the mountain's east hump, darkness coagulates, and
> Already, where sun has not touched for hours, the new
> Ice-crystal frames its massive geometry.

Once again, the poet must start over. Searching for stability, he has exhausted every prop in sight. Now he is down to last resorts. He rummages in his hope chest and comes up with an old, forgotten pair of galoshes: his blood connections with the human race; his hitherto overlooked status as one who has replenished the family stream.

B: The vision of the human stream itself conforms to the affirmative Dionysian pathos; in fact, since what recurs is never the same (as against Nietzsche's desperate theory of exact recurrence), the pathos is peculiarly sharp. Even should a son's face change unrecognizably, be wrecked by time, he must be blessed, for to bless this oddly familiar stranger is to bless all human continuance, new life succeeding to, by replacing, the old. "The loving vigilance of death" is the only moral form "an ecstatic affirmation of the total character of life"—of human life—can take. Only in this vigilance does life remain "the same . . . through all change," as powerful and blissful as is reasonable to expect, given the dark nature of things. The poet must be given credit for a heroic resolve to see fearlessly and, having done so, to conquer the evil of nothingness by courage and faith.

A: What does the literal stream care about vigilance, or love, or death? There is more fret in this humanistic "immortality" than genuine tragedy can tolerate. The tragic is nonethical; the vigilant human group, an ethical huddle.

B: Warren evokes a tragic trust in the destiny of the generations: their successive leaps, as from stone to stone, across the abysmal transitoriness of time. Here the ethical swells with an unwonted confidence, which is yet not complacency, but a trust in the cohesive properties, the masculine preparedness, of vigilance. In the "deep certainty" of this trust, which a strong soul would feel as joy, the phrase "the loving vigilance of death" even hands over the caretaking responsibility to death itself (if in the equivocal form of a grammatical conundrum), as though charging the lion with watching over the lambs. Death is the father of what Heidegger (after Kierkegaard) called *Sorge*, or Care: as George Steiner sums it up, "a caring for, an answerability to, the presentness and mystery of Being itself, of Being as it transfigures beings." Man: "the shepherd and custodian of Being," vigilant because loving.

A: Vigilant because (to begin with) terrified. Only by loving the humanity of the future does man secure enough time for himself to stand for a moment without fear.

B: It is true that remorse urges the poet to this lyric love of his own kind. He wants back his lost years ("Where / Have the years gone?"), and cannot have them until excused from his history of failure, folly, ignorance, and anguish:

Now
Here stare westward, and hear only
The movement of darkening water, and from
Whatever depth of being I am, ask
To be made worthy of my human failures and folly, and
Worthy of my human ignorance and anguish, and of
What soul-stillness may be achieved as I
Stand here with the cold exhalation of snow
Coiling high as my knees.

To cast out remorse is to grow flush with "the presentness and mystery of Being." To come into time out of the briar patch of guilt is to come into the sunshine—the "unconcealment"—of love and happiness. The poet needs to take joy in the particular being he is, or all is lost, the future could have no meaning for him. Why should he wish on his son and grandson the doom of his own unworthiness?

The miraculous turn is this: the moment he has a good thought for others, he feels lightened within himself. The blessings he gives rebound back on him. After all, he is "in" the others, not only as "family" but as man. To speak them well is to speak himself well.

Unawares, he invokes others—calls for their blessing—as soon as he asks "To be made worthy." To whom is this plea addressed? Not only to the human other implicit in the use of language, but to the moral other, the injurable others who have the power to absolve him of the crime of self. Something there is beyond a man, the further and full extent of his humanity, into which his being can purifying flow, surviving the wounds slashed into it by the boulders in its path, by passing on, giving way. What impels the poet toward vision is anxiety over his own happiness; but the enlightenment of his humanity instantly transforms that anxiety into care, which is broadly custodial and thus, for the individual, freeing.

A: His metaphysical *Angst*, his "taking upon [himself]," in George Steiner's words, "the nearness of nothingness," is the black pitch with which he fuels his lamp.

B: Heidegger can always get a word in edgewise with Warren, the poet of being here, instancy, naughtening, destiny. But Wordsworth's blessing lies on this poem as well. Like the English master of joy, Warren turns sharp startlement into delight in being alive, a value flash-illuminated (flesh-illuminated) by its very frailty. Gradually he modulates a frantic chest-thump into a "grandeur in the beatings of the heart." "Thanks to the means," he might say after Wordsworth—thanks to the means nature deigned to employ, severe interventions included, to awaken "praise to the end." (As for "huge and mighty forms," like the mountain, they "do not live / Like living men.") In Wordsworth, too, soul-stillness, or "The calm existence that is mine when I / Am worthy of myself," owes as much to human error as to mighty forms:

> How strange that all
> The terrors, pains, and early miseries,
> Regrets, vexations, lassitudes interfused
> Within my mind, should e'er have borne a part,
> And that a needful part, in making up
> The calm existence that is mine when I
> Am worthy of myself! Praise to the end!

If Warren has recast Wordsworth's declarative exclamations into interrogative form, still his own praise to the end is implicit in his asking for his son and grandson what he himself has been privileged to experience: virtually the same season, hour, red west, sound of moving water, and impulse to offer a benediction. For all this is to be blessed. It is to achieve such soul-stillness as is still possible for a man.

A: Warren's fathers and sons will never stand together on the banks of the stream, as Wordsworth in "Tintern Abbey" stands with his "dear, dear Friend."* A characteristic heroic aloneness haunts—dogs—even this vision of a caring community. His instinct is ever, in Melville's words, to "take high abstracted man alone," so that "he seems a wonder, a grandeur, and a woe," and not one of a "mob of unnecessary duplicates, both contemporary and hereditary."

---

* "Wordsworth blessing his sister at the conclusion of *Tintern Abbey*, and Coleridge in many similar moments, are the ultimate ancestors of Warren's poem." Harold Bloom, *A Map of Misreading* (Oxford: Oxford University Press, 1975), p. 197.

B: And yet, more decidedly than in "Snowshoeing Back to Camp in Gloaming," he has in his own severe way echoed Wordsworth's happy discovery that "the affections gently lead us on."

Truth's Glare-Glory

Like love, glory is what a man makes himself worthy of, and what makes him worthy. But love eases the way, where glory challenges his fortitude and ingenuity and proves his genius. Save for its vigilante role, love is feminine; glory, masculine. A loved man is given admiration, a glorious man compels it—he carves it out, exacts it, coerces it into being; it is his. Love: a sometimes airy, sometimes physical "osmosis of being." Glory: a hard triumph of the will to power, proof of ontological heft, utmost distinction.

For the Greeks, glory meant standing in the light, a resplendent appearing. It was the crown of the pagan view of things: "Glory was not something additional," notes Heidegger," . . . it was the mode of the highest being." A pagan Appearance amorously coincident with Being, light and singleness and radiant bursts of time—this is no less Warren's realm, and standing in the light no less his joy. Apostate as soon as he makes to cross to the other side, into transparent purities of Being, he looks back, as in "Evening Hawk," and speaks with telltale generosity of "the gold of our error."

A love of glory is in any case a natural accompaniment, if not indeed the cause, of poetry; for, as Pindar said, the essence of the art is to glorify, to place in the light. Heidegger elaborates: "The poet always speaks as though the essent were being expressed and invoked for the first time. Poetry . . . has always so much world space to spare that in it each thing—a tree, a mountain, a house, the cry of a bird—loses all indifference and commonplaceness."

To delight in the world as Audubon does is to see now this one, now that one of its creatures glimmering in the light. He himself is in the shade of obscurity, an audience; his attention is all applause. Warren plays down this painter's presumptive need for personal glory, plays down his art. The appearances that matter are those of the

birds, whether in "air that glitters like fluent crystal" or "In our imagi-
nation." Where is the all-important middle term, the work of art it-
self, *that* glory, in "He put them where they are, and there we see
them / In our imagination"?* Nondescript, it is merely nodded to, as
a "where," a "there," a conveyance like a library shelf on which books
are placed to be taken down. Yet would Warren have been drawn to
Audubon, have written about him, had it not been for his fame, the
heroism in and behind his glory?

It is not in Warren's nature to be secretive (at least not in the long
run) about his excitement over a "name." If he took Audubon's artis-
tic splendor for granted, it was less out of rivalry or disingenuousness
about the importance of personal glory than out of fidgetiness over
the precisions and patience of his painterly eye. In Warren, an appear-
ance is above all a symbolic action (as in the great trumpeter swan's
clangorous ascent to incandescence) and not a stylishly limned, mi-
nutely lined, finely shaded, "static" intricacy. Besides, if *doxa*, which
emphasizes sight and aspect, was one of the Greek words for glory,
the other was *kleos*, which stresses hearing and calling; and in *Audubon*
when the world declares itself, it does so as—"oh, arch on arch"—a
voice. His seeing ablaze, Audubon appeases our terror of darkness,
but not our terror of silence. His voice is not distinctive enough to
stave off the "roar" of time and untime; the hooting geese over Ken-
tucky are more audibly arresting. Warren's own "spoken" work tries
to perfect their call. "Tell me a story," raise yet another forceful cry of
human destiny. Glory to the man who, like "our Milton," makes
words hum and hive in his name.

In "Old Nigger on One-Mule Cart," Warren is equivocal, yet ve-
hement, about his desire to end by "holding, / I trust, in my hand, a
name." On the one hand, he feels that his vanity rates a rebuke. Sure-
ly others—for instance, the old black man carting junk on the back-
road those many years ago, the one he almost drove into—surely oth-

---

* There is something in this of Whitman's "All music is what awakes from you when
you are reminded by the instruments," or "All architecture is what you do to it when you
look upon it." There is a tribute to the human imagination as a property common to both the
artist and his audience.

ers put down vanity. In his mind's eye, he can see the old man going home to his "askew / Shack," where he

> Unhitches the mule.
> Stakes it out. Between cart and shack,
> Pauses to make water, and while
> The soft, plopping sound in deep dust continues, his face
> Is lifted into starlight, calm as prayer. He enters
> The dark shack and I see
> A match spurt, then burn down, die.

Why does he, the poet, lack this prayerlike calm? Why does he feel he must *eat* stars? Why can't he pee in the dust and lie down in the dark, and so call a truce to his rage? Perhaps he will, at that:

> And so I say:
> Brother, Rebuker, my Philosopher past all
> Casuistry, will you be with me when
> I arrive and leave my own cart of junk
> Unfended from the storm of starlight and
> The howl, like wind, of the world's monstrous blessedness,
> To enter, by a bare field, a shack unlit?

On the other hand, his noble heart, his will to power, his love of glory, of "the grandeur of certain utterances," will not put up with such meekness. A shudder overcomes the poem at the point of "a bare field, a shack unlit," as the poet feels the pall in the old man's lack of protest. To be black as the spaces among the stars; a casualty of silence, the same that earlier in the poem, after the dance music stopped, raged in the poet's liquored ears ("it ranges the world, it will / Devour us"); to be one of Melville's "mob of unnecessary duplicates," a "nigger," even—a man without so much as a social face! (Throughout the poem, from the title on, and not least with its terrified "Man-eyes . . . white-bulging / In black face," the old man is an objectionable stereotype.) Born to revert to dust!* Intolerable. So, hardly pausing to take a breath, and casuistically, the poet continues:

> Entering into that darkness to fumble
> My way to a place to lie down, but holding,
> I trust, in my hand, a name—
> Like a shell, a dry flower, a worn stone, a toy—merely
> A hard-won something that may, while Time
> Backward unblooms out of time toward peace, utter
> Its small, sober, and inestimable
> Glow, trophy of truth.
>
> Can I see Arcturus from where I stand?

Man has created glory to save both himself and the universe from nothingness. But for Warren this pertinacious pursuit—this starting with the world and seeing how near the stars one can go—is redeemed from vanity only if consecrated, at the same time, to the truth. The "glow" of a poem, a name, a painting, is sign of its "trophy of truth." However harsh the truth may be, it is sacrosanct, all reverence is due it, because nothing is more utter, nothing else real. Truth, together with its beauty, is all we know of God, and all we know of glory. The task of the philosopher is to shine a light on the truth, that of the poet to see the truth itself as a splendor. The poet will succeed in this insofar as he can see the truth through his longing and his ability to be the medium of its beauty.

---

* When Warren wrote in his poem "Pondy Woods," "Nigger, your breed ain't metaphysical," Sterling A. Brown was provoked to respond, "Cracker, your kind ain't exegetical." In his essay, "The Briar Patch," published in *I'll Take My Stand* (New York: Harper, 1930), when he was twenty-four or twenty-five, Warren opposed "the group in the South whose prejudice would keep the negroes forever as a dead and inarticulate mass in the commonwealth—as hewers of wood and drawers of water." Yet Warren's casuistry in "Old Nigger on One-Mule Cart" might seem content to leave the old man forever part of "a dead and inarticulate mass." His tragic loneliness (partly self-obsession) wars with his liberal humanism.

"Learning to face Truth's glare-glory, from which our eyes are long hid," is distressing, and "It is hard sometimes to remember that beauty is one word for reality." But at other times it is not, especially to one with a feral thirst for glory. To see truth in a blaze of joy is less a choice than a glad and terrible compulsion.

"Red-Tail Hawk and Pyre of Youth" is another apologia, or reaffirmation, of this thirst. It is even, though far more clandestinely than that star-climbing monolith "Old Nigger on One-Mule Cart," another defense of the "name" a "A hard-won something that may"—because built on words—"utter" its "Glow, trophy of truth." In this poem the slain-and-stuffed red-tail hawk becomes a muse of the fallen glory of the word:

> Year after year, in my room, on the tallest of bookshelves,
> It was regal, perched on its bough-crotch to guard
> Blake and *Lycidas*, Augustine, Hardy and *Hamlet*,
> Baudelaire and Rimbaud, and I knew that the yellow eyes,
> Unsleeping, stared as I slept.

Eventually, the poet burns his first published poems together with this former "king of the air," this victim of his "crime of I." He also throws on the pyre his "first book of Milton, / The *Hamlet*, the yellow, leaf-dropping Rimbaud, . . . not to mention / The collection of sexual Japanese prints—strange sex / Of mechanical sexlessness." Yet, like Yeats, he would be content to live it all again—in his case because shooting the hawk, writing poems, and sexual passion were his chief share in power and glory, all the life there was. The rest was death.

This is to contradict Dave Smith's description of the poem as a "mini-Mariner in plot, vision, and construction." Granted the murder of the hawk is a parable "of man's Fall." But it is no less a parable of his "blood-marriage" with power and glory. In consequence, Warren's poet does not want the slain bird's blood washed away. For him there is no "dear God who loveth us," who "made and loveth all." Only man loves all, and man's love is by nature transgressive. You feel it as an electric irony in

How my heart sang!

Till all was ready—skull now well scraped
And with arsenic dried . . .

What binds "air-blood and earth-blood" together is, in this poem, "The old .30-.30," not prayer. "And I pray that . . . all will be as it was" is not penitence, but greed for the crime (and *its* punishment, for this crime was costly). To bring a marvelous otherness near enough for a mingling, we must destroy it, as we do each time we look at beauty, or read a poem. It is thus that we make it our own, a regalness perched on the bough-crotch we provide for it, stiff but "moulded as though . . . to take to the air." Always the rifle must swing up, our leaden eyes sink after staring at "unapprehensible purity" of silver air, for such is the destructive rhythm of the imaginative life.

The hawk is every fall the poet himself has endured, the fall that life somehow essentially is, that love is, that passion for truth and beauty is. And if at last he earns the right to address this "hot blood of the air," intimately, as "you," it is because, like any man, he has tumbled from the sky of his own expectations of himself, of life; has become shabby, bandy winged, "commensurate."

So it is that the plot of "The Ancient Mariner" is turned upside down—one might say, refuted. The sum total of the poet's wisdom is that, to taste or know a fate "Whose name is a name beyond joy," he would shoot the hawk again.

Indeed, he is eager, even rapaciously so, to do it:

And I pray that in some last dream or delusion,
While hospital wheels creak beneath
And the nurse's soles make their *squeak-squeak* like mice,
I'll again see the first small silvery swirl
Spin outward and downward from sky-height
To bring me the truth in blood-marriage of earth and air—
And all will be as it was
In that paradox of unjoyful joyousness,

> Till the dazzling moment when I, a last time, must flinch
> From the regally feathered gasoline flare
> Of youth's poor, angry, slapdash, and ignorant pyre.

What he transcribes here, in a language of ecstasy, is the rhythm of his fate. So, then, he has found it; it is clear to him now; and having found it he must love it. What else is he but what his fate is? What other chance for being does he have? The remorse accreted from this fate might require the burning of a pile of criminal evidence. But this is really no sacrifice. Neither is it the promise of a new start. It is only a ritual acknowledgment of "the cost of experience." It reduces the decayed body of what was loved to ashes, but the love itself hasn't worn. The will awaits its next occasion; the .30-.30 still hangs on the hand "As on a crooked stick"; and memory—the poem shows it—grows rank at the first drop of rain.

Numbered among the costs of experience are both metaphysical and Oedipal chagrins. The first are more distinct. Just as Goethe questioned how he could be alive if others were, this poem questions how there can be life if there is God. It chooses life. The hawk is first a forced symbol of God incarnate, spinning as it does out of the unapprehensible purity of the silver afternoon sky, its "Gold eyes, unforgiving, for they, like God, see all." Then it is shot; God is dead. Later, thinking of its wicked-yellow eyes staring in vengeance, the poet will ask: "Could Nature forgive?" So the bird has been demoted to nature. The transcendent is retained only as the thrill and terror of transgression.

In this God slaying, this God denying, there is both sorrow and elation. On the one hand a man cannot endure the white albatross of idealism, so murderously pure. Better, even, endure the predatory hawk of conscience. So he flees from innocence and toward his guilt, like Jeremiah in *World Enough and Time*. He makes "the crime of self" his familiar, "the crime of life" his passion. "If we can have knowledge, if we can know the terrible logic of life, if we can only know!" True, knowledge "is not redemption, but is almost better than redemption." Jeremiah, like Camus's stranger, "will shake the hangman's hand, and will call him my brother, at last."

Appearance, not the unapprehensible, is our sphere. And here the soul hawks, or else is mouse. The mouse squeak of the nurse's shoes will (so the poet imagines) set his soul to hawking once again. Glory here below lies in triumphs, even Zen miracles of the will:

> There was no choice in the act—the act impossible but
> Possible. I screamed, not knowing
> From what emotion, as at that insane range
> I pressed the cool, snubbed
> Trigger. Saw
> The circle
> Break.

In *Brother to Dragons*, "R.P.W." relates the story of Kent, a boy who shot a wild goose, "seized it, hugged it, ran / Three miles to town and yelled for joy and every / Step cried like a baby and did not know why." He comments: "the only thing / In life is glory," and that "knocks society's values to a cocked hat." Salvation-by-glory is a "terror." It means that ours is a "reality of decreation," in Wallace Stevens' phrase—our revelations not those "of belief" but portents "of our own powers." Fear, grief, and joy mingle in its wicked, life-justifying transgressions. Kent cries, the boy in "Red-Tail Hawk" cries ("in / Eyes tears past definition") because transgression—so congenial—yet injures the dream of innocence. This injury is a shock, worse than could ever be imagined. Blood on the albatross, on the wild goose whose flock-mates still bestride the icy altitudes, or on the king of the air, master of the element that sings to the soul, is blood on the soul.

The will shows a "fearful resolve," notes Coleridge, "to find in itself the one absolute motive of action." It weeps to do so, but does it. Clasping the bleeding body of the hawk to his bare chest, the boy would instinctively nuture it back to life:

> Heart leaping in joy past definition, in
> Eyes tears past definition, by rocky hill and valley
> Already dark-devoured, the bloody
> Body already to my bare flesh embraced, cuddled

> Like babe to heart, and my heart beating life love:
> Thus homeward.

There is more than God grief, there is father-grief, mother-grief, self-grief in this fleshy embrace. Or there is a real father in the fictitious God, the fiction of God in every father. Hate alone would not have shrieked in transgressive joy to bring this hot-blooded father down; terribly, love wanted the transgression just as much, and love weeps in the tears past definition.

As the unforgiving father-god falls, as the winged phallus plummets, the boy's heart leaps in joy—but short-lived triumph, for every son is his father's father's father, his father's fall is his own but one, his own in advance. And now that the king is dead, his eyes filmed, his "lower beak drooping, / As though from thirst," is he not the very image of Oedipal deprivation? Does he not take after his son? Hug him, then, to the maternal breast of nourishment and sympathy. The boy imitates his mother in order to succor his father, who is now himself.

None of this is real, unless as the truth that "can only be enacted, and that in dream, / Or in the dream become, as though unconsciously, action." What is real is the sad body that must be wrapped in a newspaper and hidden like a crime in an ice chest in the appallingly empty-at-afternoon family home. Shut far from the admiring airy spaces. Far from the thermal paradise of both sky and breast. And now, allowing for the demigod taxidermist's joy of scraping the skull and flesh joints, anchoring the bone joints, driving steel "through to sustain wing," and so on ("Oh, yes, / I knew my business"), the killer must begin to pay.

In time, his living father becomes bankrupt, as foretold in parable. His mother dies. As for him, he seems athirst, "whiskey / Hot in [his] throat." His heart no longer leaps, but is "slow in the / Meaningless motion of life." Almost, he might be stuffed. So out come the battered bird, the books, and the sensational, pathetic "sexual Japanese prints." But the expiatory burning does not lead to a fresh start. "What left / To do but walk in the dark, and no stars?"

What would bring back "joy past definition"? Shooting the hawk would. Writing the same bad passionate early poems. Feeling the same dirty excitement over the pictures. The only phoenix that could rise from the ashes of the pyre is the bird of his youth, all earthly will to glory.

Done, if a wish were a will.

There could be no greater happiness, so the conclusion suggests, than to experience again this passage from dazzling moment to dazzling moment, beginning and end all adazzle, chasing off the darkness in between. The line "youth's poor, angry, slapdash, and ignorant pyre" ritualizes and consecrates the period of youth, even as it deplores it. This is not anathema, but a grieving love; the pell-mell adjectives are youthfully rich and eager in number, a joyfully joyless homage. The paradox, once more, of an affirmative pathos. "My formula for greatness in a human being," Nietzsche said, "is *amor fati*: that one wants nothing to be other than it is, not in the future, not in the past, not in all eternity. Not merely to endure that which happens of necessity, still less to dissemble it—all idealism is untruthfulness in the face of necessity—but to *love* it."

The artist is helped to *amor fati* by *amor operandi, amor operis*. Discovering, as he does, the rhythms of destiny in the rhythms of his art, he can turn "even fear and disgust" into love. If in no other way, art would war on God through what Yeats called the joy of always making and mastering, which like all joy wants itself, redundantly. Burning the books along with the hawk—even the yellow leaf-dropping Rimbaud (the same Rimbaud who, notes Enid Starkie, "determined to leave God's love behind him and to keep his personal freedom at all costs")—only confesses this aspect of art, its formula of affirmation born out of its own fullness.

In the poem, life repeats itself at a gulp, at a gallop, in uncompromised passion. The same life is twice within it, mirrored back to itself, freeingly reflected to its own and the poet's glory. So it is that the love of the making overflows as love of the life it remembers—love of life as a general thing and love of a specific story. Yet *amor fati* was doubtless the soil and rain and sun in whose mingling the desire for the work originally germinated. This circularity is passion's plenty and redundance, illustrating again how joy "bites itself," "wants itself eternally."

The glory of a "name" remains too implicit to seem either an incitement or a comfort; the will to power must achieve an ecstasy without it. Elsewhere it is even more deeply implicit—merely an inference from the publication of the poem. In "Trying to Tell You Something" and "Unless," profane passion and glory consist, on the surface, only in courage and sublimity. But, as Nietzsche said, "we find remedies in our courage and sublimity as well as [in] the nobler deliria of submission and resignation." To stand beneath the unseeing stars and be drenched by their acid light, yet be happy and assured of one's individual dignity, is a kind of inverted glory, a glory *despite* . . .

Where the image of the pissing black man failed to convey this—he seemed an Uncle Tom even to the stars; lacked ferocity; carted junk—the solitary oak in "Trying to Tell You Something" and the solitary poet in "Unless" (both the "image of man") are tragic protagonists. One might say they assume the *posture* of courage—for courage is never other than a self-reflective virtue. The category of the tragic is, in great part, aesthetic; the tragic is a spectacle of will, suffering, misfortune, or endurance, with the cosmos for audience, and the viewer or reader or listener the audience of it all. The tragic exists only as a creation of art; and art cannot get around itself—around its showcasing, its foregrounding, its expectation of admiration, its calling upon everything in sight, from a comma to a context, for witness.

In "Trying to Tell You Something" the immense old Jamestown oak has been stripped of the agreeable, delusory leaves of youth and summer and is naked before "the crackling absoluteness" of the icy skies. Nonetheless, it chooses this moment to sing:

It is ten below zero, and the iron
Of hoops and reinforcement rods is continuing to contract.

There is the rhythm of a slow throb, like pain. The wind,
Northwest, is steady, and in the wind, the cables,

In a thin-honed and disinfectant purity, like
A dentist's drill, sing. They sing

Of truth, and its beauty.

In this tragic variant of the romantic trope "necessity / Blooms like a rose," what rings one round is what, in the musical sense, rings. Fate is a cadence.

Unclouded by atmospheric enrichments, past deluding thermal joy and generative fervor ("splitting / With its own weight at the great inverted / Crotch, air-spread and ice-hung"), and singing in a thin-honed voice like a very old man, reduced to being a stiff statement of its own structure and reality, the tree stands as if before the Last Judgment, without apology. It is what it is—chooses be so even in its nakedness, let all the stars crackle as they will.

True, existence is mostly impurity, the will to live hardly innocent, and these last days rightly shed off austerities as the early days shed off enticings. Welcomely "disinfectant" is this song like a dentist's drill, satisfyingly "thin-honed." Put to rest by a tragic asceticism, conscience closes the black book it has kept against the rooting, branching, and leafing will to self-activation; closes it like the December night around the oak. The spectacular white world of death under its crackling "high brightness" might be a physically daunting father who has at last succeeded in exacting conformity to his puritanical laws.

But at least this conformity has not come too soon; besides, it is not all it seems, for the tree is not esoteric but sings of its own existence, its presence as a particular thing, a fate. Just as it spreads before us in the not-quite-trapping unrhymed couplets of the poem (a thin-honed stanza form), so it stands immense on its hill—"stands alone in a world of snowy whiteness," indelible under the full moon. It is a noble instance of what R. W. B. Lewis named "the central theme of American literature, . . . *the hero in space*"—a successor to Whitman's live-oak in Louisiana, which, even "without any companion," and because of it, uttered joyous leaves—a tragic aloneness that Whitman fled (without altogether escaping it), and that Warren, at least in imagination, pursues.

In the end, the (tragic) beauty of truth is its reliable utterness, its exquisite authority. What emerges, and is beautiful, is the bedrock discovery of selfhood within a bedrock universe—the joyous, freeing certainty that the self is not the world but, in a founding tautology, precisely itself. (Lukács remarked that the longing of man for selfhood, "the deepest longing of human existence," is the metaphysical root of tragedy.)

In "Unless," the truth is said to be "fanged, unforgiving":

> All will be in vain unless—unless what? Unless
> You realize that what you think is Truth is only
>
> A husk for something else. Which might,
> Shall we say, be called energy, as good a word as any. As when
>
> The rattlesnake, among desert rocks
> And Freudian cactus tall in moonlight,
>
> Scrapes off the old integument, and flows away,
> Clean and lethal and gleaming like water over moon-bright
>   sand,
>
> Unhusked for its mission. Oh, *neo nato!* fanged, unforgiving,
> We worship you.

Slipping through the slender husks of the stanzas as it does, this fearful truth "might . . . be called energy," the only criterion for absoluteness "under the storm of the / Geometry of stars." The miracle of tragedy is that it places in perfect balance the vast, diffuse, if "fanged" energy of the cosmos and the concentrated energy of the self. This astonishing mutual deliverance is not a harmony; it is simultaneously an opposition and a consent, its atmosphere clear, cold, harsh. The joy of it is almost rasping. Still, "This is happiness":

> The mountains, in starlight, were black
> And black-toothed to define the enormous circle
>
> Of desert of which I was the center. This
> Is one way to approach the question.

All is in vain unless you can, motionless, standing there,
Breathe with the rhythm of stars.

You cannot, of course, see your own face, but you know that
it,
Lifted, is stripped to white bone by starlight. This is
happening,

This is happiness.

The lethal X-ray of the stars exposes the resistance of an individual armature, a "Freudian" will as hot as any the stars have mustered behind their light. This presence stands up to the stars as what serves to meet them. Yet, even as he discovers himself opposite the world, the tragic man sees that "all will be in vain" unless, without for a moment confusing it with himself, he allows it to world him. Where else can he glut his appetite for the real? What other utterness or fullness is possible to him, tormentingly partial as this one form is? Where else is there any true splendor, even if fearfully scattered abroad in the night, as if made by the only particles still virulent enough with original energy to have escaped the gravitational snap of the black-toothed mountains? What makes a man comical, noted Kierkegaard, is that he would gain himself, be the absolute. The tragic man would gain himself by breathing with the absoluteness of the world.

The "question" of truth might well be approached, then, through this desert-plain and compass-true geometry, this experiment with center, circumference, total context, and relativism, with nowhere to hide in the great circle and the pointed foot fixed in the crumbling sand. In any case, the approach had best be physical, a "happening." For the body itself knows truth through its sixth sense, the knit of the other five. And the imagination had best add its own peculiar slant on reality, standing off but turned back to it as an excited spectator. The tragic man's "glory" is to picture his own face stripped to white bone by starlight, shining once in the undistinguishing, destructive starlight and again in the distinguishing rays of his own mind's eye—a seeing that is chorus to his tragic destiny. In the center of a vast and hungry circle, the prey at once of earthbound and stellar elements, in the face of this mania, the tragic hero triumphs over the impulse both to flee (hysteria) and to repine (melancholia). He bears the brunt of the light, and himself becomes part of the surrounding circle; his are the conscious, watching eyes within it; he is the discoverer of its wonder, and of his own in relation to it.

There is a mutuality implicit in this meeting of the upraised face and the scouring starlight. The light might be thought to rub and rub at the face till not only the vain impurities are gone but its fundamental reality is exposed (as with the stripped oak), even if in the process it approaches its mortal limits.* On the other hand, what is the appearingness of even the finest of phenomena, light, if there is nothing sentient in all its fall and field, no one to whom it can appear?

Tragic happiness is a final reconciliation with the father, or Law, in an atmosphere of terrible beauty, the mother's legacy of a passionate attachment to the world's body, of the need to bask in the light. That the encircling mountains are "black-toothed," like mountains in a tale, or that they "seem abstract" in the morning light, like the old translucent skin of truth, does not make them less real. Here, the Dionysian is not belied by Appearance; there is only Appearance; the snake is now in this skin, now in a new one. Truth need not be enacted "only . . . in dream." Tragedy, as Nietzsche argued, reconciles energy with appearance. The face lifted to starlight is energy confronting energy and—because visualized by the one whose face it is—appearance at one with appearance. The dregs of nightmare remain inactive. Tragedy is the loving triumph of Appearance, even in the last alarm of energy.

The Joy of Living, the Joy of Dying

If a spiritual development can be discerned in Warren's recent volumes, it is only by effort and abstraction, as with picture-puzzle books

---

* The image may remember Rilke's "O und die Nacht, die Nacht, wenn der Wind voller Weltraum uns am Angesicht zehrt" (O and the night, the night when the wind full of cosmic space consumes our face). Kathleen Komar, in an unpublished manuscript, comments: "Along with our name (which Rilke uses in Elegy I, l. 74), our face is the clearest sign of our self and of our self-consciousness . . . (Rilke's *Malte* contains many scenes in which a person's face is figuratively or literally torn away to reveal a more essential being beneath it.)"

that require you to pick out, from a diabolic profusion of forms, the hiding hare, the elusive fox. For a "man like me," Warren has said, philosophy is not "a finished product . . . It's a way of thinking about your life as you live." Impulse has continued to flout impulse. One view alights, flies off; another alights. Vitality upsets rational stabilities; abstention sets up a sensual reaction.

The tragic balance between the individual and the all is but one of Warren's reconciliatory "thoughts" about life. Another is the ravenous absorption of "Have You Ever Eaten Stars?" A third is the death-love of "Paradox of Time." And still a fourth, the aesthetic but charitable harmony of "Dead Horse in Field," which, however, differs from the fate-love of "Unless" by the merest softening. If in the next section I close the book by examining certain recent poems on death, and now consider a poem "transitional" to those, the beautiful "Acquaintance with Time in Early Autumn," it is not to deny that the death-hungry poems are few in number, their creeping night-flowers by day offset by towering sunflowers (even if many of these nod dreamily over the flaking fence of the past).

"Acquaintance with Time in Early Autumn" hypnotically crosses the line between life and death, then comes to, feels duped, grows angry, and scrambles back; yet it remembers the *air* of beauty on the other side, and ends in a moving suspension between the rival joys of life and death. Redoubtably, the poem begins with an authoritative evocation of the utmost physical vitality. It seesaws from one extreme to the other, before trembling, poignantly, in the balance.

Even if Warren had not been a weathered seventy-five when the poem was published, the opening lines would be astonishing for their warm-blooded gusto:

> Never—yes, never—before these months just passed
> Had I known the nature of Time, and felt its strong heart,
> Stroke by stroke, against my own, like love,
> But love without face, or shape, or history—
> Pure Being that, by being, our being denies.
>
> Summer fulfills the field, the heart, the womb,
> While summerlong, infinitesimally,

Leaf stem, at bough-juncture, dries,
Even as our tireless bodies plunge,
With delicious muscular flexion and heart's hilarity,
White to the black ammoniac purity of
A mountain pool. But black
Is blue as it stares up at summer's depthless azure,
And azure was what we saw beneath
At the timeless instant hanging
At arc-height.

The lines lend persuasiveness to E. M. Cioran's words that "we actually exist only when we radiate time itself, when suns rise within us and we dispense their light." With its plenitude of short phrases following stroke by stroke, the first little paragraph, whorled with caesuras, asks for an excited complicity with the poet's bliss at having struck a mother-lode of radiant moments in a Dickinsonian splendor of summer. The emphatic rhetoric of "Never . . . never" insists on our astonishment, as on his own. How extraordinary to have, and to have so late, a carnal knowledge of "the nature of time," experienced as a millennial coincidence of its heartstrokes and one's own. Here the terror of the primordial heartbeat bursts into an unexpected apocalypse, a divination of the rhythm of "Pure Being," that total Being our consciousness of our individual being denies. Here paradise is of the body, the animal body in its unselfconscious play.

Yet as that exultant "never . . . before" dwindles into "these months just passed," "never" gains the undertone "never more." Instancy (Heidegger thought *Inständigkeit* the word that most beautifully designates existence, and Warren uses "instancy" elsewhere in *Being Here*, as earlier in *Brother to Dragons*)—instancy has already fled; "just" watches it disappear with a slight sinking feeling. In "Pure Being that, by being, our being denies," the syncopation almost subdues the snub-nosed fact of denial, together with the snub-nosed nasal of "denies." Yet what began as a celebration has clearly slumped into an elegy.

An immediate attempt at the recovery of a joyful plenitude sounds in the generalized present and the syllabic fullness of "Summer fulfills." (The second half of each word clings fast to the first, by repeating something.) But again the sense of the matter seesaws: "While . . . / Leaf stem . . . dries." Vacillation is the small, as it is the large, structural principle of the poem—a poem on its mettle to be cognizant of contradiction and ambivalence. Could not the drying have been overlooked in the interest of lyrical nostalgia? As a perception isn't it a touch forced? The poet seems to be conducting a post mortem.

In another reversal, the "tireless bodies" arc again in the present tense of "Pure Being": "Even as our tireless bodies plunge." This is a comfort, but a trick of imagination or mere speech, and the ruse collapses: the reflection "But black / Is blue" shifts the present tense out of certain instancy and back into the ambiguous general case of "Summer fulfills." Every summer fulfills, and the black mountain pool is blue every summer. In the discrepancy between blue and black, the difference between summer and autumn, past and present, opens once again: "And azure was what we saw."

There is blue seeming, and black actuality. Under every arc-height, a black depth. Is joy, then, deception? Now that it is fall, the poet is lucid, but lacks joy. His lucidity is that of the lone—the sexless and loveless—man:

> Voices of joy how distant seem!
> I float, pubic hair awash, and gaze
> At one lone leaf, flame-red—the first—alone
> Above summer's bulge of green,
> High-hung against the sky.
>
> Yes, sky was blue, but water, I suddenly felt,
> Was black, and striped with cold, and one cold claw
> Reached ghostly up
> To find my flesh, to pierce
> The heart, as though
> Releasing, in that dark inwardness,
> A single drop. Oh, leaf,
> Cling on! For I have felt knee creak on stair,
> And sometimes, dancing, notice how rarely
> A girl's inner thigh will brush my own,
> Like a dream. Whose dream?

If "Pure Being" is physical exuberance, heart pressed to heart, then this fall from "our tireless bodies" and "azure is what we saw" to a bereft "I," to this floating flesh with "pubic hair awash," rehearses nonbeing. Rising to metaphysical poetry, Freud cast the idea of the intrinsic death of the *single* into his grandest theory. For him, notes Paul Ricoeur, "sexuality is the great *exception*" in a world of death. "The sexual instincts are 'the true life instincts.' They operate against the purpose of the other instincts, which lead by reason of their function, to death," Hence,

> If the living substance goes to death by an inner movement, what fights against death is not something internal to life, but the conjugation of two mortal substances. Freud calls this conjugation Eros; the desire of the other is directly implied in the emergence of Eros; it is always with another that the living substance fights against death, against its own death, whereas when it acts separately it pursues death through the circuitous paths of adaptation to the natural and cultural environment. Freud does not look for the drive for life in some will to live inscribed in each living substance: in the living substance *by itself* he finds only death.

The poet's body, his oracle, has felt the unmistakable fatal cold as sharply as ever the first red leaf of autumn has; he himself is like a leaf left high and dry above summer's massive sexual bulge of green, in a mockery of once hanging in heart's hilarity at arc-height. Not only "Pure Being" is gone; his "being" itself grows faint, his dreams maybe another's, his body a faint dispelling, the inner thigh already a cloud on the horizon. The poet understandably becomes a one-man cheering section for the leaf: "Cling on!" Yet when "The sun / Pours down on the leaf its lacquer of Chinese red," the leaf becomes an exotic from the point of view of nature; it departs from the vital and enters the decorative realm; its fate is sealed. There is nothing for it, now, but to fall:

> Then, in the lucent emptiness,
> While cries of joy of companions fade,

I feel that I see, even in
The golden paradox of air unmoving
Each tendon of that stem, by its own will,
Release
Its tiny claw-hooks, and trust
A shining destiny. The leaf—it is
Too moorless not to fall. But
Does not. Minutely,
It slides—calm, calm—along the air sidewise,
Sustained by the kiss of under-air.

The fading of the cries of companions is mentioned once again, as if obscurely connected with this peculiar magnifying vision, in which the releasing tendons of the leaf-stem, the trust in a shining destiny, and the sliding along the air sidewise limn the poet's sudden peace with death. In the reversal signed by the lacquer metaphor, he himself now hankers for the aesthetic calm of being unmoored from vitality, all concluded, no longer in the "dimension of Time." His, too, would be (but to whose eyes?) a glorious leave-taking, as sanctified by the valedictory golden air as the noble head of the quarry in *Audubon* is by its "halo of gold leaves."

This trust in the air is the far-end-of-life counterpart to the figure "necessity / Blooms like a rose." In the latter, the organism itself is a summation of freedom and beauty; in the former, it abandons its own "being" to rest in the arms of a beautiful necessity. The descent of the leaf is as trusting as that of an expertly partnered ballerina or a babe laid to rest by its mother's arms. The support and kiss of the air is the exquisite attention of Thanatos, who, in this moment, seems to be imitating Eros. Freud himself noted between the two "a dramatic *overlapping of roles.*"

It may be the intrusion of Eros that accounts for the element of "paradox," the unexpected "glory" of this "shining destiny." Something there is, however, that the poet suddenly suspects and repulses:

While ages pass, I watch the red-gold leaf,
Sunlit, descend to water I know is black.
It touches. Breath

> Comes back, and I hate God
> As much as gravity or the great globe's tilt.

The gravity, the seasonal tour, the contingency and fate that tilt us into death—these design for us a "shining destiny"? What, then, of our inglorious disappearance, that antispectacle? To one who loves the world of appearances, what greater catastrophe than descending into "water I know is black"? This last phrase alerts us to the coming reaction: the leaf has but to touch the surface of the pool to break the spell of its shining destiny and remind the poet of the black water-claw of cold that had just now pierced his heart, ghost to ghost. Just as the writing rose to partner the "shining destiny," doubly extending "slides," for instance, in "sidewise," and humming a resonant calm in "calm, calm—along," and gallantly placing "under-air" under "air," while in sibilance after sibilance the last breath lingeringly suspired, so now the contraction of breath is felt in short "It touches," in the flinch from "black" to "back," and the clutch of those close-packed *g*'s in "God . . . gravity . . . great globe's." In a painful rebirth, breath bursts back. The poet will dig his claw-hooks in again; he will not trust destiny; he will draw Eros away from its head-bent collusion with Thanatos, and stay on his guard, and refuse to kiss the void.

But isn't this a cold and lonely position? Is he, this poet of joy, to do without joy?

In still another vertiginous rotation, he discovers that, on the contrary, he yet means to take the full measure of joy, even if it lies, as momentarily it had seemed to, in the instinctual swoon of death. "Shall gratitude run forward as well as back?" is now his revolutionary question. More fully, "How shall we know the astrolabe of joy? / Shall gratitude run forward as well as back?" Having deliberately returned among the living, he again speaks as "we," if now for the community of the perplexed, not of tireless bodies. Distracted between Pure Being, which has become a memory, and erotic Nonbeing, which is still a promise, he must stop and question. How shall he determine where joy lies, and its motions, and its time of day? Which is the more shining, life or death? Is death or life the instrument by which to navigate a course to joy?

"Astrolabe," naming an outdated navigational device for finding latitude, longitude, and time by taking the altitude of stars, imputes to joy, not least through its austere lusciousness as a word, a sublime, old-fashioned glamor, a legendary, zodiacal magnitude. The very phrase "astrolabe of joy" renews the delirium of language, dispels the "lucent emptiness" (itself, however, a magnetizing phrase), and solaces the heart. It returns romance to the early autumn moment.

Can the phrase be remembering not the brilliant light of summer's splashes but the "golden paradox of air unmoving," so beautiful though dying, soft from overripeness? Or Eros' part in the germinative regression of the leaf, the kiss of the under-air? Somewhere the "life drives" find a roundhouse and begin the journey back, the loop of the "long compulsion," closing "the circuit hope." Doesn't dying mean, simply, *more* pleasure? Isn't sexuality at work, as Freud thought, wherever death is at work?

For whatever reason, joy, which had been at diver's arc-height above false azure, then a leaf sliding gently through the golden air, borne up as much as lifted down by a still caressing thermal universe, is now, of an instant, stellar: a glittering fixed point in the cosmos itself. What has the heart learned if its questions can still leap past reason in this way?

But a third and final question (one the questioner cannot go beyond) wonderfully restores a balance between lucidity and rapture, by peculiarly and touchingly intermingling them. Long, periodic, poised, heartfelt, wise, humorous, it forms a perfect finish:

> Who once would have thought that the heart,
> Still ravening on the world's provocation and beauty, might,
> After time long lost
> In the tangled briars of youth,
> Have picked today as payday, the payment
>
> In life's dime-thin, thumb-worn, two-sided, two-faced coin?

Excited like the first two questions, this one yet raises to an ironic pitch their mumurs of inhibitory doubt about the nature and substantiality of joy. Youth gambled that there would be berries as well as briars on the summer fields of life. And tokens of joy have indeed clattered out of the gaming device of the basic drives—or, at least on this day, bits of wisdom-hard questions have. But this coinage in the name of joy is perturbingly "two-sided." Self-divided, facing both forward and back, it is thin from ambivalence.

Ambivalence, it is certain now, plagued pleasure from the start. Life and death are so near allied that if you rub one with your thumb, the tip of your finger is on the other. On payday, the coins, every one stamped "all is death" on one side and, on the reverse, "sex is everywhere," arrive already "thumb-worn." They've been secretly handled all along—besides, are of ancient, universal, and ubiquitous mintage. When was the heart ever innocent? Always having known everything, it even picks its own payday.

But what use is this subtle knowledge? What can you buy with a dime? Coins are reliably firm; a use can always be found for them; a heap of them is a treasure. But payday is notorious for dealing out less than one feels one deserves. "Payday": what a word! It would seem that gorgeous "astrolabe" has been pulled down. Irony has contracted the just-now dilating heart.

But unequivocal, if uninsistent in its subordinate clause, "Still ravening on the world's provocation and beauty" contradicts this. The heart is a prehistoric animal, it knows only "to seize." Its taste for pleasure is indefatigable. The poet is in part still as he was in his youth, at the heart's ignorant, hopeful, and stubborn beginning.

Passion and humane irony thus set the beautifully cast question spinning like a two-faced coin. Each says to the other "convince me," in a runaround it takes all the poet's reflective self-detachment to control. He affects, he needs, "the philosophical mind"; before him lies, marked out as a subject for contemplation, the eternal perplexity of "the heart," about which everyone has heard so much, knows so little. As a thinker, he might be a lone leaf above life's bulge of green; but he is also "the heart," and we note the strength of feeling in the lines, the way they chase and wind across the fields of life, their syntax in search of fulfillment—emotional lines in which the fruit of sense must be rather carefully sought out and picked.

Joy wishes to be joy, not mere gratitude. But in a lean time, gratitude itself must count as joy. The ravening heart will count it so, if only to keep the beat till . . . Still, the sense of a mere handful of returns casts its pall. The occasion might be dreary indeed if "payday" were not just another of the tales the self tells itself, another of its punctuation marks, a way of wresting the tireless pen from destiny and writing *finis* in its own hand. *Wouldn't* the heart like a rest, though. Then again, it would not. It intends, and it knows it intends, to go on ravening—remembering summer, growing acquainted with early autumn.

The Beauty So Long Withheld

Life begins in demand, ends in an acceptance of necessity—demand proving superfluous before what starts to demand *us*, even though death is not at all what we thought we had raged to possess or to be possessed by. Passion is originally a grasping, finally a handing over, grateful for being done. It begins by provoking fate, concludes by suffering it.

Yet even the line between life and death can be stormed in rage, as "Heart of Autumn" delights to imagine. To take the initiative from death—Warren's Audubon dreams of someday waking to do this—to be all passion to the last, is one of passion's most extravagant schemes of transgression.

In "Heart of Autumn" the climactic, freeing, explosive energy of departure is ambiguous in that, bent on the peace of the inanimate, it makes itself the opposite: an unbearably ecstatic rage of animation. What is life that it takes a godlike will to power to outstrip it? What is death that life should never be so alive as when soaring to meet it?

An eschatological blaze of "now," "Heart of Autumn" brings to mind an arresting but random phrase published in an earlier volume, *Tale of Time:* "the fierceness of last joy." After casting mournfully about for some point to life, it builds to an unsurpassable climax when it receives the bulletin that we are here to die. After all, nothing is so directive, so conclusive, as death. Life? A beating about the bush.

Above all, death is the climax, the clue, to destiny. "We long for the *branding*," Denis de Rougemont writes; "we long to grow *aware* of what is on fire inside us . . . death and self-awareness are in league." Emerson's lovely thought, that the soul *is* revelation (and nothing else), is revised, in the absence of earlier disclosures, and in the tingling approach of death, to "death is revelation," "death is the soul."

The geese instruct the poet in how to die: by taking to distance. The story of destiny: a "story of great distances," or so the geese hooting northward over Kentucky, at the end of *Audubon*, give the boy listening below in the dust to understand. Here, flying southward, the sky-striders, star-striders, "rise, and the imperial utterance, / Which cries out for distance, quivers in the wheeling sky." Distance has always been for Warren a sign of what has been "denied." Distance is the death in life, by definition never near, never surmountable. Here even the sky, that greatest circumference, wheels as if toward a far and consummate destination. Is the heart to lag behind? Is a wild goose to stride stars and a man not even to know his path through life?

To close the distance between himself and the *X* that distance conceals, the *X* that may be an as yet undisclosed part of himself, the poet imagines he has become (but a sky-strider must be more definite: he becomes) a kind of human wild goose flying at a great height toward sunset. If truth is "the only thing that cannot / Be spoken," what further need has he for human speech? If truth "can only be enacted," then the final hour is "the hour . . . for the great wing-beat." Death is an affair of the animal body. The latter has first title to its own death— has always known it most intimately.

The poet seems to have asked himself, "Is my imagination so weak that it cannot simply leap into a knowledge of destiny?" And thereupon leaped, the more convincingly for moving into the metamorphosis without any astonishment of his own, and so relieving us of an accompanying embarrassment. Besides, he could scarcely have remained as he was; we could not have borne it. If ever a soul could be described as pasty-faced:

Now, today, watching
How tirelessly V upon V arrows the season's logic,

Do I know my own story? At least, they know
When the hour comes for the great wing-beat. Sky-strider,
Star-strider—they rise, and the imperial utterance,
Which cries out for distance, quivers in the wheeling sky.

That much they know, and in their nature know
The path of pathlessness, with all the joy
Of destiny fulfilling its own name.
I have known time and distance, but not why I am here.

In self-pity, with doleful, mesmerizing double strokes, the poet plucks the string of the enviable word "know" as he maunders in deadbeat, dragging verse. *Of course* he had to pick up the bow of his passion and notch himself into it, or we should all of us have been left mouldering. He must *not* stand stock still on this wind-tossed autumn day, in total ignorance of his destiny.

And so the miracle happens:

Path of logic, path of folly, all
The same—and I stand, my face lifted now skyward,
Hearing the high beat, my arms outstretched in the tingling
Process of transformation, and soon tough legs,

With folded feet, trail in the sounding vacuum of passage,
And my heart is impacted with a fierce impulse
To unwordable utterance—
Toward sunset, at a great height.

A poet of strong-arming imaginative suasion—"This is happening. / This is happiness"—Warren has no trouble convincing us of this transformation. He does the simple thing, and concentrates, first, on physical sensation—which, given the circumstance, is like understatement, a technique opposed to hysteria. After "tingling / Process," "tough legs," "folded feet," and "the sounding vacuum of passage," *then* "my heart . . . impacted with a fierce impulse / To unwordable utterance"—the Dionysian impulse the more credible after the matter-of-fact description. The resonant "sounding vacuum of passage" prepares for it, but the tough legs and folded feet trail in it as homely as those of the next wild goose, if sublimely surrendered to desuetude.

Brother to Dragons states that "man must love his own necessity," a necessity that could be nimbused only by "that perfect certainty of self" that all life long is "yearned for." It is against reason that we should be strapped with a hunger for utterness and "peace of definition" in a world itself relative, obscure, changeable, and passing. Necessity must lie in getting out of this absence of it. To know as "the bee knows," or as "the eel's cold ganglia burn," or as the goose that "hoots north where the starlit marshes are" is, according to "The Ballad of Billie Potts," to know by *carrying* knowledge—to know something that time itself does not know.

Best, perhaps, to know as the goose knows—to cut, through the "long compulsion," blaze-lines of literal vision and fill the "vacuum" of the world with impatient echoes of the inner impulse to unwordable utterance. For the world, as a vast tangled visual hieroglyph of beauty and as a sonorous echo-chamber for the vocables of being-as-will, can be loved even in its pathlessness. "And love is a hard thing to outgrow." Immanence, then, by way of immensity. Truth by way of beauty. Death by way of sublimity.

The poet's sensation of destiny (for it is that, rather than an idea) announces itself as a physiological impulse and flow. It is caught as a contagion from the "high" beat of the flying geese, as if from a Dionysian awakening of the heart of the sky, all Immanence having suddenly come alive with demand. Once again in Warren, destiny means a physical sympathy with the world (breathing with the rhythm of stars, feeling the strong heart of time stroke by stroke against one's own, being consumed away at sunset), but by way of prelude: an embrace preceding a departure. This closeness seems a necessary consummation; for the otherness that death is to life, the body has always been to the mind, and the physical world to the body. Dying closes the gaps.

The physical world is a fluid that finally cannot buoy or sustain us; we head through cloud-scut to a "land of warm water," and are heard from no more. The sun, inexorably, is setting. You would think: the flight lies beyond equivocation—pure annihilation really is the aim.

Yet not only is the water "warm"; the chill glory of the stars is replaced by the golden glory of the sun. Both the sun and the water bear the memory of the mother's body. Then, too, wheeling in the wheeling sky, the sun is still a series of seminal combustions, even if burning low. If there is any name for death besides transformation, it is home. Nothingness can make no radical inroads here. The only "vacuum" is the one shed by the physical rush of being.

Elevated to the highest pitch, passion becomes pure motion toward the source of all being. At the heart of this motion is an impulse to travel back by means of the voice itself: the motive for poetry, but galvanized into a Dionysian urge to a metasaying, one that stops mere utterance because, as Emily Dickinson said, "Size circumscribes—it has not room / For petty furniture." Speech, therefore, is "folded"; what is now needed would be to speech what wings are to feet.

The syntax is impatient: "And my heart is impacted with a fierce impulse / To unwordable utterance— / Toward sunset, at a great height." The whole being, not just the heart or the impulse to utterance, is "Toward sunset" and "at a great height." The meaning of the elliptical word order is tri-fold: *Being is now motion. It has a destination* (destiny). *It is pressing the limits of the hitherto denied* ("a great height").

The last two lines contract, in a propositional as well as linear arrowing:

> To unwordable utterance—
> Toward sunset, at a great height.

There are three short prepositional phrases here, each impatient to detonate beyond the brink of discourse. The dentals in "Toward sunset, at a great height" would bite the matter off.

For all that, the writing *is* discourse—is not nearly so rhapsodic as it could be. (The rhapsody is largely one of conception.) It plainly chooses to be writing, not a simulated oral imperious ejaculation. It is thereby the more persuasive (expressive and well calculated as the compressed syntax is). If a commensurate "utterance" would be "unwordable," it would be folly to attempt to word it; it would be bad faith. Like a mask, the lines fascinate and at the same time enforce distance from what the "unwordable impulse" contains. The grunted *uh* heard four times in "unwordable utterance" is unapologetically conveyed through polysyllabic—practiced—articulation. Yeats's astonished perception that the supreme aim of tragedy is to arrive at the conviction that nothing can injure us is oddly realized by these unexcited, somberly autumnal lines.

The as yet uncollected "Caribou near Arctic" is another spell-binding poem about the destiny of departing from life; only here the rage to die (to *live death*) is beautifully slowed to a cold-benumbed life-long entranced resignation. As if magnetically drawn to the icily eternal pole under a sky in which even the moonlight "in shadowless vastness breathes northward," the caribou seem to move out of nothing (they "drift from the white purity of forest"), across nothing (a "moon-shaven distance, . . . once . . . a lake, / Now, long ages, ice-solid"), toward a zero-point of being, nothingness dogging their every step:

> each hulk
> Lurching, each lifted leg leaving a blackness as though
> Of a broken snowshoe partly withdrawn.

(Each step repeats, in dumb refrain, a truth stated in *Brother to Dragons:* "All life lifts and longs toward its own name, / And toward fulfillment in the singleness of definition"). These cumbrous animals do not wait for the fated "hour" to come; their whole existence is a laborious step-by-step leave-taking at the remote summit of the planet.

How enviable they are, how superior to the delusions of thermal fantasy. Theirs must be the clear joy of an ice crystal:

> The shoulders
> Lumber on forward, as though only the bones, inwardly,
>   could
> Guess destination. The antlers,
> Spoon-awkward are carved by some primitive craftsman.
>
> We do not know on what errand they are bent, to what
> Mission committed. It is a world that
> They live in, and this is their life.

> They move through the world and breathe destiny.
> Their destiny is as bright as crystal, as pure as
> A dream of zero

The trance of monosyllabism ("We do not know on what . . . they are bent . . . It is a world that / They live in, and this is their life. / They move through the world and breathe") betrays the poet's wish to share their destiny. These stiff words march toward death quickened only by the cadence of "errand," "mission," "committed," "destiny," "crystal," and "zero," with their fatal conceptual pushes and rhythmic beckonings. The snowshoe-pull of the monosyllables against their own gravity, the paratactic step by step of word and sentence, make the writing "guess destination" in its very bones.

How awkward these antlers, these heaving heads, these beards of frozen spittle, this bulk, these bench-knees, these lurchings. And how endearing; for clearly these homely beings belong elsewhere, there perhaps in the direction in which their lumbering shoulders are bent. Their ungainly adaptation, their crudeness in the realm of appearances, testifies to their essential unworldliness, an inner remoteness. They might have been assigned to the drawingboard of some impatient novice who had little sympathy with comely disguises for the "long compulsion." All the more reason, then, to cheer them on their way. They are the vagrancy of death, death's lost separation from itself.

The poet had been watching the herd (more imagining than watching) from a small plane passing in the eerie blue moonlight overhead. Although he does not speak of how free of vainglory their pilgrimage is, his astonishment at it, his admiration, can be inferred from his awed absorption in their isolated sojourn, which calls nothing in the world to witness, which just *is*, and is its own reward. To witness it, even, he must pry and spy, using binoculars.

To lose sight of these blessed, unearthly creatures ("What they know must / Resemble happiness, even though / They do not know its name") is to be recalled, forlornly, to the sole self:

> I lay the binoculars on the lap of the biologist. He
> Studies distance. The co-pilot studies a map. He

Glances at mysterious dials. I
Drink coffee. The binoculars
Courteously come back to me.

I have lost the spot. I find only blankness. But
They must have been going somewhere.

Here the parataxis chinks, where before it was all instinctual pull: "I
lay . . . He / Studies . . . The co-pilot studies . . . He / Glances . . .
I / Drink," and so on—the poet has indeed "lost the spot." Imagining
the happiness of the caribou, he had discovered his own need for a
motion "committed" to distance; but now, while the others continue
to study distance and abstraction in their own worldly way—the bi-
ologist distance, the copilot a map and mysterious dials—he has lost
his clairvoyance, his delicate inner knowledge of destiny. His closing
remark, "They must have been going somewhere," is calculated to
hide his anguish behind dullness. With this remark he seems to rub his
eyes a bit roughly, as if to spite them for mistaking a dream for a vi-
sion. In a defeated mood he returns to his ordinary superficial relation
to destiny—his well-equipped human knowing, which knows not the
one essential thing.

The buried root of "noble" is *noscere,* "to come to know," and the
final nobility, for Warren, is to know death as (in Heidegger's words)
"that *possibility which is one's own most, which is non-relational, and
which is not to be outstripped.* " So it is that in *Audubon* "The quarry lifts,
in the halo of gold leaves, its noble head." "Paradox of Time," in *Ru-
mor Verified,* calls knowledge of what is not to be outstripped the "pu-
rity of being that may / Be had past all ambition, and the frivolous
hope." Where "Caribou near Arctic" locates it in animals, "Paradox
of Time" (a sequence of three poems) first uses minerals, then (taking
the full challenge) a man dying of cancer.

"Gravity of Stone and Ecstasy of Wind," the first and weakest
poem, doubtless intended as a prologue, yearns for "wild words
sprung / From vision," words to "atone / For all folly now left be-
hind." This feverish wish for prophecy reeks of the vanity of con-
science. It jars with the hortatory conclusion: "Learn the gravity of

stone. / Learn the ecstasy of wind." These urgings are Zen; they leave rage of vision behind.

"Law of Attrition"—the next poem—hymns the gravity of what is first a particle of "crag-jut" and aeons later (so it is supposed) a grain of sand on an unmapped strand. The poem is cast as a guide to meditation:

> Learn the law of attrition,
> Learn that the mountain's crag-jut,
> In the altitude of pride,
> Knows the sledge and gnaw of seasons,
> Each in its enmity.
> Do you know how a particle,
> Now rain-washed downward, and down,
> Is seized by the stream that boils
> And roils in tumultuous white
> Of flung spray, down the chasm
> To reach falls that, airward, leap,
> Then plunge, in incessant thunder,
> To the swirl of blind mist below?
> Do you know how . . .

With its strenuous short lines and passionate concentration, the writing is all exalted inspiration; an ascetic fervor speeds the unusual odyssey along. How excited the poet is by this fall from "altitude of pride." His intensity belies the gravity of stone.

He is avid for "a self that is not-self," and only the aim of leaving "folly . . . behind" explains why. But then he goes on to evoke the joy of what is splendid, benign, arrogant: the nonselved physical world, reigned over by "The western star" in the first poem, the star disdaining "You, and your tenement / Of flesh." The particle is to become part of this arrogance, sharing its joy. Although "backed by shadow / And depth of rain-jungle, and / The utterance of the victim / When, in nocturnal prowl-time, / It feels the fang at the throat," the grain itself will be invulnerable, "A single self-possessed grain":

Day dawns, and then the sand-grain
Exposes the glaze of a tiny
And time-polished facet that now
Will return from its minimal mirror
The joy of one ray from above,
But no more joy for this than
When tropic constellations,
Wheeling in brilliant darkness,
Strike one ray at that same facet
That, across howling light-years,
Makes what answer it can—
With the same indifferent joy.

For safe, safe within this asylum
Of self that is non-self, it lies
On a beach where no foot may come.

This is not "altitude of pride" but a subtler form of assurance. To the
question "What am I?" Lacan chillingly answers, "'I' am in the place
from which a voice is heard clamoring 'the universe is a defect in the
purity of Non-Being.'" In the particle this voice has been stilled, the
defect of the "I" itself has been removed, leaving the universe so pure
and indifferent in its joy that whether it be called Being or Non-Being
is immaterial.

Seized and flung by the "surface agitation" of the stream, borne by
the "rapt and somnambulistic" estuary into "The dark inwardness of
sea-wisdom," the grain at length represents, self-possessed on its white
unfrequented strand, a complete freedom from agitation. "The pri-
mordial preference for agitation," notes Hubert Benoit, "is errone-
ous, and the cause of all . . . miseries." Nor is it separable from a wish
to be "affirmed as distinct." Jungle prowlings, glory prowlings, the
eating of stars—against these primal kinds of agitation, the "single"
grain forms an antisermon. Its counsel: abandon appetency, the cause
of all miseries.

Perhaps it is only language that makes the particle seem exhibition-
istic in "Exposes the glaze," or earnestly responsive in "Makes what
answer it can." Or perhaps the poet brings it thus a little way into the

animate, so as to make it the more accessible as a model to us. In any case, it must be his own fear that stresses the safety of an "asylum / Of self that is non-self." Nor can we mistake the deliberate attribution of "joy" to the sand-grain. We are required to stretch our imaginations, to conceive an "indifferent joy": the joy of a particle, the joy of mirroring. "Abstract" energy, we are to glimpse, is not essentially different from us; it is only miraculously unagitated. We gain a sense of what Robbe-Grillet calls "the poverty of the old myths of 'depth,'" by encountering a bold new literal claim.

Warren now takes the risk of turning from mineral to human "purity." "One I Knew" returns to the subject matter of "Reading Late at Night, Thermometer Falling": an aged father guarding his "precious secret," cancer. But now the cancer is both physical and—well, metaphysical:

> It was as though he leaned
> At a large mysterious bud
> To watch, hour by hour,
> How at last it would divulge
> A beauty so long withheld

The simile is grotesque until its basis in the poet's experience is explained:

> As I had once sat
> In a room lighted only by
> Two candlesticks, and
> Two flames, motionless, rose
> In the summer night's breathlessness.
> Three friends and I, we sat
> With no conversation, watching
> The bud of a century plant
> That was straining against the weight
> Of years, slow, slow, in silence,
> To offer its inwardness.
> The whisky burned in our throats.

With this proselike anecdote, the "bud" gains sublimity: the natural light, falling through the glass shade of the comparison, arrives as miracle.

The old man is a "true" father, pure, abstract. There is a tension between what he says—"To deny / The self is all"—and what the poet, with his old-Adam attachment to appearances, says: "beauty," "bud," "divulge," "summer night's breathlessness," and, finally, "The shimmering / White petal—the golden stamen":

> At last, the injection.
>
> I saw the end. Later,
> I found the letter, the first
> Paragraph unfinished. I saw
> The ink-slash from that point
> Where the unconscious hand had dragged
> The pen as he fell. I saw
> The salutation. It was:
> "Dear Son."
>   The shimmering
> White petal—the golden stamen—
> Were at last, in triumph,
> Divulged. On the dusty carpet.

Whom should we believe, the father with his austerity or the son with his trembling excitement? We are left to imagine (and again the poet enforces a new perception) the agreement between them, the point where "purity" and "beauty" converge.

If the old man has ceased "ravening on the world's provocation and beauty," a feeding that aggrandizes our own being, may he not be ravening, instead, on death's provocation and beauty, perhaps in the hope of graduating into the gigantism of Being itself? To consider death the blossom a life has labored to produce is both to convert it into the ultimate aesthetic experience and to chasten life. The father lacks the gravity of stone, has the ecstasy of expectation. Prizing what is "non-relational" and yet himself, grateful for approaching at last what "is not to be outstripped," he is prepared to die.

Or so the son is moved to suppose. With his relative youth and aesthetic adhesion to life, he would shield the old man from the unimaginable, unappearing abstractness of death. His mollifying gift: the figurative plant, an eschatological promise, with which he belatedly brightens up the dreary rest home ("He sat alone in that spot / Of refuge for life's discards"). The son cannot really know that the white petal and golden stamen were finally divulged; his imagining merely completes his gift giving, reaffirms his loving wish for his father.

What might the old man have been about to write to his son? News of death? The son would have it so. He must complete this last of his father's gifts to him, must have it all written out. There is only one way to have it, and that is to write it out himself, as the poem.

He thus bestows on the two of them at once the "triumph" of the exquisite divulgence of the beauty so long withheld. He and his father share (in a sympathetic succession harmonious with the one conceived in "Sunset Walk in Thaw-Time in Vermont") the secret of the loving immortality of death. The white petal and the golden stamen, the first all tenderness, the second all seminal prod, represent, respectively, the soft surrender of self and the radical emergence of the "nonself," the projection of "one's ownmost" that death is. Death is not only the antithesis of "dust"; it is itself a complete sexual figure, in which Oedipal agony is allayed. The father and the son reach a perfect accord in its abstract beauty, its tender severity, its mysterious merging of the masculine and feminine.

"Dead Horse in Field," in the same volume, reintegrates death into life through process, closing the movement left eschatologically linear in "Paradox of Time"—affirming the full circle. Process, here, is the decaying and stinking carrion of a thoroughbred with shattered foreleg and a "30.06 in heart." It is the "beneficent work of crows" and buzzards. It is (in a temporal projection) bones "white now / By weather and sun," and later "The green twine of vine." It is really the most reasonable system of losses and gains; and though the heart grieves for the two-year-old, it cries out at the vital beauty of change—even exclaiming, of the buzzards, "How beautiful in air!" Harshness and beauty are austerely reconciled; bleakness and verdure, accident and necessity, ugliness and vim, combine to confuse yet pacify the heart. The disinfecting impulse behind "Paradox of Time" is replaced by a tragic equanimity before both life and death. Process emerges as richly endowed, if greatly entangled. Recovering its own losses, it breaks up the rigidity of the famous dichotomies: life and death, creation and destruction, the beginning and the end, power and fate. It pours the contents of each pitcher back into the nondistinguishing well. It gives all to circulation.

Here we find a difficult appreciation—human and tragic—of what towered above even the mirroring particle in "Law of Attrition": the physical world as the "Beautiful Necessity":

> A week later I couldn't get close. The sweet stink
> Had begun. That damned wagon mudhole
> Hidden by leaves as we galloped—I found it.
> Spat on it. As a child would. Next day
> The buzzards. How beautiful in air!—carving
> The slow, concentric, downward pattern of vortex, wing-glint
> On wing-glint. From the house,
> Now with glasses, I see
> The squabble and pushing, the waggle of wattle-red heads.
>
> At evening I watch the buzzards, the crows,
> Arise. They swing black in nature's flow and perfection,
> High in sad carmine of sunset. Forgiveness
> Is not indicated. It is superfluous. They are
> What they are.

It is motion in and mastery of air (always, for Warren, the most exhilarating of sights) that turns the tone away from the bitterness touching it earlier:

>   The day
> After death I had gone for farewell, and the eyes
> Were already gone—that
> The beneficent work of crows. Eyes gone
> The two-year-old could, of course, more readily see
> Down the track of pure and eternal darkness.

If "beneficent" is not altogether ironic here, the sore heart is not yet ready to look into the justice of the word. The contiguous stresses of "I now see gorged crows rise ragged in wind" disagreeably weights the birds with what they have eaten, and checks the impulse to exclaim at the vital motion. The poet is just unforgiving enough to wince back into the sentimental conceit of "the track of pure and eternal darkness." He sides with the thoroughbred; the ragged crows are vital refuse by comparison.

Now, with the gleaming vortex carved by wing-glints comes the involuntary cry of appreciation. "That damned wagon mudhole" certainly need not have been "Hidden by leaves": this is hateful contingency. By contrast, what the buzzards' wings inscribe is as fated as the "closing vortex" drawn in Pacific waters by the sinking Pequod. It is a "pattern" of Necessity, in whose slow, concentric, and downward rhythm ("They swing black in nature's flow and perfection") "Forgiveness / Is not indicated." Beneath this awesome configuration, the rotting horse is diminished to a detail in a canvas; it becomes the anchor of an aerial ballet. At the same time it gains a new importance, though one too gruesome to be dwelt on—that of nurturing the living, a role it will sustain even when, as bare bones, it lattices and provides meal for the green twine of vine.

That the thoroughbred was beloved the clipped title and stern-lipped "A 30.06 in heart" betray. But to carve a space for oneself in thin air, to sculpt the sky, to be a vital monarch! Admiration of appearances and of power produces a certain elated flightiness; with a slightly nauseated lurch, the poet's allegiance, hence ours, shifts, for a time, to the whirlpool of wing-glints, which is not only a passionate instance but a symbol of the weaving and unweaving of forces that, as Pater said, both waste and repair the eye, and rust iron, and ripen corn.*

---

* Victor Strandberg also calls brief attention to the affinity between Warren and Pater. Strandberg is correct, I think, in stressing the distinguishing religious tonality in Warren's passionate love of the world, but perhaps overcredits Warren's religious rhetoric (for example, "We must try / To love so well the world that we may believe, in the end, in God"). Then, too, to say that "In his epiphanies, Warren obviously shares Pater's thirst for 'getting as many pulsations as possible into the given time' " makes the somewhat lumbering, bearlike Warren sound too much like a butterfly. See Strandberg, *The Poetic Vision of Robert Penn Warren* (Lexington: University of Kentucky Press, 1977), p. 235.

So hard-hitting a detail as "The squabble and pushing, the waggle of wattle-red heads" qualifies the Paterian breathlessness of attention with a rude admixture of (breath-stopping) shock. Fieldglasses have that tendency, anyway: the enlargement startles, feels strange. Voyeurism lends its tingle. The eyes pry. The vehement physicality of the buzzards, of what they do and how they look, offsets, like a mocking antithesis, the repressed sexuality of spying. The sight smites the act of peeking. But the text bears the brunt of it with equanimity. From the beginning, with its notation of "left foreleg shattered below knee, / A 30.06 in heart," it has steeled itself to fact; and in its clear shot of "barberry bushes red-fruited," of "gorged crows [rising] ragged in wind," of the buzzards' "squabble and pushing," its language stands in an eager, enactive relation to its subjects. This acceptance of the world at the level of rhythm and timbre, this syllabic pushing and gorging and waggling, preludes and parallels the mental accord expressed by "They are / What they are." The moral peace available in the knowledge that (as Nietzsche said) "everything breaks, everything is integrated anew" remains an unemphatic undertone to the aesthetic delight afforded by the breaking and reintegrating; it is largely as an aesthetic phenomenon that process (whether running, flying, physical decay, gorging, squabbling, or twining) is justified.

The thoroughbred's bones will live not in themselves, but in the life they quicken—the beholder's delight in their abstract structural beauty; the green spurt of vine; the beholder's delight in the vine:

> How long before I go back to see
> That intricate piece of
> Modern sculpture, white now
> By weather and sun, intricate, now
> Assuming in stasis
> New beauty! Then,
> A year later, I'll see
> The green twine of vine, each leaf
> Heart-shaped, soft as velvet, beginning
> Its benediction.

Just as the wings had sculpted a mobile in the air, so decay will sculpt this "New beauty"—Nature charitably turning what had been an inside into an external object fit to behold. The pointing pronoun "That" ("to see / That intricate piece") prizes the visual draw; and "intricate" is twice repeated in caressing wonder. "Now" is also repeated, so as to wrest a future pleasure into a present one. If motion can be beautiful, so can stasis—necessity requiring this dialectic, appearance admitting it, and aesthetics exploiting it.

"By law and process of great nature," that intricate piece of sculpture will be "Freed and enfranchised" (*The Winter's Tale*). There is an art that nature makes, purging all infection from our air. Well might Warren join his dear enemy Emerson in wondering at "the necessity of beauty under which the universe lies; that all is and must be pictorial," that an "indwelling necessity plants that rose of beauty on the brow of chaos, and discloses the central intention of nature to be harmony and joy." "Not only to bear necessity, . . . but to *love* it" is the aesthetic and philosophical juncture, and injunction, that brings Emerson, Nietzsche, and Warren alike to their knees.

Guy Murchie has written that "the living body is sculptured by dying cells, by the simple wasting away of no-longer-wanted cells as surely as a statue is shaped by the departing chips of chiseled 'dead' marble." Life, then, is death's sculpture; "death helps life" is a name for "nature's flow and perfection." Born out of death, the vine will shape itself into signs of love. Each "Heart-shaped" leaf will intimate that shape itself is love, the love of necessity for the things of this world. It will speak well of the conditions of being, well of the dead.

Warren's chosen course—to start with the world to find God—may be thought to climax in this poem, in which the green vine "thinks it is God. / Can you think of some ground on which that may be gainsaid?" The sacralizing "art" of nature, the benevolence in its process, is as much as we shall ever have of God, but nonetheless adequate (so it is the grace of this poem to suggest) for the total reverence of the heart.

Sympathy with process, gratitude that "the world is real. It is there," has kept Warren young. He is like the hydra that, as Murchie says, "metabolizes so fast . . . the tissue [flows] straight through like gas in a candle flame . . . and diffuses into the surrounding water like smoke." Warren has balanced his firm awareness of fate and his sensory flow and refreshment, with the result that he is as passionate now as when, a young man, he spoke in "Picnic Remembered" of "Joy, strongest medium" and is less ready now to turn against that medium as a "bright deception . . . , for fears have fructified." He has since grown larger than his fears. "In the heart's last kingdom," he was later to say, "only the old are young."

Notes
Acknowledgments
Index

Notes

These notes annotate the poems and other works cited in the book, with the exception of items perhaps sufficiently identified in the book itself. The numerals at the left refer to page numbers in this text. Those at the right of the entries list pages in the sources cited.

The citations from Robert Penn Warren's works are from the following editions:

Poetry

Brother to Dragons: A Tale in Verse and Voices. New York: Random House, 1953.

Brother to Dragons: A Tale in Verse and Voices. A New Version. New York: Random House, 1979. (Unless otherwise noted, this is the version referred to in the notes.)

Selected Poems: 1923–1975. New York: Random House, 1975. (This volume contains selections from *Selected Poems: 1923–1943; Promises: Poems 1954–1956; You, Emperors, and Others: Poems 1957–1960; Tale of Time: Poems 1960–1966; Incarnations: Poems 1966–1968; Audubon: A Vision; Or Else—Poem/Poems 1968–1974;* and *Can I See Arcturus from Where I Stand? Poems 1975.*)

Now and Then: Poems 1976–1978. New York: Random House, 1978.

Being Here: Poetry 1977–1980. New York: Random House, 1980.

Rumor Verified: Poems 1979–1980. New York: Random House, 1981.

Chief Joseph of the Nez Perce: A Poem. New York: Random House, 1983.

Novels

Night Rider. New York: Random House, 1939.

At Heaven's Gate. New York: Harcourt, Brace, 1943.

All the King's Men. New York: Harcourt, Brace, 1946.

World Enough and Time. New York: Random House, 1950.

Band of Angels. New York: Random House, 1955.

The Cave. New York: Random House, 1959.

Flood. New York: Random House, 1964.
Meet Me in the Green Glen. New York: Random House, 1971.
A Place to Come to. New York: Random House, 1977.

Other Works

American Literature: The Makers and the Making. Compiled with Cleanth Brooks
   and R. W. B. Lewis. 2 vols. New York: St. Martin's, 1973. (For a discussion of
   Warren's contributions see R. W. B. Lewis, "Warren's Long Visit to American
   Literature," *Yale Review 70* (Summer 1981): 568–591.
Democracy and Poetry. Cambridge, Mass.: Harvard University Press, 1975.

Introduction

3   the fume-track: "Natural History I," *Incarnations,* in *Selected Poems,* p. 106.
4   knowledge based: *Democracy and Poetry,* p. 48.
4   the world: Ibid., p. 47.
4   the Individual: *The Modern Tradition,* ed. Richard Ellmann and Charles Fei-
     delson, Jr. (Oxford: Oxford University Press, 1965), p. 409.
4   contumely: "Dark Night of the Soul," *Promises,* in *Selected Poems,* p. 248.
5   To write: *Journal of Katherine Mansfield,* ed. J. Middleton Murry (New
     York: Ecco, 1983), p. 197.
5   Kafka said: Quoted in Max Brod, *Franz Kafka: A Biography* (New York:
     Schocken, 1963), p. 78.
5   tragedy: Georg Lukács, "The Metaphysics of Tragedy," in *Soul and Form,* tr.
     Anna Bostock (Cambridge, Mass.: MIT Press, 1978), p. 154.
5   the un-uprootable ferocity: *Brother to Dragons,* p. 33.
5   Ibsen's question: quoted in Lukács, *Soul and Form,* p. 152.
5   Truth's glare-glory: "Infant Boy at Midcentury," *Promises,* in *Selected Poems,*
     p. 250.
5   Question: "Have You Ever Eaten Stars?" *Rumor Verified,* p. 89.
6   To know: "Patriotic Tour and Postulate of Joy," *Tale of Time,* in *Selected
     Poems,* p. 161.
6   You / must eat: "The Interim," ibid., p. 148.
6   we may endeavor: "Ransom," *Selected Poems: 1923–1943,* in *Selected Poems,*
     p. 398.
6   the bosom's nocturnal disquiet . . . the fanged commotion: "Eidolon,"
     ibid., p. 300.
6   an unreviving benison: "The Garden," ibid., p. 314.
7   "Go it, Granny—Go it, Hog!":   *Promises,* in *Selected Poems,* p. 262.
7   rage of joy: "Saul at Gilboa," *Tale of Time,* in *Selected Poems,* p. 181.

7   At the hour: "The Ballad of Billie Potts," *Selected Poems: 1923–1943*, in *Selected Poems*, p. 279.

7   The salmon heaves: Ibid., p. 283.

7   creature: *Robert Penn Warren Talking: Interviews 1950–1978*, ed. Floyd C. Watkins and John T. Hiers (New York: Random House, 1980), p. 234.

7   deep delight . . . nobility: *Brother to Dragons*, p. 128.

8   his greatest: James R. Justus, *The Achievement of Robert Penn Warren* (Baton Rouge: Louisiana State University Press, 1968), p. 33.

8   reviews of *Promises*:   Leonard Casper, "The Founding Fathers," *Western Review* 22 (Autumn 1957): 69–71. James Wright, "The Stiff Smile of Mr. Warren," *Kenyon Review* 20 (Autumn 1958): 645–655; rpt. in *Robert Penn Warren: Critical Perspectives*, ed. Neil Nakadate (Lexington: University Press of Kentucky, 1981), pp. 262–269. James Dickey, "Robert Penn Warren," in *Babel to Byzantium* (New York: Farrar, Straus and Giroux, 1968), pp. 75–77.

9   But at your laughter: "To a Little Girl, One Year Old, in a Ruined Fortress," *Promises*, in *Selected Poems*, p. 220.

9   We must try: "Masts at Dawn," *Incarnations*, in *Selected Poems*, p. 115.

11   Dawn: *Audubon*, I, in *Selected Poems*, p. 85.

11   he embodies: *The Cave*, p. 238.

11   love knowledge: *Democracy and Poetry*, p. 48.

11   starward . . . stared: "Snowshoeing Back to Camp in Gloaming," *Being Here*, p. 28.

12   I would . . . start: *Robert Penn Warren Talking*, p. 234.

12   What has been denied: *Audubon*, II, in *Selected Poems*, p. 92.

13   In the deep certainty: "Sunset Walk in Thaw-Time in Vermont," *Or Else*, in *Selected Poems*, p. 76.

13   Time's irremediable joy: "Lullaby: A Motion Like Sleep," *Promises*, in *Selected Poems*, p. 268.

13   Man lives: "Reading Late at Night, Thermometer Falling," *Or Else*, in *Selected Poems*, p. 69.

13   lift our eyes: *Brother to Dragons*, p. 62.

14   Tell me: *Audubon*, VII, in *Selected Poems*, p. 100.

14   What was: "What Was the Promise," *Promises*, in *Selected Poems*, p. 227.

15   This is happening: "Unless," *Now and Then*, p. 36.

15   Continue to walk: *Audubon*, III, in *Selected Poems*, p. 93.

15   on the one hand: "Heart of Autumn," *Now and Then*, p. 74.

16   vital image: *Robert Penn Warren Talking*, p. 16.

17   image of man: "Knowledge and the Image of Man," *Sewanee Review* 63 (Spring 1955): 187–188.

17   failures . . . folly: See, for instance, "Sunset Walk in Thaw-Time in Vermont," *Or Else*, in *Selected Poems*, p. 77.

17   The awful responsibility: *All the King's Men*, p. 438.

18   to give the impression: *Flood*, p. 127.

18   There's a lot: *Night Rider*, p. 193.

19   the real begins: "The Mad Druggist," *Tale of Time*, in *Selected Poems*, p. 142.

19   Tramps: "Blackberry Winter," *The Circus in the Attic and Other Stories* (New York: Harcourt, Brace, 1947), pp. 63–87. "Dark Night of the Soul," *Promises*, in *Selected Poems*, p. 245. "Convergences," *Rumor Verified*, p. 37.

20   past contumely: "Dark Night of the Soul," *Selected Poems*, p. 245.

20   with the rhythm: "Unless," *Now and Then*, p. 35.

20   the film director: *Flood*, p. 127.

20   total reverence: "The Interim," *Tale of Time*, in *Selected Poems*, p. 144.

21   all that heightens: William Butler Yeats, "J. M. Synge and the Ireland of his Time," *Essays and Introductions* (New York: Macmillan, 1961), p. 327.

His Mature Manner

25   But that secret: *Meet Me in the Green Glen*, p. 182.

25   October: *Audubon*, I, in *Selected Poems*, p. 85.

26   And they came: *The Cave*, p. 80.

26   Wind finds: "Heart of Autumn," *Now and Then*, p. 74.

27   One group: Sigmund Freud, "Beyond the Pleasure Principle," in *A General Selection from the Works of Sigmund Freud*, ed. John Rickman (Garden City: Doubleday Anchor, 1957), p. 162.

28   It is impossible: Walter Pater, "Style," in *Appreciations* (London: Macmillan, 1924), p. 37.

29   People nowadays: Boris Pasternak, quoted in Donald Davie, *Thomas Hardy and British Poetry* (New York: Oxford University Press, 1972), p. 49, where the reader is referred to Pasternak, *Sochineniya* [Works], vol. 3 (Ann Arbor: University of Michigan Press, 1961), p. 152.

29   We live: "Bearded Oaks," *Selected Poems: 1923–1943*, in *Selected Poems*, p. 308.

29   Go to the clinic: "Pursuit," ibid., p. 287.

29   sun-torment: "Original Sin: A Short Story," ibid., p. 290.

29   Or it goes: Ibid., p. 289.

30   the hunchback: "Pursuit," *Selected Poems: 1923–1943*, in *Selected Poems*, p. 286.

30   All day: "Foreign Shore, Old Woman, Slaughter of Octopus," *Promises*, in *Selected Poems*, p. 244.

31   lip-biting: "Switzerland," *You, Emperors, and Others*, in *Selected Poems*, p. 197.

31   Suddenly: "Two Poems about Suddenly and a Rose," *Tale of Time*, in *Selected Poems*, p. 186.

32   What makes: Nietzsche, *The Gay Science*, tr. Walter Kaufmann (New York; Vintage, 1974), p. 219.

32   the use of power: Martin Heidegger, *An Introduction to Metaphysics*, tr. Ralph Manheim (Garden City: Doubleday Anchor, 1961), p. 134.

32   From behind: "Sila," *Being Here*, p. 38.

32   The flashlight: "Speleology," ibid., p. 8.

32   Stared long: "Looking Northward, Aegeanward: Nestlings on Seacliff," *Rumor Verified*, p. 7.

32   But / Cannot: "Sila," *Being Here*, p. 40.

32   One moment: "Preternaturally Early Snowfall in Mating Season," *Being Here*, p. 36.

32   the *groan-swish*:   "Youthful Truth-Seeker, Half-Naked, at Night, Running Down Beach South of San Francisco," *Being Here*, p. 26.

32   While the heart: "Language Barrier," ibid., p. 72.

32   the irremediably dark: Karl Jaspers, *Reason and Existenz*, tr. William Earle (New York: Noonday, 1957), p. 62.

32   Never: "Acquaintance with Time in Early Autumn," *Being Here*, p. 89.

32   I warily handled: "The Only Poem," ibid., p. 19.

32   Is light: "Two Poems about Suddenly and a Rose," *Tale of Time*, in *Selected Poems*, p. 186.

33   Bowl-hollow: "No Bird Does Call," *Being Here*, p. 66.

34   Paradox coils: "Marble," *New Yorker*, October 24, 1983, p. 46.

35   Like substance: "Why You Climbed Up," *Georgia Review* 37 (Fall 1983): 565.

35   The wind: "Trying to Tell You Something," *Can I See Arcturus from Where I Stand?* in *Selected Poems*, p. 10.

36   Path of logic: "Heart of Autumn," *Now and Then*, p. 74.

36   and saw: *Audubon*, IV, in *Selected Poems*, p. 96.

36   I / Stopped: "Snowshoeing Back to Camp in Gloaming," *Being Here*, p. 28.

36   Got back: "Folly on Royal Street before the Raw Face of God," *Or Else*, in *Selected Poems*, p. 74.

36   Spat on it: "Dead Horse in Field," *Rumor Verified*, p. 59.

37   The great coin: "Youth Stares at Minoan Sunset," *Now and Then*, p. 25.

37   *Tap-tap*:   "Waking to Tap of Hammer," ibid., p. 51.

37   Her eyes: "Marble," *New Yorker*, October 24, 1983, p. 46.

37   Raw-ringed: "Folly on Royal Street before the Raw Face of God," *Or Else*, in *Selected Poems*, p. 74.

37   A crow: "Chain Saw at Dawn in Vermont in Time of Drouth," ibid., p. 39.

37   Are you: "Dawn," *Rumor Verified*, p. 79.

37   But what use: "The Cross," *Being Here*, p. 60.

37   The door: "Marble," *New Yorker*, October 24, 1983, p. 64.

37   And flesh: "Auto-Da-Fé," *Being Here*, p. 85.

38   But / Cannot: "Sila," ibid., p. 40.

38   Yes, sky: "Acquaintance with Time in Early Autumn," ibid., p. 89.

38   like a hurricane: "Folly on Royal Street before the Raw Face of God," *Or Else*, in *Selected Poems*, p. 73.

38   That voice: *Audubon*, IV, in *Selected Poems*, p. 95.

38   Off in Wyoming: "Little Boy and Lost Shoe," *Or Else*, in *Selected Poems*, p. 62.

38   Years later: "Fox Fire: 1956," *You, Emperors, and Others*, in *Selected Poems*, p. 204.

40   bloom: *Audubon*, IV, in *Selected Poems*, p. 95.

40   natural medium: Hugh Kenner, "Something Nasty in the Meat-House," in *Hudson Review* 6 (Winter 1954): 605–610.

40   From plane: "Evening Hawk," *Can I See Arcturus from Where I Stand?* in *Selected Poems*, p. 4.

43   Through / Air: "I Am Dreaming of a White Christmas: The Natural History of a Vision," *Or Else*, in *Selected Poems*, p. 26.

43   The cave: "Speleology," *Being Here*, p. 7.

44   Song is lost;   "Another Dimension," *Rumor Verified*, p. 70.

45   Night comes: "When Life Begins," *Being Here*, p. 10.

45   What left: "Red-Tail Hawk and Pyre of Youth," *Now and Then*, p. 20.

45   More snow: "Snow out of Season," *Rumor Verified*, p. 73.

45   I can: "Dawn," ibid., p. 80.

45   And it is not certain: "Love Recognized," *Now and Then*, p. 52.

46   twists and compacts: George Steiner, *Martin Heidegger* (New York: Penguin, 1980), p. 86.

46   Nothing / But: "Time as Hypnosis," *Or Else*, in *Selected Poems*, p. 24.

47   He enters: "Old Nigger on One Mule Cart," *Can I See Arcturus from Where I Stand?* in *Selected Poems*, p. 16.

47   inorganic: F. W. Dupee, quoted in Leonard Casper, *Robert Penn Warren: The Dark and Bloody Ground* (Seattle: University of Washington Press, 1960), pp. 62–63.

48   picked today: "Acquaintance with Time in Early Autumn," *Being Here*, p. 89.

48   The blessedness: *Audubon*, IV, in *Selected Poems*, p. 94.

49   Then / In widening: "Red-Tail Hawk and Pyre of Youth," *Now and Then*, p. 17.

49   When the tooth cracks: "When the Tooth Cracks—Zing!" ibid., p. 45.

49   the earth: *Brother to Dragons*, p. 90.

49   the sun: "Prairie Harvest," *Being Here*, p. 74.

49   the lips: "A Way to Love God," *Can I See Arcturus from Where I Stand?* in *Selected Poems*, p. 3.

49   But what can you say: "American Portrait: Old Stlye," *Now and Then*, p. 6.

50   She wept: "Amazing Grace in the Back Country," ibid., p. 9.

50   Never: "Old Flame," ibid., p. 13.

50   unless: "Unless," ibid., p. 35.

50   the city: "Love Recognized," ibid., p. 52.

51   Enormous: "Boyhood in Tobacco Country," "*Being Here*, p. 11.

51   Think hard: "Loss, of Perhaps Love, in Our World of Contingency," *Can I See Arcturus from Where I Stand?* in *Selected Poems*, p. 5.

52   Flesh: "Old Nigger on One-Mule Cart," ibid., p. 13.

53   The heart, like a trout: "Language Barrier," *Being Here*, p. 72.

54   The trail: "Sunset Scrupulously Observed," *Rumor Verified*, p. 31.

54   The evening: Ibid., p. 32.

54   With the tire song: "Going West," *Rumor Verified*, p. 25.

54   From plane: "Evening Hawk," *Can I See Arcturus from Where I Stand?* in *Selected Poems*, p. 4.

55   Warren was to learn: Stanley Plumly, "Warren Selected," in *Robert Penn Warren: A Collection of Critical Essays*, ed. Richard Gray (Englewood Cliffs: Prentice-Hall, 1980), p. 134.

55   and at / Dawn: "The Interim," *Tale of Time* in *Selected Poems*, p. 147.

55   The red cabooselight: Ibid.

55   Over the green interstices: "A Problem in Spatial Composition," *Or Else*, in *Selected Poems*, p. 80.

55   With what painful deliberation: "English Cocker: Old and Blind," *Rumor Verified*, p. 78.

56   Now with glasses: "Dead Horse in Field," ibid., p. 59.

56   What I have: "Rattlesnake Country," *Or Else*, in *Selected Poems*, p. 45.

58   knowledge: Georg Lukács, *The Theory of the Novel* (Cambridge, Mass.: MIT Press, 1973), p. 88.

58   Matter is supposed to be: Henri Bergson, *Matter and Memory* (Garden City: Doubleday Anchor, 1959), p. 218. See also p.6: "Now the phenomena of memory, in which we believe that we can grasp spirit in its most tangible form," etc.; and p. 237: "With memory we are in very truth in the domain of spirit."

59   Since prehistoric times; a return to the pre-formal: Mircea Eliade, *Patterns in Comparative Religion* (New York: Meridian, 1963), p. 189.

61   severe responsibility: Sergei Eisenstein, *Film Form*, ed. and tr. Jay Leyda (New York: Meridian, 1957), p. 115.

62   Montage: Sergei Eisenstein, *Film Sense*, ed. and tr. Jay Leyda (New York: Meridian, 1957), p. 11.

62   was glad: *Flood*, p. 57.

63   Joy flickers: *Brother to Dragons*, p. 100.

63   Slashed: "Ballad of Your Puzzlement," *Being Here*, p. 80.

63   We ourselves: "On Death and Its Relation to the Indestructibility of Our
       True Nature," *The Will to Live: Selected Writings of Arthur Schopenhauer,* ed.
       Richard Taylor (Garden City: Doubleday Anchor, 1962), p. 126.

64   the orgiastic moment: William Butler Yeats, "J.M. Synge and the Ireland of
       his Time," *Essays and Introductions* (New York: Macmillan, 1961), p. 325.

64   imperially: *A Place to Come to,* p. 168.

65   It is essential: Eleanor Clark, *The Oysters of Locmariaquer* (New York: Vin-
       tage, 1966), p. 7.

65   In poetry: Robert Graves, *The Common Asphodel: Collected Essays on Poetry,
       1922–1949* (London: Hamish Hamilton, 1949), p. 3.

66   The idea: Virginia Woolf, *A Writer's Diary* (London: Hogarth, 1954),
       p. 139.

66   Criticism: *Robert Penn Warren Talking: Interviews 1950–1978,* ed. Floyd C.
       Watkins and John T. Hiers (New York: Random House, 1980), p. 145.

66   There isn't much: Ibid., p. 32.

66   *Rip:*   "Sunset Walk in Thaw-Time in Vermont," *Selected Poems,* p. 76.

67   going out: Walter J. Ong, *Orality and Literacy: The Technologizing of the
       Word* (London: Methuen, 1982), p. 71.

67   pure perception: Bergson, *Matter and Memory,* p. 220.

71   an affirmation; the abstraction: "Knowledge and the Image of Man,"
       Sewanee Review 63 (Spring 1955): 192.

72   What other need: "Have You Ever Eaten Stars?" *Rumor Verified,* p. 88.

72   regrets its absence: Paul Breslin, review of *Being Here,* in *New York Times
       Book Review,* November 2, 1980, p. 12.

73   Below all: "Youthful Truth-Seeker, Half-Naked, at Night, Running Down
       Beach South of San Francisco," *Being Here,* p. 26.

73   We find the poet: James Wright, "The Stiff Smile of Mr. Warren," *Kenyon
       Review* 20 (Autumn 1958): 645–655; rpt. in *Robert Penn Warren: Critical Per-
       spectives,* ed. Neil Nakadate (Lexington: University Press of Kentucky, 1981),
       pp. 262–269.

74   And your heart: "Convergences," *Rumor Verified,* p. 37.

74   you have lain: "Ah, Anima!" *Now and Then,* p. 33.

76   drunk: "Rumor at Twilight," *New Yorker,* July 19, 1982, p. 32.

76   spirit's narrative: Josephine Miles, "The Romantic Mode," in *Romanticism
       and Consciousness: Essays in Criticism,* ed. Harold Bloom (New York: Norton,
       1970), p. 180.

77   A flycatcher: "Sunset Scrupulously Observed," *Rumor Verified,* p. 31.

77   a grand style: Charles Molesworth, "Plain Abstractions," in *Partisan Re-
       view,* 49 (Autumn 1982): 620–624.

78   a form of the tragic: Quoted in Nancy Marmer, "Clayfford Still: The Ex-
       tremist Factor," *Art in America* 68 (April 1980): 102–112.

78   about Stephen Crane: *American Literature: The Makers and the Making*, vol. 2, p. 1640.

78   In an author's lexicon: Roland Barthes, *Roland Barthes*, tr. Richard Howard (New York: Hill and Wang, 1977), p. 129.

79   Scraggle and brush: "Snowshoeing Back to Camp in Gloaming," *Being Here*, p. 27.

80   Geometries and orchids: "Evening Hawk," *Can I See Arcturus from Where I Stand?* in *Selected Poems*, p. 4.

81   Still ravening: "Acquaintance with Time in Early Autumn," *Being Here*, p. 89.

81   Hunger of the Word: Roland Barthes, *Writing Degree Zero*, tr. Annette Lavers and Colin Smith (New York: Hill and Wang, 1968), p. 48.

81   a collage: Donald Hall, "Easy Lines," *New York Times Book Review*, November 8, 1981, p. 13.

82   And you: "Immanence," *Rumor Verified*, p. 62.

82   Have you ever seen: "Questions You Must Learn to Live Past," ibid., p. 54.

82   I have seen: "Going West," ibid., p. 25.

83   As for the characters: Robert Lowell, "Prose Genius in Verse," *Kenyon Review* 15 (Autumn 1953): 619–625.

83   Once one has faced: Delmore Schwartz, "The Dragon of Guilt," *New Republic*, September 14, 1953, p. 17.

84   the day's finicking shamelessness: *Brother to Dragons* (1953), p. 121.

84   the impudent: *Brother to Dragons*, p. 77.

84   Bombast: Leslie Fiedler, "Seneca in the Meat-House," *Partisan Review* (March–April 1954): 208–212.

84   virtuoso: Louise Bogan, "Verse," *New Yorker*, October 24, 1953, p. 141.

84   It's just his blues: *Brother to Dragons*, p. 73.

84   And I wanted: Ibid., p. 23.

84   And blackberry: Ibid.

84   A fellow: Ibid., p. 20.

85   We must: Ibid., p. 64.

85   every act: Ibid., p. 39.

85   When ice breaks: Ibid., p. 65.

86   Into a dark place: *Chief Joseph of the Nez Perce*, p. 10.

87   Their ponies: Ibid., p. 3.

87   a sense of vital relations: *Democracy and Poetry*, pp. 28 and 25.

88   Spirit of a people: G.W.F. Hegel, "History as the Self-Realization of Spirit," in *The Modern Tradition*, ed. Richard Ellmann and Charles Feidelson, Jr. (New York: Oxford University Press, 1965), p. 461.

88   The ground: Chief Seattle, quoted in *American Literature: The Makers and the Making*, vol. 2, p. 1185.

Sunny Particulars

91 The broad, sometimes sweeping: Stanley Plumly, "Warren Selected," in *Robert Penn Warren: A Collection of Critical Essays*, ed. Richard Gray (Englewood Cliffs: Prentice-Hall, 1980), p. 141.

91 In reading: Vladimir Nabokov, *Lectures on Literature*, ed. Fredson Bowers (New York: Harcourt, Brace, Jovanovich, 1980), p. 1.

91 paleface pathology: *Democracy and Poetry*, p. 50.

99 language of sexuality: Michel Foucault, "A Preface to Transgression," *Language, Counter-Memory, Practice*, tr. Donald F. Bouchard (Ithaca: Cornell University Press, 1980), p. 31.

99 Worlds on worlds: Percy Bysshe Shelley, "Hellas," ll. 197–200.

100 rich slime: *A Place to Come to*, p. 218.

100 appearances: Hannah Arendt, *The Life of the Mind* (New York: Harcourt, Brace, Jovanovich, 1978), pp. 28–29.

103 focal word; Quoted in Gerald Bruns, *Modern Poetry and the Idea of Language* (New Haven: Yale University Press, 1974), p. 54.

109 the world: "Court-Martial," *Promises*, in *Selected Poems*, p. 232.

112 Yeats and Warren: Cleanth Brooks, *The Hidden God: Studies in Hemingway, Faulkner, Yeats, Eliot, and Warren* (New Haven: Yale University Press, 1978), p. 98.

112 I can contain: Gustave Flaubert, *Flaubert in Egypt*, ed. and tr. Francis Steegmuller (Boston: Little Brown, 1972), p. 50.

114 went forth every day: Walt Whitman, "There Was a Child Went Forth."

115 the light: Emily Dickinson, "Dare you see a Soul *at the White Heat?*" poem no. 365 in *The Complete Poems of Emily Dickinson*, ed. Thomas H. Johnson (Boston: Little, Brown, n.d.), p. 173.

115 Being in: Martin Heidegger, *Being and Time*, tr. John Macquarrie and Edward Robinson (New York: Harper & Row, 1962), p. 80 and passim.

116 We are blest: William Butler Yeats, "A Dialogue of Self and Soul."

His Varying Stance

121 the "they": Martin Heidegger, *Being and Time*, tr. John Macquarrie and Edward Robinson (New York: Harper & Row, 1962), p. 346 and passim.

122 a dark cave: "Sunset Walk in Thaw-Time in Vermont," *Or Else*, in *Selected Poems*, p. 76.

122 Percy Bysshe Shelley, "Mont Blanc."

122 into nullity: Quoted in Lionel Trilling, "James Joyce in His Letters," *Commentary* 45 (February 1968): 53.

122 Of truth: "Trying to Tell You Something," *Can I See Arcturus from Where I Stand?* in *Selected Poems*, p. 10.

122   first dark: *Audubon,* VII, in *Selected Poems,* p. 100.

122   Tell me: Ibid.

122   There can be: Herman Melville, *Moby-Dick; Or, the Whale* (Berkeley: University of California Press, 1981), ch. 125, p. 525.

123   immanence of meaning: *Robert Penn Warren Talking: Interviews 1950–1978,* ed. Floyd C. Wakins and John T. Hiers (New York: Random House, 1980), p. 234.

123   peace of definition: *Brother to Dragons,* p. 39.

123   last kingdom: "In the Turpitude of Time: N.D.," *You Emperors, and Others,* in *Selected Poems,* p. 206.

123   all hearing;   Walter J. Ong, *Orality and Literacy: The Technologizing of the Word* (London: Methuen, 1982), p. 72.

124   Why did I stand: "Why Have I Wandered the Asphalt of Midnight?" *Being Here,* p. 29.

124   And taciturn: "On into the Night," ibid., p. 64.

126   Gorgias: Quoted in Hannah Arendt, *The Life of the Mind* (New York: Harcourt, Brace, Jovanovich, 1978), p. 25.

126   Since we live: Ibid., p. 27.

126   profound philosophy: William Butler Yeats, "Modern Poetry," *Essays and Introductions* (New York: Macmillan, 1961), p. 502.

126   the last kiss: *W. B. Yeats and T. Sturge Moore: Their Correspondence 1901–1937,* ed. Ursula Bridge (London: Routledge and Kegan Paul, 1953), p. 154.

126   In the star-pale field: "Boy's Will, Joyful Labor without Pay, and Harvest Home (1918)," *Promises,* in *Selected Poems,* p. 267.

127   eczema: "August Moon," *Being Here,* p. 31.

127   we can only obey: Ralph Waldo Emerson, "Fate," *in Conduct of Life* (Boston: Houghton Mifflin, 1904), p. 3.

127   dear redemption: *Brother to Dragons,* p. 39.

127   We must learn: "Loss, of Perhaps Love, in Our World of Contingency," *Can I See Arcturus from Where I Stand?* in *Selected Poems,* p. 5.

127   stripped: "Unless," *Now and Then,* p. 36.

127   To be alive: Emily Dickinson, "To be alive is Power," poem no. 677 in *The Complete Poems of Emily Dickinson,* ed. Thomas H. Johnson (Boston: Little Brown, n.d.), p. 335.

128   cost of experience: "What Is the Voice that Speaks?" *Being Here,* p. 71.

130   but petals paler: "Sila," *Being Here,* p. 37.

131   Man eats: "Knowledge and the Image of Man," *Sewanee Review* 63 (Spring 1955): 187.

131   two things: "Two Studies in Idealism," *You, Emperors, and Others,* in *Selected Poems,* p. 215.

132   part of all: "Red-Tail Hawk and Pyre of Youth," *Now and Then,* p. 17.

132   instancy: "Youthful Truth-Seeker, Half-Naked, at Night, Running Down Beach South of San Francisco," *Being Here,* p. 25.

132 the poor world's abstract storm: "Lullaby: Smile in Sleep," *Promises*, in *Selected Poems*, p. 252.

132 mission: "Synonyms," *Being Here*, p. 97.

132 distance drowses: "Butterflies over the Map," *Selected Poems: 1923–1943*, in *Selected Poems*, p. 302.

133 fanged: See, for instance, "Part of What Might Have Been a Short Story, Almost Forgotten," *Being Here*, p. 51; and "History," *Selected Poems: 1923–1943*, in *Selected Poems*, p. 296.

133 sun's heel: "A Vision: Circa 1880," *You, Emperors, and Others*, in *Selected Poems*, p. 207.

133 Slick . . . blood: "Inevitable Frontier," *Now and Then*, p. 61.

133 Rages: "Old Nigger on One-Mule Cart," *Can I See Arcturus from Where I Stand?* in *Selected Poems*, p. 14.

133 garbled: "Safe in Shade," *Being Here*, p. 92.

133 We are the blade: "History," *Selected Poems: 1923–1943*, in *Selected Poems*, p. 296.

133 paradox of fate: *American Literature: The Makers and the Making*, vol. 2, p. 1640.

133 pants and clanks: "Evening Hour," *Now and Then*, p.14.

133 Bootheels: "A Way to Love God," *Can I See Arcturus from Where I Stand?* in *Selected Poems*, p. 3.

133 one death: "Heat Lightning," *Now and Then*, p. 60.

133 the worst: Arthur Schopenhauer, *The Will to Live: Selected Writings of Arthur Schopenhauer*, ed. Richard Taylor (Garden City: Doubleday Anchor, 1962), p. 210.

133 must be some kind: Ibid., p. 232.

133 beast: Ibid., p. 283.

133 a world: *Audubon*, V, in *Selected Poems*, p. 98.

134 the crime of self: *World Enough and Time*, p. 505.

134 the dream: "What Happened," *Tale of Time*, in *Selected Poems*, p. 142.

134 labor: "Saul at Gilboa," *Tale of Time*, in *Selected Poems*, p. 180.

134 lust: *Audubon*, V, in *Selected Poems*, p. 96.

134 our werewolf thirst: "Man in Moonlight," *Promises* in *Selected Poems*, p. 253.

134 *I caught:* *Audubon*, epigraph, in *Selected Poems*, p. 83.

136 a total stranger: Martin Buber, *I and Thou*, tr. Ronald Gregor Smith (New York: Scribner's, 1958), p. 32.

136 Oedipal guilt: Sigmund Freud, *Totem and Taboo*, tr. A. A Brill (New York: Vintage, n.d.), p. 199.

137 sublimated murder: Susan Sontag, *On Photography* (New York: Farrar, Straus and Giroux, 1977), pp. 14–15.

137 each element: *Robert Penn Warren Talking*, p. 276.

137 intellect as a box: Henri Bergson, *Creative Evolution*, tr. Arthur Mitchell (New York: Modern Library, 1944), pp. 151–203.

139 the mouth is opened: Elias Canetti, *Crowds and Power*, tr. Carol Stewart (New York: Seabury, 1978), p. 223.

139 What a stench: See George F. Butterick, *A Guide to the Maximus Poems of Charles Olson* (Berkeley: University of California Press, 1978), p. 63.

139 blood: "Safe in Shade," *Being Here*, p. 92.

143 A mother: Elias Canetti, *Crowds and Power*, p. 221.

145 the real reason: Ibid., p. 347.

145 reborn to love: T. R. Hummer, "Robert Penn Warren: *Audubon* and the Moral Center," *Southern Review* 16 (Autumn, 1980); 799–815.

145 The emotions: F.W.J. von Schelling, quoted in Hannah Arendt, *The Life of the Mind*, p. 32.

145 Man lives: "Reading Late at Night, Thermometer Falling," *Or Else*, in *Selected Poems*, p. 268.

146 In this world: Arendt, *The Life of the Mind*, p. 19.

147 Perhaps the superior: Philip Rieff, *Freud: The Mind of the Moralist* (New York: Viking, 1959), p. 126.

147 Audubon's work: Helen Vendler, *Part of Nature, Part of Us* (Cambridge, Mass.: Harvard University Press, 1980), p. 88.

148 first of all: Arendt, *The Life of the Mind*, p. 22.

149 your mother: "Loss, of Perhaps Love, in Our World of Contingency," *Can I See Arcturus from Where I Stand?* in *Selected Poems*, p. 5.

150 we never seek: Blaise Pascal, *Pensées*, tr. W. F. Trotter (New York: Dutton, 1958), p. 38.

150 the dream: "What Happened," *Tale of Time*, in *Selected Poems*, p. 142.

150 air that kills: A. E. Housman, "Into my heart an air that kills."

150 energy: "Lullaby: Smile in Sleep," *Promises*, in *Selected Poems*, p. 252.

150 Whiteness ablaze: "Folly on Royal Street before the Raw Face of God," *Or Else*, in *Selected Poems*, p. 73.

151 concrete sexual desire: Arthur Schopenhauer, *The Will to Live*, p. 177.

152 man has been subjected: Norman O. Brown, *Life against Death: The Psychoanalytical Meaning of History* (Middletown, Conn.: Wesleyan University Press, 1959), p. 31.

152 demand: Jacques Lacan, *Ecrits: A Selection*, tr. Alan Sheridan (New York: Norton, 1977), pp. 286–291.

154 The freedom: Buber, *I and Thou*, pp. 39 and 54.

158 In art: Boris Pasternak, *Safe Conduct* (New York: New Directions, 1959), p. 49.

158 the metonymical texture: Roman Jakobson, "Concluding Statement: Linguistics and Poetics," in *Style in Language*, ed. Thomas A. Sebeok (Cambridge, Mass.: MIT Press, 1960), p. 375.

158   You do not live: *Band of Angels*, p. 134.

160   Star-triumphing: *Brother to Dragons*, p. 15.

160   circuit hope: "The Ballad of Billie Potts," *Selected Poems: 1923–1943*, in *Selected Poems*, p. 283.

160   Why, all the years: "Why Have I Wandered the Asphalt of Midnight?" *Being Here*, p. 29.

160   Where is the Truth: "Safe in Shade," ibid., p. 92.

160   And whatever / Vision: "Identity and Argument for Prayer" *Now and Then*, p. 66.

160   Man's mind: Ibid., p.68.

161   Moon-walking: "Night Walking," *Being Here*, p. 104.

161   Have you ever: "Old Nigger on One-Mule Cart," *Can I See Arcturus from Where I Stand?* in *Selected Poems*, p. 16.

161   A man: "Tires on Wet Asphalt at Night," *Being Here*, p. 68.

161   The body: "Birth of Love," *Or Else*, in *Selected Poems*, p. 79.

161   Running: "Youthful Truth-Seeker, Half-Naked, at Night, Running Down Beach South of San Francisco," *Being Here*, p. 25.

161   embrace / The world: Ibid.

162   Why should the heart leap: "Snow out of Season," *Rumor Verified*, p. 74.

162   What tongue: "What Is the Voice that Speaks?" *Being Here*, p. 71.

162   If I set muzzle: "Vermont Ballad: Change of Season," *Rumor Verified*, p. 50.

162   The painful bellows: "Paradigm of Seasons," *Ploughshares* 9, nos. 2–3 (1983): 11.

162   The Moments: Emily Dickinson, "The tint I cannot take is best," poem no. 627 in *The Complete Poems of Emily Dickinson*, p. 309.

163   White Election: Emily Dickinson, "Mine—by the Right of the White Election," poem no. 528, ibid., p. 258.

163   mission: "The Mission," *Now and Then*, p. 42.

163   Catskill eagle: Melville, *Moby-Dick*, ch. 96, p. 436.

163   gaze of blaze: "Part of What Might Have Been a Short Story, Almost Forgotten," *Being Here*, p. 51.

163   like an image: "On into the Night," ibid., p. 64.

164   feather-fine brush: "Vision," ibid., p. 47.

164   You've looked up: "Little Black Heart of the Telephone," *Now and Then*, p. 55.

164   worship Death: *All the King's Men*, p. 160.

164   the smallest particles: Saint Augustine, *The Confessions of Saint Augustine*, tr. Edward B. Pusey (New York: Washington Square Press, 1960), p. 226.

164   But is there: "Sister Water," *Now and Then*, p. 47.

164   What, ah: "Heart of the Backlog," ibid, p. 63.

164   our arbitrary illusions: "Identity and Argument for Prayer," *Now and Then*, p. 64.

164 only the fantasy: "Old Nigger on One-Mule Cart," *Can I See Arcturus from Where I Stand?* in *Selected Poems*, p. 16.

164 bright emptiness: "Questions You Must Learn to Live Past," *Rumor Verified*, p. 54.

164 The absolute: "Debate: Question, Quarry, Dream," *You, Emperors, and Others*, in *Selected Poems*, p. 211.

164 blind, blunt: *A Place to Come to*, p. 138.

164 life-beyond-Time: *A Place to Come to*, p. 221.

165 the old: "Tires on Wet Asphalt at Night," *Being Here*, p. 68.

165 Into the black: *Flood*, p. 335.

165 cruelly: Ibid., p. 362.

165 begins at the moment: Georg Lukács, "The Metaphysics of Tragedy," in *Soul and Form*, tr. Anna Bostock (Cambridge, Mass.: MIT Press, 1978), p. 155.

165 Then heels: "Heat Lightning," *Now and Then*, p. 60.

166 But your body: "Platonic Drowse," *Being Here*, p. 20.

166 Look: "Evening Hawk," *Can I See Arcturus from Where I Stand?* in *Selected Poems*, p. 4.

167 the basis: Miguel de Unamuno, *Tragic Sense of Life*, tr. J. E. Crawford Flitch (New York: Dover, 1954), p. 34.

167 And love: "American Portrait: Old Style," *Now and Then*, p. 3.

167 Freud: See Lacan, *Ecrits: A Selection*, p. 310.

167 like philosophy: "The Mad Druggist," *Tale of Time*, in *Selected Poems*, p. 142.

167 to hold position: "The Leaf," *Incarnations*, in *Selected Poems*, p. 116.

167 shoulders like spray: "Fall Comes in Back-Country Vermont," *Tale of Time*, in *Selected Poems*, p. 162.

168 true father: *Robert Penn Warren Talking*, p. 183.

168 The truth: *All the King's Men*, p. 354.

168 the testicles: "The Ballad of Billie Potts," *Selected Poems: 1923–1943*, in *Selected Poems*, p. 273.

168 Jed Tewksbury: *A Place to Come to*, p. 187 and chs. 1 and 2.

168 burden of every story: Roland Barthes, *The Pleasure of the Text*, tr. Richard Miller (New York: Hill and Wang, 1975), p. 10.

168 the father / Of [his] father's father's father: "The Leaf," *Incarnations*, in *Selected Poems*, p. 118.

168 when the end comes: Plato, *The Dialogues of Plato*, tr. B. Jowett (New York: Random House, 1937), pp. 259–260.

169 and I stand: "Heart of Autumn," *Now and Then*, p. 74.

169 blast, wheeze: "Preternaturally Early Snowfall in Mating Season," *Being Here*, p. 35.

170 The canoe: "Antinomy: Time and Identity," ibid., p. 81.

170   Had light: "Speleology," ibid., p. 7.
170   land of Platonic ice: "Snowshoeing Back to Camp in Gloaming," ibid., p. 27.
173   Tooth: Dickinson, "This World is not Conclusion," poem no. 501 in *The Complete Poems*, p. 243.
173   We cannot regard: Martin Heidegger, *An Introduction to Metaphysics*, tr. Ralph Manheim (Garden City: Doubleday Anchor, 1961), p. 90.
173   The salmon heaves: "The Ballad of Billie Potts," *Selected Poems: 1923–1943*, in *Selected Poems*, p. 271.
173   infinite immensity: Pascal, *Pensées*, p. 61.
174   Nostalgia: Gaston Bachelard, *The Psychoanalysis of Fire*, tr. Alan C. M. Ross (Boston: Beacon, 1968), p. 38.
174   Oh gently: Rainer Maria Rilke, "The Third Elegy," *The Selected Poetry of Rainer Maria Rilke*, ed. and tr. by Stephen Mitchell (New York: Random House, 1982), p. 167.
175   the darkening wooded landscape: "Sunset Walk in Thaw-Time in Vermont," *Or Else*, in *Selected Poems*, p. 76.
175   ego affinity: "Waking to Tap of Hammer," *Now and Then*, p. 51; "Night Walking," *Being Here*, p. 103.
175   a slow / And pitying happiness: "Youth Stares at Minoan Sunset," *Now and Then*, p. 25.
177   wants what is happening: Elias Canetti, *Crowds and Power*, p. 20.
177   tragic pathos: Friedrich Nietzsche, *Ecce Homo*, tr. R. J. Hollingdale (New York: Penguin, 1979), p. 100.
177   formula of supreme affirmation: Ibid., p. 80.
178   The word 'Dionysian':   Friedrich Nietzsche, *The Will to Power*, tr. Walter Kaufmann and R. J. Hollingdale, ed. Walter Kaufmann (New York: Random House, 1967), p. 539.
179   a caring for: George Steiner, *Martin Heidegger* (New York: Penquin, 1980), p. 100.
180   the nearness: Ibid., p. 105.
181   Thanks to the means: William Wordsworth, *The Prelude*, bk.1.
181   take high abstracted man: Melville, *Moby-Dick*, ch. 107, p. 475.
182   osmosis of being: "Knowledge and the Image of Man," p. 186.
182   glory was not something: Heidegger, *An Introduction to Metaphysics*, p. 87.
182   the poet always speaks: Ibid., pp. 21–22.
183   air that glitters: *Audubon*, VI, in *Selected Poems*, p. 99.
183   holding / I trust: "Old Nigger on One-Mule Cart Encountered Late at Night When Driving Home from Party in the Back Country," *Can I See Arcturus from Where I Stand?* in *Selected Poems*, p. 13.
184   the grandeur: "Waiting," *Now and Then*, p. 40.
186   learning to face: "Infant Boy at Midcentury," *Promises*, in *Selected Poems*, p. 250.

186 It is hard: "Synonyms," *Being Here*, p. 100.

186 Year after year: "Red-Tail Hawk and Pyre of Youth,"*Now and Then*, p. 17.

186 mini-Mariner: Dave Smith, "He Prayeth Best Who Loveth Best," *American Poetry Review* 8 (January/February, 1979): 4–8.

188 the cost: "What Is the Voice that Speaks?" *Being Here*, p. 71.

188 Jeremiah: *World Enough and Time*, pp. 505–506.

189 story of Kent: *Brother to Dragons*, pp. 15–16.

189 reality of decreation: Wallace Stevens, *The Necessary Angel: Essays on Reality and the Imagination* (New York: Vintage, 1951), p. 175.

189 fearful resolve: Quoted in Robert Penn Warren, "A Poem of Pure Imagination," in *Selected Essays* (New York: Random House, 1951), p. 228.

191 My formula: Nietzsche, *Ecce Homo*, p. 68.

191 even fear and disgust: "Knowledge and the Image of Man," p. 192.

191 determined to leave: Enid Starkie, *Arthur Rimbaud* (New York: New Directions, 1968), p. 291.

192 bites itself: Friedrich Nietzsche, *Thus Spake Zarathustra*, tr. Thomas Common (New York: Modern Library, n.d.), p. 364.

192 we find remedies: Friedrich Nietzsche, *The Gay Science*, tr. Walter Kaufmann (New York: Vintage, 1974), p. 256.

192 the crackling absoluteness: "Trying to Tell You Something," *Can I See Arcturus from Where I Stand?* in *Selected Poems*, p. 10.

193 necessity: *Audubon*, IV, in *Selected Poems*, p. 95.

193 R. W. B. Lewis, *The American Adam: Innocence, Tragedy and Tradition in the Nineteenth Century* (Chicago: Phoenix, 1955), p. 49.

193 Whitman's live-oak: Walt Whitman, "I Saw in Louisiana a Live-Oak Growing."

194 the deepest longing: Lukács, "The Metaphysics of Tragedy," p. 162.

194 fanged, unforgiving: "Unless," *Now and Then*, p. 35.

195 What makes a man comical: Soren Kierkegaard, *Either/Or*, vol. 1, tr. David F. Swenson and Lillian Marvin Swenson (Garden City: Doubleday Anchor, 1959), p. 143.

196 only . . . in dream: *Audubon*, IV, in *Selected Poems*, p. 96.

196 reconciles energy with appearance: Friedrich Nietzsche, *The Birth of Tragedy*, tr. Francis Golfing (Garden City: Doubleday Anchor, 1956), p. 102 and passim.

197 man like me: *Robert Penn Warren Talking*, p. 155.

197 Never—yes, never: "Acquaintance with Time in Early Autumn," *Being Here*, p. 89.

198 We actually exist: E. M. Cioran, *The Temptation to Exist*, tr. Richard Howard (Chicago: Quadrangle, 1968), p. 218.

198 instancy: "Youthful Truth-Seeker, Half-Naked, at Night, Running Down Beach South of San Francisco," *Being Here*, p. 25; *Brother to Dragons*, p. 5.

200 sexuality is the great *exception*: Paul Ricoeur, *Freud and Philosophy: An Essay*

on Interpretation, tr. Denis Savage (New Haven: Yale University Press, 1970), p. 291.

201   a dramatic *overlapping:* Ibid., p. 292.

203   long compulsion: circuit hope: "The Ballad of Billlie Potts," *Selected Poems: 1923–1943*, in *Selected Poems*, p. 283.

205   line between life and death: "Heart of Autumn," *Now and Then*, p. 74.

205   the fierceness: "Saul at Gilboa," *Tale of Time*, in *Selected Poems*, p. 179.

206   We long: Denis de Rougemont, *Love in the Western World*, tr. Montgomery Belgion (Garden City: Doubleday Anchor, 1957), p. 42.

206   the soul *is* revelation: Ralph Waldo Emerson, "The Over Soul," *Essays: First Series* (Boston: Houghton Mifflin, 1903), p. 282.

206   the only thing: *Audubon*, IV, in *Selected Poems*, p. 96.

207   This is happening: "Unless," *Now and Then*, p. 36.

208   man must love: *Brother to Dragons*, p. 101.

208   And love: "American Portrait: Old Style," *Now and Then*, p. 7.

209   Size circumscribes: Emily Dickinson, "Size circumscribes—it has no room," poem no. 641 in *The Complete Poems of Emily Dickinson*, p. 318.

210   supreme aim of tragedy: William Butler Yeats, *The Letters of W. B. Yeats*, ed. Allan Wade (London: Rupert Hart-Davis, 1954), p. 838.

210   in shadowless vastness: "Caribou near Arctic," *New Yorker*, November 30, 1981, p. 46.

210   All life lifts: *Brother to Dragons*, p. 77.

212   that possibility: Heidegger, *Being and Time*, p. 294.

212   purity of being: "Paradox of Time," *Rumor Verified*, p. 13.

214   The primordial preference: Hubert Benoit, *The Supreme Doctrine: Psychological Studies in Zen Thought* (New York: Viking, 1959), p. 77.

215   the poverty: Alain Robbe-Grillet, *Snapshots* and *Towards a New Novel*, tr. Barbara Wright (London: Calder and Boyars, 1965), p. 56.

215   an aged father: "Reading Late at Night, Thermometer Falling," *Or Else*, in *Selected Poems*, p. 67.

217   30.06 in heart: "Dead Horse in Field," *Rumor Verified*, p. 59.

218   Beautiful Necessity: Emerson, "Fate," p. 49.

219   both waste and repair: Walter Pater, *The Renaissance* (New York: Meridian, 1961), p. 220.

220   everything breaks: Nietzsche, *Thus Spake Zarathustra*, p. 244.

221   the necessity of beauty: Emerson, "Fate," p. 48.

221   Not only to bear: Nietzsche, *Ecce Homo*, p. 68.

221   the living body: Guy Murchie, *The Seven Mysteries of Life: An Exploration in Science and Philosophy* (Boston: Houghton Mifflin, 1978), p. 527.

221   the world is real: "Court-Martial," *Promises*, in *Selected Poems*, p. 232.

222   metabolizes so fast: Murchie, *The Seven Mysteries of Life*, p. 528.

222 Joy, strongest medium: "Picnic Remembered," *Selected Poems: 1923–1943*, in *Selected Poems*, p. 309.

222 In the heart's last kingdom: "In the Turpitude of Time: N.D.," *You, Emperors, and Others*, in *Selected Poems*, p. 206.

Acknowledgments

Parts of the poems "Caribou near Arctic," "Rumor at Twilight," and "Marble" are reprinted by permission; copyright © 1981, 1982, 1983 by Robert Penn Warren. Originally in *The New Yorker*.

Part of "Paradigm of Seasons" is reprinted by permission; copyright © 1983 by Robert Penn Warren. Originally in *Ploughshares*.

Part of "Why You Climbed Up" is reprinted by permission; copyright © 1983 by Robert Penn Warren. Originally in *The Georgia Review*.

The author gratefully acknowledges the permission granted by Random House, Inc., to quote from the following volumes of Robert Penn Warren's poetry: *Selected Poems: 1923–1975*, copyright 1936, 1940, 1941, 1942, 1943, 1944, © 1955, 1957, 1958, 1959, 1960, 1963, 1965, 1966, 1967, 1968, 1969, 1970, 1971, 1972, 1973, 1974, 1975, 1976 by Robert Penn Warren—copyright renewed 1964, 1968, 1969, 1970, 1971, 1972 by Robert Penn Warren; *Now and Then: Poems 1976–1978*, copyright © 1976, 1977, 1978 by Robert Penn Warren; *Being Here: Poetry 1977–1980*, copyright © 1978, 1979, 1980 by Robert Penn Warren; *Brother to Dragons: A Tale in Verse and Voices*, copyright 1953, © 1979 by Robert Penn Warren; *Rumor Verified: Poems 1979–1980*, copyright © 1979, 1980, 1981 by Robert Penn Warren; *Chief Joseph of the Nez Perce*, copyright © 1982, 1983 by Robert Penn Warren.

Part One of this book appeared in an altered form as "Greatness and Robert Penn Warren," in *The Sewanee Review* 89 (Summer 1981), copyright © 1981 by Calvin Bedient.

Index